KEEP TRUE

KEEP
TRUE
A LIFE IN POLITICS

To Vdand,
I appreciate for contribute to
progressive causes
Howard Pawley
Sept 8, 2015

HOWARD PAWLEY

Foreword by Paul Moist

University of Manitoba Press

University of Manitoba Press
Winnipeg, Manitoba
Canada R3T 2M5
uofmpress.ca

16 15 14 13 12   2 3 4 5

Printed in Canada
Text printed on chlorine-free, 100% post-consumer recycled paper

Cover design: Doowah Design
Interior Design: Karen Armstrong Graphic Design

Unless otherwise noted, photographs are taken from the personal collection of the
author. Every effort has been made to contact copyright holders for the materials
appearing in this book. Photo 6, courtesy Interlake Publishing, originally appeared in
the Selkirk Enterprise, 13 June 1969; Photos 7 and 11, courtesy University of Manitoba
Archives and Special Collections; Photos 10 and 14, courtesy Western Canada Pictorial
Index; Photo 15, Andrews-Newton Photographers; Photo 17, Concacan Inc.; Photos
16, 20, 21, 22, Government of Canada photos, reproduction not produced in affiliation
with, or with the endorsement of, the Government of Canada; Photo 23; Office of the
Governor General of Canada.

Library and Archives Canada Cataloguing in Publication

Pawley, Howard, 1934–
Keep true : a life in politics / Howard Pawley ; foreword by Paul Moist.

Includes index.
ISBN 978-0-88755-724-8 (pbk.)
ISBN 978-0-88755-404-9 (PDF e-book)

1. Pawley, Howard, 1934–. 2. Premiers (Canada)—Manitoba—Biography.
3. Manitoba—Politics and government—1969-1977. 4. Manitoba—Politics and
government—1977–1988. I. Title.

FC3777.1.P39A3 201   971.27'03092   C2010-906076-8

The University of Manitoba Press gratefully acknowledges the financial
support for its publication program provided by the Government of Canada
through the Canada Book Fund, the Canada Council for the Arts, the Manitoba
Department of Culture, Heritage, Tourism, the Manitoba Arts Council,
and the Manitoba Book Publishing Tax Credit.

FSC
www.fsc.org
MIX
Paper from
responsible sources
FSC® C016245

CONTENTS

Photographs follow pages 86 and 182.

"KEEP TRUE, NEVER BE ASHAMED OF DOING RIGHT;
DECIDE ON WHAT YOU THINK IS RIGHT,
AND STICK TO IT."

—George Eliot

"IF YOUR CAUSE IS JUST AND RIGHT,
SOONER OR LATER YOU WILL WIN.
IT MUST TRIUMPH BECAUSE IT IS PART OF THE
WARP AND WOOF OF THE UNIVERSE.
NO MATTER HOW MANY SETBACKS THERE MAY BE
ALONG THE ROAD, YOU MAY BE SURE
THAT SOME DAY THE RIGHT AND JUST
WILL PREVAIL."

—Tommy Douglas

Foreword

HOWARD PAWLEY PRESIDED OVER MANITOBA POLITICS during a significant period of Canada's history. His insider view is both fascinating and instructive in terms of explaining the contemporary national political scene.

First elected in the historic 1969 election, the NDP's first victory in Manitoba, Pawley played a key role in altering the province's political landscape. His political memoirs offer insight into the success of his party in winning seven of the past eleven elections held in Manitoba. Of equal importance, we gain a glimpse of Howard Pawley himself as a dedicated social democrat, MLA, cabinet minister, party leader, and premier.

As a front-bench minister during the Schreyer years, Pawley had a hand in critical legislation that introduced public auto insurance, the province's first human rights code, and the Marital Property Act, a landmark achievement for women's equality. These and other key issues demonstrate the passion and diligent attention to duty that Pawley brought to each file that hit his desk.

From the vantage point of his long political career, Pawley gives us unique insights into the key economic and political issues on both the provincial and national scenes during this tumultuous period in Canadian politics. His perspective on the French Language Services debate, the CF-18 fiasco, and the Meech Lake Accord expose fault lines in federal-provincial relations and the seeds of the rise in western discontent, birth of the Reform Party, and the rejection of the Liberal Party of Canada by the west.

The success of Howard Pawley's economic policies is his greatest legacy. Assuming power in the midst of a recession with both high unemployment and interest rates, the Pawley administration was an activist one. Pawley questions today's fixation on tax-cutting when unemployment is high and communities are suffering. The Manitoba Jobs Fund was a success as Manitoba weathered the recession better than most. The agreements Pawley's administration struck with public employees are in stark contrast to the failed strategies of the Rae government a decade later. The Pawley government's management of the economy offers important lessons which contrast with the less activist role adopted by many governments in the current global recession.

But Howard Pawley's story also shows that, despite a strong vision, political careers always are at the mercy of circumstance. The 1988 demise of the Pawley administration in mid-term at the hand of one of its own disgruntled MLAs marked the end of Howard Pawley's elected political career. Yet even at this low point, Pawley remained an energetic and committed social democrat. In March 1988, just after the defeat of his government's budget, Pawley accepted my invitation to address over 600 Winnipeg Labour Council members at the University of Winnipeg at the Council's annual spring school. Despite the unexpected events that had just ended his government, Pawley's speech that day was riveting and upbeat. As he was leaving public life, his message to the assembled crowd was to never abandon the goal of social justice, to reject the neo-liberal agenda, and for the assembled workers to remain active politically.

Two decades later, I again called upon Howard Pawley, this time to address over 1000 civic workers on strike in the City of Windsor in June 2009. As always, he did not disappoint in offering encouragement and support to a group of workers in their time of need.

His words on both occasions, and no doubt countless others, were unselfish, inspiring, and heartfelt, which is perhaps the best way to describe the life and times of Howard Pawley.

Paul Moist
Ottawa, Ontario
September 2010

Acknowledgements

This memoir is a journey along the path of my life and it would not have been possible without the generous assistance from many friends and colleagues. Party members, former caucus members, and cabinet ministers were always available. Without them, these memoirs would have never been possible.

Federal and provincial archives were most beneficial. The research was aided by newspaper articles from Manitoba and from across the country. Brian Cowan, Sina Naebkhi, Victoria Cross, Jake Soderlund, Tracy Kosa, and Bob Krause from the University of Windsor and David Wilson from the University of Toledo facilitated the intricate work of editing the preliminary chapters. David Woodbury, James Eldridge, Errol Black, Gail Whelan Enns, Raymond Hiebert, William Regehr, Paul Thomas, Gerry Friesen, and Saul Silverman, my former classmate from United College days, aided and supplied important information and research. Richard Cleroux, once a reporter for the *Globe and Mail*, provided me with extensive assistance.

The staff at the University of Manitoba Press, including David Carr, Glenn Bergen, and Cheryl Miki, provided invaluable help on the organization of this book.

To all those I have mentioned and countless others who provided me with support, I express my appreciation and gratitude.

*To my wife Adele, to Chris and Charysse,
and to my grandchildren.*

KEEP TRUE

CHAPTER 1

My Early Years

ON 20 NOVEMBER 1934, the evening before I was born, my mother attended a meeting in Brampton, Ontario, where Co-operative Commonwealth Federation (CCF) leader J.S. Woodsworth spoke. Always supportive of my father, she had accompanied him to the meeting. She confided years later that she had been so nervous that she sat in the back row of the crowded meeting hall; in those times, pregnant women were shy about being seen in public. Nonetheless, because of her deep reverence for J.S. Woodsworth, she was not going to miss one of his speeches. Afterwards, as my mom and dad drove home, she felt her first labour pains. The following day, 21 November, in Brampton, in Peel County, Ontario, I arrived. I was named Howard after Norman Howard Pawley, who had won the Military Cross at Vimy Ridge in World War I. I would be my parents' only child.

Then, as in the present day, one of the county festivities was the annual fair. My mother entered me into the Best-Looking Baby Contest in the Cooksville Fair for two years running, 1935 and 1936, and twice I won the first prize. The prize in each instance was a silver cup and a dollar. The contest got me my first public appearances, and I was featured in the Crown Syrup advertisements. The company gave my mother a coloured portrait of me in remembrance. It was, you might say, the beginning of my public life.

My father, Thomas Russell Pawley, was born in Ontario, in an agricultural community, in 1903. He was one of four sons born to Thomas and Eliza Pawley. Hoskin, the eldest, served in the First World War and then was employed by Ontario Hydro; John became the secretary to the Ontario Milk Board before his retirement; and Robert served as the director of the Veterans' Land Act. My mother, Velma, was born in Marlborough County to Henry and Priscilla Medill. Being born in rural areas, both of my parents were active in the local CCF, and the national leader or MPs would visit our home on occasion. When he visited the Pawley farm while in the vicinity, M.J. Coldwell would babysit as my parents tended to the milking of the cows. Political discussions were the norm around the dinner table. Then known as one of the most politically Conservative areas in the Peel constituency, their poll received but three CCF votes. It was no secret in the neighbourhood who had cast them. In 1937, in the early years of the CCF, my father ran in the Ontario provincial election; he did not fare well.

As the second oldest of four sons, my father remained on the family farm near Brampton, Ontario, to assist his father and mother. He was influenced by an early and unfortunate experience arising from his father's having heavily mortgaged their home farm to assist in financing a farm purchase for Hoskin near Moorefield, Ontario. When the 1929 financial crash came, and with it the global depression, my grandfather's mortgage encumbrance resulted in foreclosure of the family farm. My father and mother were forced to venture to another farm. It was a tragic incident that left a lifelong impression on my father, especially in his business dealings. Some good did come of these events, however: my father had gone to Moorefield to help his brother with the farm, and it was there that he met my mother.

My father proved successful in every field of his future endeavours, both as a farmer and as a businessman. Starting without a nickel, he achieved relative prosperity as a farmer, and later as a manager and businessman in Manitoba. He was especially gifted when it came to carpentry or anything mechanical.

Since I was an only child and living on a farm, my playmates were the cats, the dog, the cattle, and the chickens. When I was little more than a toddler, I once ran unannounced into the barn at the exact moment that my father was slitting the throat of a rather fat chicken. The unfortunate bird was hanging by its legs from the ceiling by a cord, a steady trickle of blood dripping from its slashed throat. This childhood experience would later deter me, even on special family occasions, from enjoying meals where chicken was served— which would prove occasionally awkward for me in my political life when I attended banquets where chicken was on the menu. Still, I never touched it. Rarely did anybody notice. During my years as premier, my executive secretary, Georgette Dragan, would frequently phone ahead and ensure I would be served a vegetarian dish or some other alternative.

My paternal grandfather, Thomas Pawley, lived with us during my formative childhood years. Being very religious—he was a strict "old school"

Methodist and the Sunday school superintendent for thirty years of the local United Church—he did not tolerate any deviation from the strict literal teachings of the Bible. Sunday, the Sabbath, was not a day for sports or any other activity. Playing games was prohibited. And of course, alcohol, tobacco, dancing, and cards were banned on all days. Once, while I was listening to the Charlie McCarthy and Edgar Bergen radio program, he turned it off. This and other radio programs were the works of the devil, and not for Sunday evening entertainment. My mother served for a time as the chair of the local temperance board for the local United Church that we attended.

One Saturday night my parents took me to Brampton to watch the then famous movie *How Green Was My Valley*. It vividly portrayed the horrendous working conditions of Welsh coal miners. As a youngster, I was deeply taken by the film (and it would leave a lasting impression on me). The next morning, as we gathered around the breakfast table, I carelessly blurted out "what a good movie we saw last night." Taken by surprise, Grandfather Pawley stormed from the kitchen, accusing my parents of setting a bad example for their son. After all, they had taken me to the theatre. I blamed myself for provoking such an outburst.

It was in this atmosphere that I received an early upbringing in the church and the Christian faith. Later in my teens, I questioned much of what I had learned, but the moral teachings of Jesus Christ in the Sermon on the Mount played a major role in providing guidance in my later life.

I attended S.S. 7 Chinguacousy, a one-room school, located nearly two miles from our home, a substantial distance for any six-year-old to walk. My mother helped with my homework daily, especially my atrocious spelling and arithmetic. The school had only twelve or thirteen students, and for most of my elementary school career, there was only one other pupil, Jack Judge, in the same grade as myself. We became close friends, although his interest was mainly sports while mine was reading. He was certainly more proficient on the hockey rink and on the baseball diamond, but I managed to achieve higher grades in school. Early on, I gained an interest in history.

My former teacher, Betty Hutchinson, recalled in a 1982 *Winnipeg Free Press* interview that square dancing wasn't my forte in those days. She recalled, however, that I excelled "in spelling bees and geography matches" and loved to "do plays and recite." I suppose she summed up my early childhood character well when she said, "he was very quiet and shy but enthusiastic about things. He was always reading and was very interested in the social side." About my love of speaking, she said, "Howard talked and talked, the children were interested so I let him ... But I finally had to tell him to stop."

Sometimes, I would bicycle to school; other times, I took a shortcut through a wooded area. During the winter months the distance would often prove difficult to walk. A severe blizzard once compelled me to seek refuge overnight with hospitable neighbours who lived some distance from my own home. I doubt that I would have survived had I continued to make my way home. I never did learn to ride a pony, despite growing up on a farm. The only time I dared to ride one it threw me, and that was the end of that. After, I stuck to bicycling or walking to school.

Among the highlights of my early school career were the annual Christmas party, the baseball tournaments, the lacrosse games, and the annual county music festival. I was not, to say the least, outstanding in sports, but it was my lack of musical talent that would be the main cause of my personal undoing. In this I differed radically from my mother, who was generally considered the most talented soloist at the local Home United Church as well being quite proficient with the church organ. I, by contrast, am tone deaf. Understandably, my total inability to sing distressed the music teacher who visited our school on a weekly basis. If she permitted me to sing in the choir, the school would certainly fail to win the coveted Harris Cup, awarded in the annual music competition. Consequently, she instructed me to only *pretend* that I was singing; under no circumstances was I to permit any notes to escape my lips. I willingly complied. Year after year in the competition I stood, usually in the front row, pretending. It was an early lesson in the importance of ensuring discipline and team solidarity.

As the son of a farmer, I kept busy during the summer months tending to the livestock and working in the fields. Although it was hard work stretching over long hours and leading to nasty sunburns, I still recall those summer days with pleasure.

My Early Interest in Politics

I have some early political memories, mainly because of the interest in politics shown by my parents and Grandfather Henry Medill. The first was the night of the 1943 Ontario provincial election, which saw a tight electoral race, right down to the final radio reports. With excitement growing and tension rising, my parents and I huddled together around the radio listening as first the CCF and then the Tories took the lead. That evening, I recall, my parents could not resist the temptation to "eavesdrop" on the telephone party line, on which their Conservative neighbours were calling each other to share their anguish about the potential takeover of their farms the next morning by a socialist CCF government. I was only nine, but that night left a lasting impression upon me.

As a youngster I remember a visit to our farm by three MPs, two CCF members (Scotty Bryce from the Selkirk constituency and Claire Gillis from Cape Breton), and Gordon Graydon, our own Conservative MP from Peel. Graydon wanted to introduce the two CCF members he was hosting for the weekend to one of the few CCF farm families residing within his constituency. The emotional impact of that meeting with these parliamentary representatives left an indelible imprint upon my childhood mind. Their simple humility and their manner of relating to me as a child inspired me. I thought to myself, "I would like to be like one of them when I grow up." Shortly afterwards, I was delighted when the CCF under the leadership of Tommy Douglas won the election in the distant western province of Saskatchewan.

Our family farm was only seven miles from Brampton, a town with fewer than 7000 residents when I attended high school there in 1948. Interestingly, one other student attending Brampton High at the same time eventually became an Ontario premier. He was Bill Davis. In 1948, he was finishing Grade 13 while I was just starting my first year. Unlike Bill Davis, the son of the local Crown prosecutor, I was just a country kid travelling each morning to the town high school, on board a school bus.

Years later, at my initial first ministers' meeting in 1982, Premier Davis introduced me by commenting on how fortunate Canada was to have two former students of Brampton High School as premiers. This may have helped Brampton Billy's popularity in Ontario, but it certainly didn't boost my ratings in Manitoba, where a traditional and healthy distrust of Canada's largest and wealthiest province prevails. On another occasion Agriculture Minister Eugene Whelan, when questioned on a Brandon hotline program about the unfairness of having an agriculture minister from Ontario, replied by pointing out that Alberta Premier Getty came from Ontario, Saskatchewan Premier Blakeney from Nova Scotia, and Manitoba Premier Pawley from Ontario. If they're good enough for Westerners, he argued, then surely I am too.

Grandfather Henry Medill arrived to live with us on the farm after the sale of his own farm in Moorefield. He gave me three Aberdeen Angus heifers, which I would greatly treasure. Looking back, I'm amazed that I had such an interest in cattle, because I suffered from severe allergies, including an allergy to grain dust, which made daily chores difficult. Nonetheless, my personal mission was to raise purebred Aberdeen Angus, and I read every book and magazine about black Aberdeen Angus cattle I could find. I never shared my father's skill with farm machinery or his exceptional carpentry talents. From time to time, I believe, that disappointed him just a little.

It was from my conversations with my maternal grandfather, Henry Medill, that my interest in both cattle and politics was derived. As a young man, he had remained on the farm while putting his three brothers through medical college. Ironically, it was Henry who was to become the lifelong scholar, reading on every imaginable topic and all the books that he could get his hands on. Thousands of hours were spent reading. Sometimes, in the early hours of the morning, my mother heard my grandmother call to him to come to bed so that he could do the farm chores the following day. Grandfather Medill inspired me to read about all manner of things. He played a large part in my social and political thinking.

Grandfather Medill suffered from a lifetime of diabetes and by this time had lost a leg to gangrene and was restricted to a wheelchair. I was his principal means of moving about; it was my job not only to push his wheelchair but also to assist him in and out of it and then put the wheelchair away. Because of his failing eyesight, it was my job, as well, to read to him. This meant many discussions about politics, economics, world affairs, farming, and even religion. He was my mentor, generating in me an unquenchable thirst, for knowledge. Frequently, after my chores were completed, my spare time was spent in his company. Sometimes we would go to the movies. Grandfather would refuse to stay for the playing of "God Save the King" at the end of the film, because his family had emigrated to Canada from Ireland. It was ironic that his only daughter would be married to someone of British extraction.

Sometime in early 1952, my life underwent a sudden change. The Cockshutt Plow Company, located in Brantford, sought out my father and made a proposition to him. They offered him the position of service manager for Manitoba and eastern Saskatchewan. He accepted the job and arrangements were made to place our possessions for auction and sale. I was heartsick. I did not want to move. It meant selling my young Angus heifers and travelling a long distance from my childhood home—to western Canada—where, except for some cousins at Oak Lake in Manitoba, I did not know anyone. It also meant a new start at a different high school.

The summer of 1952 was a difficult transition for our family. First, there was the sale, an old-fashioned country auction, followed by the large farewell gathering at a local hall of neighbours and other family friends. With the sale of the farm, my father left a few months ahead of us to do custom combining on the plains area of the United States, commencing in northern Texas and gradually moving northward to North and South Dakota. A month or two after my father's departure, my mother, Grandfather Medill, and I headed off for the unknown West. I reached Winnipeg just a few days late for the start of the 1952 fall high school term. We purchased a home at 1141 Ingersoll Street, in the city of Winnipeg. Daniel McIntyre would be the high school where I would complete my grade 12. I soon became entrenched in an urban life, and my earlier disappointment about our move from the farm quickly subsided.

My parents would do well in Winnipeg. A few years after Dad's arrival he left Cockshutt Plow Company and formed what proved to be his own very successful real estate business, known as Lynn Agencies Ltd. He also served for a time as school board trustee and councillor for the City of St. James, where he and my mother had moved in 1954. During the 1970s, he also served for several years on the Manitoba Land Value Appraisal Commission. Both Mom and Dad were active in the NDP and served as executive officers of the Sturgeon Creek NDP Association. They resided for a time at 121 Sunnyside Boulevard, in the Woodhaven area, then spent their final years in the Middlechurch Home in West St. Paul. My father died in 1986, in the final days of a provincial election that I, as premier, was involved in. My mother passed away in 1987.

Politics in Manitoba in the 1950s

Like the rest of Canada in the 1950s, Manitoba was enjoying the prosperity of the post–World War II era. The province's premier, D.L. Campbell, governed in a conservative and tight-fisted manner. This was symbolized by actions that sometimes appeared trivial. Years later, for instance, when I was premier, I heard stories (perhaps true) that before calling it a day's work Premier Campbell would personally check the lights throughout the premier's offices at the legislature to ensure that they had been turned off, the better to lower the provincial Hydro bill. There is no question that he exercised sound financial management of the province's expenditures. By the time of my family's arrival in 1952, however, there was a view that he was unduly conservative and behind the times, despite post-war economic growth—a view especially prevalent in urban Manitoba.

It was not the CCF that politically benefited the most from this trend which developed during the Campbell administration, but the Progressive Conservatives (PCs), led by an urban and progressive leader, Duff Roblin. His Progressive Conservative party, with an emphasis upon the progressive, was steadily making inroads within the city of Winnipeg and other provincial urban centres, where it might have been expected that the labour-based CCF would be strong as a result of the movement away from the Campbell Liberals. One difficulty confronting the CCF was an internal war, a toxic brew of demoralization and disorganization, partly the result of internal bloodletting that had occurred several years before. Prior to my arrival in Manitoba, three MLAs— Berry Richards, Dr. D.L. Johnson, and Wilbert Doneleyko—had been ousted for their alleged Labour Progressive Party leanings, and the party had suffered a bitter split. Membership had consequently declined as inter-party strife took its toll.

But internal squabbling was not principally responsible for the difficulties confronting the CCF; rather, it was external problems arising from postwar prosperity in the Eisenhower era. There was a general disinclination to attempt what might be considered radical solutions. The Cold War hysteria and the evil influence of McCarthyism next door, in the United States, did not work to the benefit of the CCF.

In 1954 I made my first contact with the CCF in Manitoba, at the annual fundraising tea for the Winnipeg North Centre CCF Association. I had been invited by Edith Cove, a hard-working supporter for Stanley Knowles. Of course, Stanley Knowles was in attendance. Other local CCF celebrities were also there, including Andy Robertson, a colourful Scot who was a trustee on the Winnipeg School Board. He had arrived as a young man from Scotland in the early 1920s, and was almost immediately thrust into Winnipeg's left-wing politics when he heard the fiery oratory of members of the local socialist and independent labour community. A committed socialist himself, he was always the life of any group. I was also instantly impressed with the firm commitment, integrity, and sincerity shown by Knowles. Before leaving that day, I purchased my first CCF membership card.

About this time, my Grandfather Medill died from gangrene at 85 years of age. My mother had been his main caregiver—and indeed the main caregiver for both my grandfathers—for over twenty years in the last stage of life. I recognize now how much this demonstrated her compassion and love.

Continuing with My Education

In 1953, I attended the Manitoba Normal School to obtain a teaching certificate. While there I was a house captain for Frontenac House and made some lifelong friendships with people attending the School. A brief spell teaching in a one-room school in Dugald, Manitoba, followed. Then I decided upon a legal career. I enrolled in the liberal arts program at United College in Winnipeg. There, I had the good fortune to be taught political science by Michael Oliver and history by Harry Crowe and Kenneth McNaught. History would come alive when these truly inspiring professors lectured. They helped motivate me to enter politics.

I particularly recall Harry Crowe's discussions in his classes on American history. These included topics like Senator Joe McCarthy (who was then at his outrageous height), civil rights, and school desegregation (the U.S. Supreme Court had just made its key decision and the struggle over implementation was beginning). Crowe's lecture on the causes of the American Civil War was especially memorable to me. He relied on a well-known American historian, Charles A. Beard, who viewed the Civil War as being fought not so much to free slaves in the South as to permit the migration of cheap labour for emerging manufacturers in the North. This interpretation revealed the power of economics in the development of history. It was an important lesson that followed me in life! I, along with many other students, was shocked and angered when Harry Crowe was fired for some outspoken comments he had written to a colleague while on sabbatical leave about the influence of religion in church-run universities. His letter had mysteriously ended up in the president's office. As a law student, I joined with others who were protesting the actions of the university's president.

During my time at United College I was elected to the chair of the student Debating Society. I can vividly recall a visit to Stony Mountain Penitentiary with Mel Myers, Graeme Garson, and Harry Backlin. The occasion was to demonstrate a debate on the topic "there's one law for the rich and another for the poor." Stony Mountain Penitentiary, which stands like a huge fortress just north of Winnipeg, is the maximum security prison in Manitoba, the prison where criminals serving major sentences are sent. When the demonstration was over, I nearly got out of the penitentiary before I realized that Ken Leishman, the chair of the debate, had forgotten to return my watch, which he had borrowed from me to time the participants. He was apologetic about the incident. Years later, in 1966, Backlin was implicated with Leishman and others in the great gold robbery that took place at the Winnipeg International Airport.

During the two years I pursued my studies at United College, I became quite active in student politics. The United College Youth Parliament included five parties—Progressive Conservatives, Liberals, CCF, Social Credit, and Labour Progressives. All participated enthusiastically. Most important for me was hearing T.C. Douglas, premier of Saskatchewan, in the college auditorium, when he urged us to commit ourselves to "the construction of a more equitable world ... the new Jerusalem." I was so impressed by this tremendous orator that there was no turning back. For me, the dispersal of both power and wealth was fundamental to the eventual achievement of a socialist society.

In the College Youth Parliament, I was one of the leaders of the CCF group and developed some modest oratorical skills of my own. Among the other leaders of our group were Mel Myers, an extremely able debater; Saul Silverman, a brilliant history student; Don Swainson, very enthusiastic and reasonable; and Bill Bedwell, tall and well spoken. I learned from this diverse group the importance of creating a convergence across a wide variety of people's needs in order to meet those needs, and to do so to the greatest extent possible without surrendering your core values. Friendship transcended party politics, as I developed close relationships with three young Conservative opponents who sat in the mock parliament: Joe Martin, Trevor Anderson, and Wally Fox-Decent.

In those years, a youth parliament existed for the entire university community. Voting would take place at various polls, including one at United College. In student voting, the CCF carried United College with a heavy majority. The reason for this, one of the university's young Liberals (who in later life became a judge of the Queen's Bench of Manitoba) told me, was my organizational efforts: "Why, you would even drag your fellow students out of the washrooms to vote CCF." I relished the accusation. While it was a bit of an exaggeration, it reflected the energy for organizing that I displayed as a young man. Too frequently, left-wingers prefer to philosophize rather than do the practical work essential to build a movement and a political party. Later, as a young man, I gained a reputation for my organizational work within the Manitoba CCF, which resulted in my rise within party circles throughout the 1950s.

In the summer of 1957, when I was twenty-two, I took on the challenge of organizing for the CCF and was soon propelled into an even larger contest. I agreed to be the sacrificial candidate in the Lisgar riding in the 1957 federal general election when Progressive Conservative John Diefenbaker ousted the Liberals. I was soundly defeated; in fact, the vote in Lisgar was the lowest tally garnered by any CCF candidate in the province in that general election. For all that, the Lisgar experience was a valuable one. During the campaign I attended my first all-candidates' forum, and I recall feeling really good about my performance. During the same year I attended a CCF convention in Winnipeg where I joined a small number of other delegates, including Andy Robertson (a Winnipeg School Board member) and Fred Tipping (of 1919 General Strike fame), in opposing the adoption of the Winnipeg Declaration. I had considered it a watering-down of the anti-capitalist principles of the Regina Manifesto which had attracted me to the party in the first place. Some laughingly referred to us as "the terrible trio." At the same convention, I took over the helm as president of the Co-operative Commonwealth Youth Federation for Canada.

The following summer I again organized for the CCF, and as luck would have it, found myself once more running for the party as a sacrificial candidate in a provincial election. This time it was in the northern riding of The Pas. I didn't do as badly this time, coming in second in an election where Progressive Conservative Duff Roblin replaced the government of Liberal premier D.L Campbell. Indeed, as in Lisgar, although I was a sacrificial candidate, I did considerable door-to-door canvassing and discovered after the first few doors how much I enjoyed meeting people this way.

In the fall of 1957 a group of young Turks and young rebels, of whom I was one, achieved an upset at the annual Manitoba CCF convention. I would become the party's new president, upsetting the incumbent, and commit myself to building a renewed and stronger provincial party. What motivated me most (alongside parliamentary advocacy) were the agrarian roots of the CCF and its emphasis on building cooperative institutions as a path toward socialism.

Recruitment was centred at the local level (various clubs, associations, etc.), to which the party granted considerable independence. Indeed, the CCF's initial constitution set in place a formal apparatus that attempted to enlarge local autonomy—and thus increase participation—even as it endeavoured to maintain organizational harmony.

The party provided members with a way of life that reminded some of belonging to a church group. It had a strong rural presence and enjoyed a great deal of support for the co-operative and credit union movement. The party culture was best summed up by Woodsworth: "making converts—yes, after all that is our job—leading people to seek a new way of living, the cooperative way through which alone a true world brotherhood may be established."[1]

It was this basic characteristic of the CCF that most attracted me: I have always been energized by interaction with other people.

Shortly after this convention, over coffee at the Parkview Drugstore in St. James, I met my future wife and my lifelong partner. Adele Schreyer was a bookkeeper and loan officer with the Household Finance Company, located on the same street as the law office where I was articling as a third-year law student. By the time I was in my fourth year, Adele was advising her mother that she would be marrying me; indeed, she went so far as to forecast that I would be a future premier of Manitoba. This was to reassure her mother that I would be in a position to support her.

Adele was born on a farm near Tyndall, Manitoba, one of six children born to Joseph and Stella Schreyer. Her father was a farmer and general merchant, and the family lived for a few years in the village of Tyndall, then on a farm nearby. She attended elementary school in Tyndall, in Golden Bay, and, finally, in a one-room school in the Greenwich school district. Her high school years were spent at St. Mary's Academy in Windsor and at Dryden High School in Ontario. Later, she moved to Winnipeg, where she attended the Manitoba Commercial College for her secretarial certificate.

Adele supported me in my political efforts and was elected as secretary of the Winnipeg South Constituency Association. In those days, having left-wing convictions could sometimes make life difficult. When her name appeared in the local urban newspapers over an issue with the national CCF office, Adele was called into her manager's office and was told that he did not wish to see her name associated publicly with "that party" again. In 1961, she was required to quit her job when it became known that she would be attending the founding convention of the New Democratic Party. She had made arrangements with the management well in advance to have that time off; however, management claimed that someone with seniority demanded the same time. Having also checked in advance that there was no schedule conflict with this senior person, Adele had no choice but to forego the convention or quit her job. Later that fall, she answered an advertisement for a loan officer position with one of the large banks. She filled out the application but was told that she would be hired only if she quit her association with the party. She turned down the job.

During this period of time, the family finances were precarious, as I was still an articling law student and our financial well-being depended largely on her remaining employed. Extremely intelligent and always practical, Adele would play a major role in the success of my later political and legal career.

On 26 November 1960, we were married in the Unitarian Church in Winnipeg. In my teens, I had become a member of the Unitarian Church, and in the early days of my membership, I had contemplated going into the ministry. The minister who performed the service was the Rev. Phillip Peturrson, later to be elected to the Manitoba legislature and appointed as Minister of Cultural Affairs in the first Schreyer government. Al Mackling, a future minister in both Ed Schreyer's and my governments, was the best man. Jack Walker, a law school friend, and Roland Otto, a friend from my Manitoba Normal School days, were the ushers.

My Campaign to Stop the Creation of the NDP

In 1959, members of the party gathered in the rural community of Anola to discuss the direction in which the party should go, given that its future at the national level seemed bleak. Some expressed the view that a socialist party should be the voice of public opinion. As a twenty-four-year-old law student, I firmly told the assembled delegates, "A socialist party should lead public opinion, even though an idea might be unpopular at a certain time."

A debate was beginning on the formation of a so-called New Party, one that would be "modern" and "pragmatic." The debate threatened to seriously split the CCF. The Manitoba party was heavily engaged in this debate, with MP Stanley Knowles and Lloyd Stinson, the provincial leader, leading the forces that were most prominent in arguing in favour of the new party's birth. I was on the opposing side, as were my friends Al Mackling and Magnus Eliason, a CCF party organizer. Labour unions provided the backbone for the new party initiative, along with much of the party hierarchy. Opposed were those of us who feared both a watering-down of the principles inherent in the CCF and the new party's domination by labour union affiliates. Most disturbing to us was the representation at party conventions of affiliates without a formula that would reflect the actual party membership. To us, this spelled power without the countervailing responsibility for building an actual membership base. Many rural members strongly supported our stand because they were worried not only about the dilution of principles but also about how labour union control of the party would be interpreted in rural areas.

That same year, Douglas Fisher, then a CCF member of Parliament for Port Arthur, had a chance meeting with me in a Chinese restaurant. He later described me as " a very thin, pale lad with a watery, hesitant smile and a shock of long, wispy hair." He also mentioned that several young CCFers had been unhappy, like him, with the idea of replacing the CCF with the NDP. Fisher considered me the most soft-spoken but also the most radical of CCFers, intent and organization–minded, with a determination to remedy social inequalities through a party with a mass, continuing, and participating membership.[2]

Today, I remain of the view that a party such as the CCF or the NDP should be one based on individual membership rather than affiliated organizations either in whole or in part. Each member should determine issues at conventions according to their own personal perspective and be freed from external dictates or pressures from any affiliated organizations. To do otherwise runs the risk of giving too much control to those who exercise special power from their leadership position in an affiliated group, for regrettably, the special interests of an affiliated group can sometimes be placed ahead of those of the party. The other difficulty with affiliate representation is the potential for placing a greater program focus on the priorities of a particular interest group rather than reducing inequality, which ought to be the foremost priority of the NDP.

The federal party was most concerned about the strength of our opposition. Des Sparham, the national organizer entrusted with the building of new party clubs, paid a visit to the CCF youth organization and attempted to disarm the apprehensions of what he described as "the very lively student movement," particularly its concern that the principles of the CCF would be watered down by "the broadening out process which the new party represents." Sparham concluded in his report to his superiors that he had made progress with this group, but "the objection remained strongly in the mind of Howard Pawley." He also advised that there was no "split" but only "a slight chip, created by the somewhat intransigent position taken by Mr. Pawley" (and perhaps to a greater extent by Mr. Mackling, with whom I had no personal conversation).[3]

Matters continued to heat up, with sharp divisions surfacing in the provincial party. Our side continued its opposition to possible domination of the New Party by affiliates and strongly supported the principle of membership without group distinction as to fees, rights, and privileges. At the provincial convention of 1960, the "Mackling-Pawley group submitted a number of resolutions," which were criticized by Knowles as a "shocking display of ignorant and incredibly narrow-minded self-interest. Manitoba will have to be purged," he warned.[4]

We attempted at the Manitoba convention to delay formation of a provincial section of the New Party until one year after the national New Democratic Party's founding convention. This resolution was defeated by a three-to-one margin. At the same convention Ed Schreyer, who was the MLA for Brokenhead in the Manitoba legislature (and a first cousin to my wife), defeated Mackling's bid for re-election as provincial chairman by only a few votes. But I was elected vice-chair over Fred Tufford, the candidate for the pro–New Party forces, by an equally narrow vote.

Events provincially and federally would eventually cement the emergence of the New Party, replacing the CCF. Adele and I were delegates to the founding convention of the NDP. Our members, despite our reservations, remained loyal members of the New Democratic Party.

It was as a member of the party's left wing that I served as president of the Winnipeg Fair Play for Cuba Committee in the aftermath of the failed Bay of Pigs invasion. I was proud that, after a number of weeks of intensive preparation, we successfully packed the Winnipeg Playhouse Theatre with a protest rally opposing the U.S.-sponsored fiasco. We delivered a clear message to the American administration from Winnipeg.

Practising Law in Manitoba's Interlake

My political activity lessened somewhat for a few years as Adele and I proceeded to open a law office in the town of Stonewall. We began the law practice in the basement of the Stonewall Credit Union, without a single client and in need of a loan for supplies to get started. Before we even got settled in, Adele's father died from stomach cancer, at a relatively early age. Somehow, though, our law office grew so quickly that within three months we were fully busy. Not too long after the business got off the ground, I received a telephone call from the mayor of Arborg requesting that I take on the appointment as solicitor for the village of Arborg; this was soon followed by a similar request from the municipality of Bifrost. I began to visit the village of Arborg each Friday at the North Star Co-op Creamery to meet clients, the numbers of whom were to swell in numbers within a brief period of time.

While we were in Stonewall, some key Liberals approached me in the then Rockwood constituency to run for the Liberals provincially in the 1963 election. They thought that they could convince Adele to talk me into it, but she was shocked that anyone would think that I would switch parties. It didn't take any thought to reject the overture.

One of the roles of a lawyer which I enjoyed immensely was to defend accused clients in the Provincial Court. I remember one particular case that propelled me into the local limelight. My client, a not-so-well-regarded individual in this small rural town, was charged with theft of an expensive rug, the property of a woman from an old, established family. After the Crown presented its case, I moved for a dismissal. Although the Crown could have proven possession—the rug had been located in the front porch of my client's home—they had nonetheless failed to establish *theft*. A charge of possession of stolen property would have been more appropriate. Judge Darichuck therefore dismissed the case; and with the evidence now back in his possession, my client and his friend made off together, the rug over their shoulders. The owner understandably yelled at the judge to prevent them from exiting the courtroom, but to the owner's anguish, the judge refused to intervene. Rumours soon began to circulate that I had become owner of the carpet for my fees: this was of course untrue.

Nothing gives a small-town lawyer more visibility than fighting to protect the rights of a defendant against a criminal charge. I enjoyed the challenge of taking on these pro-bono cases. The fees were nothing compared to the work.

Stonewall had a small population in the early 1960s. Situated near Winnipeg, the town served the surrounding rural area and was conservative in nature. I could identify very few New Democratic supporters locally during those years. I do recall, in the provincial election of 1966, Harry Enns strolling into office and asking me to sign his nomination papers. As I was busy establishing my law practice, both Adele and I joined the Kinette and Kinsmen service clubs. During our association with the service clubs, we were involved in raising funds to construct and maintain a senior citizens residence.

It was in 1964 that we had our first child, Christopher Scott, and in 1966 our daughter Charysse Crystal was born. Adele was able to continue working in the law office, as we succeeded in locating an excellent housekeeper who lived only a street away. The office swiftly grew with the responsibility for all the Farm Credit Corporation work in the Interlake region, providing us with a major financial boost. Adele also established an income tax practice, dealing mainly with people in the Interlake region.

In 1965, I made my third bid for federal political office when I agreed to run as the NDP candidate in the Selkirk-Interlake constituency. I thought I stood some chance of winning, but it proved not to be. I lost to the popular incumbent, Progressive Conservative Eric Stefanson. I recall one joint candidates' meeting in Arborg when all hell broke loose. The CBC had undertaken to do a film on the election campaign of an individual candidate, and in this case it was the Liberal, Graeme Garson, a friend from my university days. Every time Graeme answered a question, the quite conspicuous camera crew would spring into action, filming his every word. On the other hand, they ignored both Stefanson and me. An angry member of the audience—loudly though eloquently—brought the media bias to the attention of the audience, which thundered their own hostility in response. The camera crew quickly fled the hall amid ever-louder protest from the audience. It was a perfect example of a media plan gone terribly astray.

I was still residing in Stonewall at the time. Upon hearing of my nomination to run as an NDP candidate, one of my clients, a Conservative, advised my wife to tell me to withdraw because if I did not, I would lose a lot of legal business in Stonewall. That didn't happen; indeed, my legal practice increased due to my name being better known in the Interlake region. There was, however, one fallout of my candidacy: I lost the work of the Farm Credit Corporation. Later, during the 1968 federal election, I received a call from Archie Mackay, the Liberal fundraiser, asking me for a donation to the Liberal party because I had briefly been the Corporation's solicitor. The answer was an emphatic no.

The federal campaign was to have another important impact on both our law office and our future. During the campaign I had gotten to know several Selkirk councillors and town officials. One day they paid me a visit in Stonewall and offered me the town solicitor's position if I would relocate my law office to Selkirk. The town was larger than Stonewall and would provide a very substantial base to our business, so Adele and I decided it only made sense to make the move. Before the end of 1967, the move was completed. Most of our clients followed us to Selkirk, and to our surprise, Stonewall town representatives offered us their business after our move. We now represented four municipalities: Arborg, the Rural Municipality of Bifrost, Stonewall, and Selkirk. The law office was rapidly expanding.

The success of the business would not have been possible without the skill and support of Adele. It was her astuteness with legal work pertaining to estates, real estate, and the municipalities that made the law office thrive. Much of my time was spent in pursuing social justice in the rural court circuit of the Interlake region. Again and again, and in most cases successfully, I was representing clients before Legal Aid was in existence. I worked pro bono for clients in the Interlake region, or charged below the going fee rate.

Fate was, however, soon to intervene.

The Unexpected Launch of a Political Career: The 1969 Victory

In May 1969, while Adele and I were driving with our children to Winnipeg from Selkirk, we were struck in the rear by another auto. During the accident I suffered injury to my vertebrae and was confined to a bed in the Selkirk General Hospital.[5] The newly elected provincial leader of the NDP, Ed Schreyer, visited me and told me that a candidate for the Selkirk riding was urgently required for the June 25 provincial election. He asked me to at least permit my name to appear on the ballot, since not much time remained before the official nomination day when a candidate's papers had to be filed. Apparently other efforts to recruit a candidate had been fruitless. Ed had previously worked with me politically, and as a member of Parliament he regularly used my law office for his constituency purposes. When I warned him that, incapacitated as I was, I would be unable to do much campaigning, he retorted that the NDP were unlikely to win the Selkirk riding anyway. Provincially the riding had never gone NDP or CCF, nor had it ever come close to winning. Still, he believed my running would help generate visibility for me if I should decide later to seek the federal Selkirk riding seat he had vacated.

Ed Schreyer had good reason for doubt about any possible win. For over forty years, only two MLAs had represented Selkirk. The first had been James McLenaghan, a Progressive Conservative and a former Manitoba Attorney General; the second, Selkirk lawyer Tommy Hillhouse, a popular and respected Liberal, first elected in 1953. It was widely believed that Tommy had been passed over for a cabinet post by former premier D.L. Campbell because of his liberal social views. During all these years, neither CCF nor NDP candidates had ever saved their deposits; indeed in 1962, no CCF candidate had run for election in the constituency.

I was enjoying the challenge of the courtroom in 1969, including my pro-bono work for those without resources. It was for this reason that the Interlake Crown prosecutor Jack Montgomery—later the province's director of criminal prosecutions—nicknamed me "the Abe Lincoln of the Interlake." Moreover, I had no intention of saying goodbye to my law office, which was emerging as an increasingly lucrative practice. But for all that, my major reason for entering law had been to make possible a switch into politics at a future time of my choosing. It had always been my intention to pursue a political career, especially at the federal level. So, I half-heartedly agreed to run in the provincial election.

Adele spoke on my behalf to a handful of people—eight, as I recall—who were present at the riding nomination meeting a few days later. The speech contained the following words: "I make the same pledge to you as I shall make to every citizen in the Selkirk riding, namely that I will devote my experience, my enthusiasm, and my heart to building a better way of life in this area. This is not an empty political promise. I make it sincerely, believing that I can be of genuine service to the citizens of this riding and to our province." I then added, "It has been a difficult decision. A recent automobile accident has kept me on my back for the past two weeks ... my doctor has indicated that I should be able to return to full activity by July 1st."

Adele attended to the business of the law office during the day and then visited me in the late afternoon at the hospital, bringing correspondence and sharing whatever questions had arisen during the day at the office. It was Adele who went door to door canvassing on my behalf. It was she who would find an increasingly sympathetic electorate at the doorsteps. Later, I playfully suggested if it had been left to me to go door to door I would not have won. I needed Adele's determined support, coupled with the efficiency displayed by Eugene Laye, my campaign manager, and dozens of volunteers, including Doug and Leona Hacking, Lorna Morriseau, Amy Clemons, Al Scramstad and his parents, Mr. and Mrs. Nick Penner and their son Kurt, Nick and Marie Yusark, Tom Kopp, and many others.

In Selkirk, the PCs had nominated a strong candidate in Bud Oliver, later to become Selkirk's respected mayor. However, a local schism would hurt this party when Tom Norquay, president of the Selkirk Progressive Conservative Association, decided to run as an independent. He argued that the Selkirk PC nomination meeting was unconstitutional because some who voted at the meeting were not residents of their constituency, and because of this and other alleged irregularities, he attempted to declare the meeting invalid. As an independent candidate, Norquay would muster only fifty-seven votes on election day. Nonetheless, the Progressive Conservatives were not helped by such friendly fire, as some called it.

Moreover, George Sigurdson, the Liberal candidate, failed to garner the previous Liberal party support, polling only 835 votes. Hillhouse's decision not to seek re-election, coupled with the last-moment nomination of his replacement, proved to be a severe blow to Liberal fortunes in the riding. Most of their traditional support shifted over to us. Lying on my hospital bed, I was flabbergasted by the faltering campaigns of my opponents

I was released from the hospital shortly before the election. It didn't hurt that my departure from the hospital would be prominently featured in a front-page picture in the local weekly; it showed me being greeted by my loving wife and being hugged by our two children, ages five and three. I have always considered the timing and positioning of this photo amazing.[6] The *Selkirk Journal* was not known to be sympathetic to the NDP, but on this occasion, politics were apparently outweighed by sympathy for my injury. On 25 June 1969, the election produced an upset victory for the NDP, not just in Selkirk but also provincially. My elected political career was launched.

The party claimed twenty-eight of the fifty-seven constituencies in Manitoba. Premier Walter Weir had greatly miscalculated the electorate, assuming that a well-publicized national confrontation at a recent federal-provincial conference with Canada's new prime minister, Pierre Elliott Trudeau, had enhanced his popularity. Although he had disputed the use of the federal government's spending power to implement a national health care program, he failed to recognize the commotion that would result from the imposition of health insurance premiums, even going so far as to mail the billings to taxpayers during the election campaign. Premier Weir also mishandled the mounting anger over the auto insurance issue, at a time when debate raged about the deplorable state of the auto insurance system in Manitoba. This issue was to play a very important role throughout my political career in Manitoba. Indeed, since my departure from public life, it has followed me into my private life, as I have been called upon to campaign in other provinces in Canada for publicly owned auto insurance.

Another campaign issue in some parts of the province was the flooding of South Indian Lake by Manitoba Hydro, which angered environmentalists and Aboriginal people. The Aboriginal population accused the government of interfering with their opportunities for fishing and hunting. The environmentalists objected to the damage that resulted from the flooding.

Added to these issues was a residual anger at the failure of a former premier, Duff Roblin, to honour a 1966 election campaign promise not to introduce a provincial sales tax, which he did implement before seeking the leadership of his national party. There were also mounting suspicions about the Manitoba Development Fund's financial support of millions of dollars (although the full extent of the payout was not fully known at the time) to Churchill Forest Industries, a private company in The Pas, Manitoba. This, too, was to play a role in my future.

By 1969, the collapse of the Liberal Party under its right-wing leader, Bobby Bend, had left a void in the centre left of the province's political spectrum. The electorate had no alternative but to elect Ed Schreyer if they wished to avoid a right-wing Progressive Conservative administration. That was exactly what happened. At the time, the result was surprising; although it was a minority government, few had expected the NDP to win at all. With 28 seats out of 57, the newly elected Manitoba government was one seat short of a legislative working majority. Majority was finally achieved when the maverick St. Boniface Liberal Larry Desjardins, attracted by the youthful and charismatic premier-elect Ed Schreyer, joined the NDP caucus after first designating himself in the legislature as a Liberal-Democrat. The premier rewarded him by appointing him as his legislative assistant. The popular vote for the NDP, at 38 percent, led the opposition and the business community to challenge the new government's mandate. The modest levels of popular support for the NDP became a refrain that was echoed repeatedly by the powerful insurance industry in its unrelenting campaign to derail the new government's public automobile insurance initiative.

With this background, I was understandably awed when, a few days after the 1969 election, I was invited by the premier-elect to serve in the cabinet as his Municipal Affairs Minister, Commissioner of Northern Affairs, and Government Affairs Minister, and also was assigned the responsibility of dealing with the red-hot auto insurance issue. At the time, I was rather surprised to receive this responsibility, as I had no previous legislative experience. Perhaps my past experience in the party and my legal experience were the persuasive factors. After accepting the Schreyer telephone request, I thought long and hard about what I had just agreed to undertake. Did it make sense that a person without legislative experience could deal with the most important and contentious issue in the first term of the new and minority government? Should I have declined this part of my cabinet responsibility? I immediately realized that this challenge would either make or break my future political career. A good performance would undoubtedly enhance my stock, while an inept one would ruin it.

To this day, I remember my embarrassment upon arriving to assume my ministerial responsibilities—and nervously asking a legislative security officer for the directions to Room 333, the office of the Municipal Affairs Minister.

CHAPTER 2

Baptism by Fire

The Battle to Implement Public Auto Insurance

THE 1969 ELECTION, like previous Manitoba election campaigns, prompted much debate about the merits of government auto insurance. The province had a highly unsatisfactory auto insurance system at the time. Large numbers of uninsured drivers were enrolled in an Unsatisfied Judgment Fund, a fund established by the Manitoba government and used to compensate those suffering damages caused by uninsured motorists. The number of uninsured motorists exceeded 10 percent. Ever-increasing premium hikes and poor service in the claims process by private companies only exacerbated the problem. A legislative committee on auto insurance had failed to come up with any worthwhile recommendations.

In Saskatchewan, Premier Tommy Douglas had implemented a highly successful public auto insurance program. Since 1946, the New Democratic Party, and the CCF before it, had committed itself (should the Party come to power) to a similar plan. We received a boost on this issue not only from the inaction of the Progressive Conservative government but also from the insensitivity of the insurance industry, which had shown no concern about reform, believing that the traditional third party in Manitoba, the NDP, could never gain power.

The public insurance debate illustrates how many factors determine whether a government pursues the successful enactment of policy and fulfills its potential: the environment of the time and place, financial constraints, ideology, leadership, personalities, institutions, the power base of the government in question.[1]

Within weeks of the election, Ed Schreyer, reeling from a heavy barrage of criticism from the business and insurance industry, attempted to assuage the fears of those powerful interest groups. The reaction to Schreyer's win was similar to that experienced by Bob Rae's successful NDP twenty years later, when Rae attempted to reassure his powerful and hostile antagonists. Schreyer advised the insurance industry that the NDP government would move for a public agency or public ownership, but only if it could be demonstrated that such a system would be feasible: "We will not move for it simply for the sake of having a nationalized corporation."[2] Such post-election comments may have given the Insurance Bureau of Canada and its allies some expectation of a possible reversal in policy, or at least a compromise of the solemn pledge to enact a public auto insurance scheme.

Shortly after my cabinet appointment, Ed and I met with representatives of the insurance industry in the premier's office. Discussion ensued about the establishment of a committee to investigate the auto insurance system. The industry was visibly eager to play a role by sharing information and by enjoying some representation on this committee.

Within days of this meeting, the premier reported the results to cabinet. Their reaction was strongly averse to any close collaboration with the industry, which was correctly seen as a special interest group. Powerful cabinet members such as A. Russ Paulley, a former leader of the NDP and a one-time Opposition auto insurance critic, and Sid Green, a former contender for the party's leadership, were especially persuasive in reaffirming the need to follow through with the party's commitment to a public plan. They reminded us of the election pledge and conveyed sharp disapproval of any plan permitting the industry to enjoy any privilege or preferred relationship with any committee that was to be established. Dominating the mood of the cabinet was a firm resolve to avoid any equivocation and a determination to convey an unmistakable signal of the government's intention to proceed with a public system. Personally, I was delighted with the cabinet decision.

Prolonged discussion took place in that cabinet meeting about whether a task force or a Royal Commission would be most appropriate to investigate the feasibility of a public auto insurance system. Ultimately, it was agreed that a task force would be best. It could achieve the same result as a commission and accomplish its mission more expeditiously. The membership had to be such that it would not be afraid to recommend a public plan as the preferred option if that proved to be feasible.

On 29 October 1969, the cabinet approved the terms of reference for the task force, designated as a Commission of Inquiry to investigate the feasibility of instituting a program of public automobile insurance and to hear and consider representation respecting all aspects of automobile insurance.[3] The makeup of the task force demonstrated the cabinet's resolve to prevent any action that might undermine the government's plans. It consisted of R.D. Blackburn, a former Saskatchewan Government Insurance Office senior management official from Regina; Frank C. Pagan, a former insurance adjuster; and me, as chair. David Randall, former insurance adjuster and the author of *Dollars on the Highway*, a book critical of the auto insurance industry, was named as secretary to the commission.

The task force had access to the information needed to ensure the soundness of its recommendations. This included information from both the Provincial Superintendent of Insurance and any advice or data that might be desired from the Saskatchewan Government Insurance Office. The industry did not provide any data other than what was given to subsequent public hearings.

The process we chose, including the composition of the task force, clearly signalled the government's preferred choice in public policy. The industry had anticipated that a wider array of options would be examined, including adjustments to the premium structure, which would allow them to carry on privately. This was, however, a mistaken perception; it did not reflect the fundamental reality—namely, a cabinet prepared to take a very unequivocal position, one that faithfully followed the position expressed in the 1969 election campaign. The cabinet was also interested in aspects of the insurance system other than costs, such as claims service, universal coverage, a no-fault scheme, and accessibility to a ready pool of investment funds.

The announcement of the task force's makeup and mandate, not unexpectedly, evoked a sharply negative reaction from the insurance industry, as they denounced what they considered to be a gross betrayal of the spirit of the August meeting. They attempted to court me as the minister responsible.

As a youthful and idealistic social democrat, somewhat inexperienced in the ways of government and corporate business, I accepted a luncheon invitation from Harley Vannan, chairman of the Western Advisory Committee of the Insurance Bureau of Canada. We met at the prestigious and exclusive Manitoba Club. The site, while only symbolic, did not favourably impress me; in my view, other arrangements would have been more conducive to

establishing empathy between us. This may seem a minor point, but it does
show the importance of symbols in lobbying efforts and how actions, even
if they appear trivial, can create an opposite effect from that intended. I had
agreed to the meeting to enhance my limited knowledge of the insurance sector. Vannan's intent at this first meeting, and in subsequent meetings, was to
explain the complexities of auto insurance and to convince me of the benefits
of leaving it safely in private hands.

When we met for a second time, it was, at my suggestion, at a more modest restaurant. However, this occasion was soured by Vannan's threats that
the insurance industry would guarantee that the government I represented
would be destroyed if we persisted in barging ahead with our "ill-conceived
plans." Such bullying tactics did not impress me, nor was cabinet impressed
when I reported this intimidation. The insurance industry's lobby blatantly
sought to pressure the newly elected social democratic government and its
young minister to abandon all it stood for, in favour of a private system that
had not met the needs of Manitobans. From the beginning, the industry gave
the government little space or incentive for any compromise.

On 3 November 1969, I wrote to Vannan to advise him that I desired to
make use of whatever statistics they were prepared to provide and, as well,
hold regular meetings with an insurance committee representing the industry. In response, Vannan, calculating that nothing could be gained from any
further co-operation with the government, angrily released a statement to
the public in both Winnipeg daily newspapers in which he questioned the
committee's membership and its operating procedures, and chastised the
government for having made these decisions without consulting the industry.

This insurance industry strategy was based upon the assumption that the
government was politically vulnerable in our minority situation, and that if
public pressure could be brought to bear on us, we would be forced to change
our approach to the review and, perhaps, forget about the industry altogether.
Vannan also felt that the industry had been naïve about their chances of
persuading, by private communications, the members of the government
to change their minds. Vannan had been advised by Public and Industrial
Relations Ltd. of Toronto that support for the insurance industry would come
about only by generating attention-grabbing public statements. However,
the only result of this change in approach was that informal communications
among the premier, the industry, and me were terminated. Further contact
would take place only through the process established by the task force.

As the Manitoba Auto Insurance Inquiry proceeded, I announced that submissions to it could be delivered at various locations throughout the province. Presentations could be either written or oral, and they could be given in private, if the presenter specified that the details were of a personal nature (such as matters pertaining to the cancellation of auto insurance, or facts about personal injuries where the details might be embarrassing). Not all briefs would necessarily be presented at the formal hearings, as the commission wished to minimize repetition. Predictably, the industry immediately lambasted the task force, claiming that it was stacked against any chance of a fair review and that the committee was intent only on confirming a predetermined conclusion.

Our task force considered a wide array of such presentations over nineteen days of hearings, concluding on 30 December 1969. Forty-five groups or individuals presented briefs, and nearly 3000 communications were written to us. The campaigns of those for and those against the public plan were well-organized. Both the insurance agents and the government encouraged letters from their respective supporters.

At one of the first sessions, some 400 people, mainly insurance agents, turned out to hear the Insurance Agents Association of Manitoba (IAAM) present its brief in Room 254 in the legislative building. They had come from all corners of the province to demonstrate their hostility to the government's proposed action, and were clearly intent on giving their president, George Tatlock, solid backing. Tension grew when only 200 could be accommodated in the Committee Room, resulting in the remainder being compelled to stand in the legislative corridors.

Their brief warned that higher rates were in store for Manitoba's motorists if a government plan such as that in Saskatchewan was implemented. Gordon Root, the Agents Association consultant from British Columbia, recommended that the insurance agents should not link themselves too closely with the insurance industry companies in making their case to the government, and he advised them to present their case with a view to what arrangement they could make for themselves if the government did introduce a public plan. Root's pragmatic approach stressed the marshalling of concrete facts, in sharp contrast to the vast majority of presentations, which were rhetorical in style and geared more to propaganda value than to providing information. Nonetheless, his counsel was rejected by the IAAM. Their concern was that this would tend to drive a wedge between the companies and the agents. They resolutely opposed the private industry being replaced by a public plan.[4]

The rejection of Root's advice was, in my view, an egregious error on their part. If the IAAM had adopted at that stage a more constructive approach, the government might have readily reciprocated any cooperation. There was no benefit to the insurance agents in their cozy alliance with the insurance industry against the government.

The submission by the Insurance Bureau of Canada (IBC) was counterproductive; it did nothing to influence us. Assembled by the IBC staff in Toronto, Ontario, it consisted of much of the same material presented to an Alberta legislative inquiry into automobile insurance, ignoring the different political culture of Manitoba and the composition of the NDP government itself, which was very unlike that of the Social Credit government in Alberta. In short, the IBC's argument failed to reflect the political reality in Manitoba, demonstrating a lack of imagination. Again, this confirmed the wisdom of Root's advice to the insurance agents to avoid linking the two organizations in their struggle against the government's inquiry.

At another meeting, both the Flin Flon Labour Council and the Steelworkers Union in that border city came out strongly in favour of a government plan, claiming that their geographic location provided them with a unique opportunity to compare the relative merits of the private and public plans.

The mayor of Brandon suggested the City of Brandon wanted any new central headquarters of the government auto insurance corporation to be located there. Brandon was the lone area of NDP support in southwestern Manitoba, and the government was eager to respond to the mayor's request. Doing so would kill two birds with one stone, showing sensitivity for Brandon without caving in to pressure from the regional Tory sentiment, which fiercely opposed our legislation.

The Manitoba Federation of Labour and the Manitoba Chamber of Commerce predictably supported and opposed, respectively, the establishment of a public auto insurance plan. The Chamber warned that business confidence in the government would suffer and that this radical type of government intervention would be bound to undermine the efforts of the Manitoba Department of Industry and Commerce to attract business to the province. The chamber was clearly getting onside with the insurance industry, weighing in against the NDP's fulfilling its election pledge. The labour brief had more impact on the government. After all, the Labour Federation had thrown its resources behind the NDP in the recent election campaign while the Chamber of Commerce was seen, with justification, as a hostile organization, ideologically repugnant to the newly elected NDP MLAs.

A submission of the Town of Wawanesa was supported by about 250 of its 512 people. They travelled to Brandon to protest before the commission's hearings, warning that if a government auto insurance plan was instituted the Wawanesa Mutual Insurance Company head office in their community would fold. They warned that the town would be wiped from the map, for its economy was largely dependent upon the company. (A few years later, after Manitoba Public Insurance had become a reality, my turn to attend a summer fair as a member of the cabinet put me, along with my family, in Wawanesa. During the official ceremonies in front of Wawanesa Mutual's head office, my young son Chris asked my wife in a loud voice if the building was a museum. Standing nearby was the Opposition leader, Tory Sid Spivak. My wife quietly answered that it was not.)

Overall, the task force achieved a moderate success in its efforts to broaden the debate. To show that much more was involved than simply the issue of ownership, our members purposely asked questions that raised a wide array of topics—e.g., about tort vs. no-fault compensation, law enforcement, a coloured licence system vs. a demerit system, claim service, the role of the agents, and arbitration of claims through the courts vs. by tribunal. The insurance industry, by contrast, would have preferred restricting debate to issues relating to public versus private ownership of the auto insurance system.

The interaction with the public demonstrated the importance of reaching out to the public for their input on policy development. Regrettably, governments today are inclined to do too little of this. Major decisions are being made and proceeded with despite limited opportunity for the public to make representations, generating increasing levels of disillusionment among politicians and in governance.

On 22 April 1970, our report was tabled in the Manitoba legislature. Its recommendations and findings included three main points: 1) Manitoba motorists should be required to buy basic liability insurance from a Crown corporation but be allowed to purchase additional coverage from private insurance companies; 2) overall savings on auto insurance costs should be 20 percent to 25 percent; and 3) legislation to remove high-risk drivers from the road through licence suspensions must go hand in hand with a heavy government involvement in automobile insurance.

The Manitoba plan was similar to Saskatchewan's auto insurance system, but there were some basic differences.[5] Although we added some additional no-fault ingredients, we kept them relatively modest. This would avoid the industry complaint that would otherwise ensue about the public plan's higher premiums—a complaint that could not be made, naturally, without explaining that the extra cost reflected additional coverage.

The Reaction

The response from the Opposition and the insurance industry to our report was swift and intense. The gloves came off. Vannan, for the insurance industry, alleged that the government's plans demonstrated its "doctrinaire Socialist positions." He charged that the recommendations set forth were plagiarized from the Saskatchewan Government Insurance Plan. He further suggested the insurance industry was up against an unbeatable combination within the government, consisting of those who were pseudo-Marxists and felt everything should be run by the government, and others who were saying, Let's stop here.

The opposition leader, Walter Weir, referred to the task force as a Kangaroo Court, and stated that he wasn't convinced that its recommendations would result in savings for the public. He charged that "the Committee had its mind made up from the start, and the hearings seemed merely an attempt to justify its existence."

Despite the fury from our adversaries, I was encouraged by the generally favourable response from our caucus and my cabinet colleagues. Most were delighted that the government was moving to an unequivocal signal of its future intentions. This was not to say that there were no serious reservations on the part of some caucus members. However, the bulk of caucus members geared up for the prospect of a major battle with the insurance industry. We had been elected on such a promise, and this was a commitment we were going to keep. It was our belief that the NDP, a populist Left movement, often operates best when from time to time it confronts those among the most wealthy and powerful in society. It had to demonstrate that it was unlike the other parties in carrying out its promises; otherwise, it would lose credibility and cause disenchantment within its membership. Contrary to the observations of critics, this was not a purely ideological response, but rather one that illustrated the basis of power for a party like the NDP.

Ed Schreyer's initial willingness to look for a compromise had been undermined by the condescending, hard-line attitude adopted by the insurance industry. The insurance agents contributed to this impression when they mixed culture and politics one evening. One-hundred-and-forty–five sign-carrying members of their Association injudiciously picketed the Manitoba Centennial Concert Hall while the premier was inside reading some of Abe Lincoln's lines in a performance with the Winnipeg Symphony Orchestra. Placards read: "Call Schreyer when you have an Accident"; "NDP destroys 4,287 Jobs"; "Ed the Red"; "Lincoln Freed Slaves—Schreyer destroys Freedom"; "I lose my Job, I lose my home and my 15 years work gone; Auto Insurance Now Whose Job Next?" Brochures were handed out, ominously warning that while auto insurance was the current victim, this government could take your shop or your business next.

The NDP had incurred three areas of vulnerability at this stage. First and most serious was the lengthy delay in tabling legislation, which gave the Opposition more opportunity to pummel the government and generate additional uncertainty and fear about our intentions. The insurance industry organized one of the largest protest rallies that the province had ever witnessed. This was probably nurtured by a belief that the lack of legislation meant that there was still an opportunity to alter the future of the legislation.

Indeed, there was a realistic chance of this occurring. An example of the kind of modification that was possible had been debated within the committee. It involved a proposal by Ron Blackburn that would have seen the government providing accident benefit insurance but leaving collision and liability insurance for the companies, with the government eventually offering the other categories as well. Blackburn argued that the first step in the difficult transition phase would be more easily accommodated by this modification. As chair, I opposed this route, fearing that it would fall far short of our election pledge to significantly decrease rates. In fact, given that in 1969 private policies offered only optional no-fault coverage, this modification would have increased rates for most motorists. It was hardly an appealing political choice.

In addition, I believed that if we substantially reduced the package, postponing the move toward a full public auto insurance plan, we would probably never succeed in restarting the process. In hindsight, this reading of the situation was probably accurate, because the first four years of the Schreyer government turned out to be its most productive, the period in which substantial and courageous strides were taken in enacting its policies.

The second vulnerability was that the task force had not adequately considered the role of the insurance agents. Distribution of the product through the motor vehicle branches left only a minimal role for service providers who had enjoyed a fair degree of public support. To ignore this, as my committee did, was to invite difficulties. By not extending an olive branch to the insurance agents, the commission probably forfeited a chance of increasing its public approval and weaning the insurance agents away from the insurance industry.

The third cause of vulnerability was vagueness about our intentions. This problem was exacerbated by legislative and commission delays. All of this had only encouraged unhelpful speculation.

The Throne Speech of 12 March 1970 did not make clear what the government's intentions were. It said, "My Government will introduce changes in legislation affecting automobile insurance in order to bring about greater benefit to Manitobans. Systematic reviews of automobile insurance in Manitoba and in other jurisdictions in recent years have found that greater equity and efficiency can be achieved."[6] The industry was pleased with the Throne Speech and interpreted it as a weakness of our resolve to push ahead with the plan. Some argued that the deliberate ambiguity would grant the government more time to mobilize its resources for the upcoming confrontation with its adversaries. However, it can also be suggested that the commission's delay and the Throne Speech's vagueness about its intentions made the debate more difficult for the government.

In response to media demands for more detail, Premier Schreyer claimed that elaboration was impossible because we had not reached any final decision on this issue. All of these factors led Opposition leader Walter Weir to wrongly interpret the government's caucus as more undecided than it was. In his reply to the Speech from the Throne, he said, "I kind of gather from what I see in the press in recent days that the reason…for it not being definite is that the Government hasn't yet made up its mind."[7]

The delay and uncertainty gave the IAAM an opening to intensify its own campaign to generate public support.[8] In the first three months of 1970, before the government's plans were clarified and legislation was tabled, either the insurance industry or the Agents Association embarked on speeches to various organizations such as service and community groups. They began the distribution of a pamphlet to all Manitoba households, which included a reply card addressed to the IAAM favouring free enterprise in auto insurance. They also pressured municipalities to submit resolutions in opposition to government auto insurance. They began to submit advertisements to newspapers and radio stations, and to participate in radio and talk shows.[9] A process of working with the legislative opposition to prepare an alternative insurance package was also begun. Pamphlets, speeches, and letters to the editor, encouraging people to write or telephone their MLAs, were prepared as rebuttals to NDP statements.[10] Finally they participated in the meeting of insurance agents with their local MLAs and public debates with government representatives.

Adversaries of the government at this time began to redirect their attacks, raising more questions about how the public would be hurt by the enactment of a public auto insurance plan. For instance, questions emerged about potential increases in premium rates to seniors, accident-free drivers, and those engaged in farming. Adversaries argued that all of these rates would climb when a public plan lowered rates for younger and more accident-prone drivers. The no-fault aspect of the plan was attacked as a program designed to assist negligent drivers.

The IAAM printed and distributed by mail 250,000 pamphlets. Bumper stickers and car aerial banners printed with the slogan "Stop Bill 56" (which had only been tabled for first reading) were given out freely. George Tatlock, executive director of the IAAM at the time, indicated in an interview that the total campaign expenditures were probably in the neighbourhood of $250,000. The IAAM had raised about $22,000 from a voluntary contribution of $100 from each its members. This was a lot of money in 1970. It is, however, obvious that most of the campaign costs were borne by the Insurance Bureau of Canada.

A full two-page advertisement carried by both daily Winnipeg papers on 27 April 1970 proclaimed the virtues of the free enterprise system.[11] It expressed fear for Manitoba and its future in the following terms:

(1) Who will be next? Will it be the automobile body shops, drug business, the tractor manufacturers, banks and trust companies, the insurance claim adjusters, the life insurance salesmen, the real estate brokers and their salesmen? The list could go on and with it, the jobs of many taxpaying citizens will go—with an increasing government bureaucracy.

(2) Many firms will quietly relocate to a more hospitable province taking their tax dollars with them.

(3) Why should the Socialist NDP government, who expressed such concern for the South Indian Lake people, suddenly have no concern for the thousands to be affected in every part of Manitoba, especially Portage la Prairie and Wawanesa which may well become bankrupt?

(4) Why should the people of Manitoba be forced to accept a degree of compulsion and dictatorship rejected by other provinces, states and countries? If Manitobans don't stop this now, where will it end?—How secure are you?

The ad then urged Manitobans to write Premier Schreyer and their MLAs to express their views. "This is urgent," screamed the ad, and it stressed its confidence that "We do not believe you want this Province to become a Socialist community." It called for all those who believed in free enterprise to demonstrate their belief by joining the thousands coming from all over Manitoba on April 29 and meeting at 1:30 p.m. on the grounds of the legislative building in Winnipeg. Businesses were urged to close and bring their staff, for they might be next.

Manitoba radio networks also carried a similar message:

Your insurance agent has built his business on service. He values you as a customer. To him you are a real person, not just a license number! Don't turn in your name for a number. What do you do if your butcher gives you poor quality? You change butchers, right. But what will you do if the Manitoba Government takes over car insurance and gives you incomplete, expensive automobile insurance, which doesn't meet your needs? Can you change anything then? No! You'll like it or lump it, because the government doesn't intend to give you any freedom of choice.

At the rally, approximately 7000 to 10,000 people marched on the legislature with signs reading "Pawley's Folly," "Are You Next on Schreyer's List," "In Case of Accident, Call Schreyer," "Kangaroo Court decided Auto Insurance." The demonstrators assembled in close formation in front of the main entrance. There were a few counter-demonstrators, and one protester tried to burn their signs, but for the most part the rally proceeded as anticipated. Premier Schreyer, in speaking to the crowd, warned them that changing conditions often displaced people from their jobs and that this was unfortunate. Two issues confronted the government, he said: Auto insurance must become more effective and cheaper; and the government must develop policies for persons who lose their jobs. He advised them that the government knew something was amiss in the insurance industry, and, as a result, the state had the obligation to supply auto insurance at the lowest possible price, which he calculated to be at least 15 to 20 percent cheaper than the prevailing rates. He hinted that compensation plans could be designed for those who had lost their jobs in the auto insurance industry. He then concluded: "Ultimately, history and the public will decide whether we were right . . . but at the moment, we have no other course to follow but what we think is right."

Constant booing and shouts from the crowd interrupted Premier Schreyer's speech. At one point, he himself interrupted his speech to say, "It's a pity that you won't let me speak. I thought that this protest is what it's all about." The rally organizer, Dick Cooper, then pleaded that the premier be given a chance to finish his speech.

At my own suggestion, I was to play a part at the rally. I advised George Tatlock that I felt it was part of the democratic process that my thoughts be expressed. Tatlock warned me that I wouldn't be allowed to speak, and if I persisted, the microphone would be shut off. It was my intention to create a diversion in the news story to deflect from the news focus intended by our adversaries. As I walked up to the microphone with a deliberately excessive bundle of notes in hand, I was roundly greeted by a chorus of boos which, of course, succeeded, as I knew it would, in preventing me from being heard.

The following day, the media reported that I had been shouted down and that the notes for my intended address contained the following words: "I wish it, however, to be clearly understood by you so that there be no misunderstanding in the days to come, that I am of the conviction that the proposals contained in the report prepared by my committee on auto insurance would be of benefit to a large majority of the people of Manitoba."[12]

That afternoon, the legislative session opened. Clearly the demonstrators had lit a fire under the Progressive Conservative Opposition. They first called for the House to adjourn for a matter of urgent public importance—auto insurance. When the Speaker of the House ruled the motion out of order, pandemonium followed. The public gallery, filled with many of the demonstrators, joined in heckling government members, much to the consternation of the Speaker. Incidentally, as I was making my way down the halls of the legislature, a corporation lawyer from Toronto angrily waved his finger in my face, warning that he was there "to get my job." I had previously been aware

of him in the public gallery painstakingly taking notes of the legislative proceedings.

Bud Sherman, the Progressive Conservative MLA for Fort Garry and
a future vice-chair of the Canadian Radio and Television Commission
(CRTC), rose on a point of grievance as he expressed alarm about the flout-
ing, if not violation, of the due process of legislative freedom. He denounced
the government for discussing the bill at the rally before it was debated in the
House and charged that the young Lochinvar premier either had national political aspirations or was the captive of the left wing of the party.[13] He charged
that this was only the tip of the iceberg. "What comes next?" he demanded.
He claimed his party heard in the "socialist government's bill "the muffled
cadence of marching jackboots," and he warned that this would be followed by
the nationalization of "trust companies, banks, trading exchanges, newspapers,
radio and television stations and stores."

Premier Schreyer indicated quite firmly in the question period that the
auto insurance bill would not be influenced in principle by a public demonstration against the bill's proposals. Both the government and the industry
proclaimed that the rally had been worthwhile from their perspectives. My
observations are that the rally had no impact on the government resolve to
push ahead. The protest constituencies, consisting of residents of Wawanesa
and Portage la Prairie, insurance brokers and executives, and others from the
business community, were overwhelmingly anti-NDP, so the government had
little to lose by rejecting their demands. Among the government's supporters, the rally encouraged greater rather than less determination to follow this
struggle through to a successful conclusion and not to buckle before powerful
corporate pressure.

From the industry's viewpoint, the rally drew the public's attention to the
government's orientation, successfully warning them to be aware of its social-
istic nature, and it made it easier to arouse the business community against the
government. Indeed, the campaign against the proposals, now known as Bill
56, became more impassioned after the rally; it activated people. On the other
hand, the activation and polarization worked both ways, as shown by the fact
that the political middle became less tenable in Manitoba. In four subsequent
elections, the Liberals were never able to elect more than one member per
election, a small fraction of their once powerful following.

Some NDP members feared an early election on the insurance issue, given
the government's precarious position numerically in the legislature; a small

number of our members would have preferred to back off, wishing to avoid the risk. But others would have gladly gone to the people on this issue. The NDP was not inclined to retreat.

Although it was authored by Premier Schreyer, Attorney General Al Mackling, Finance Minister Saul Cherniack, and me, Bill 56 was the work of many hands. Drafting it required long hours and lengthy meetings of caucus, including some on weekends until the early morning hours.

After the April rally, Ed Schreyer and I realized that the debate on auto insurance must not be restricted to the legislative chamber. A public campaign had to be launched to invite public participation and promote our position. The Manitoba Federation of Labour and the NDP began by secretly mapping their strategies to counter the insurance industry's campaign. They encouraged the formation of a group called Citizens for Public Auto Insurance, which included NDP members, labour activists, professional groups, and even ten insurance agents. A campaign was organized to distribute brochures door-to-door, explaining the government's scheme. To muster public support, the issue would be treated very much like an election campaign. Premier Schreyer warned at the group's organizational meeting that it faced a very well-organized opposition. He added, "We will not be pushed around by any kind of highly pressured, highly financed opposition tactics. This is a golden opportunity, if we believe in participatory democracy . . . to persuade our fellow citizens of an issue of considerable importance to people."

The Citizens for Public Auto Insurance organized a non-partisan citizens committee. The intent was to attract people who were not necessarily NDP to support good legislation in the public's interest. Headed by professor of political science Michael Hicks, this group (which had originated at a special meeting of interested persons held in my office) agreed that a strategy was needed to fight the insurance industry.

A call to action was also given to various NDP constituency organizations. In Selkirk, I forwarded a letter to my constituency party members, warning them that the government could be defeated in the House. Ominously, I pointed out that the loss of only one vote there could spell our defeat. It was the first real test the new government had faced.

In retrospect, it is clear that, throughout the debate, there were election hawks and doves within the government caucus. Some wanted to find an incident that could justify the calling of an election. Several others, however, were worried about the downside of a snap election. No doubt the Opposition was just as worried about the possibility of electoral fallout from the insurance debate. But at least they had the support of the media, which speculated that the government plan would not work and that its critics would eventually be proved right.

On Sunday, 3 May 1970, I addressed approximately 150 New Democratic Party activists in the Ukrainian Labour Temple in north Winnipeg, to acquaint them with the upcoming insurance plan. It was the first round of a counter-offensive, part of a strategy for an upcoming canvass in support of the proposals. I spoke of "the first test, the first real test our government has faced." I declared that "to pass it we must become teachers and the province our classroom." The debate had reached such a feverish pitch that police chief Chris Einfeld, of the city of East Kildonan, and four constables were at the meeting to guard against trouble, and traffic barricades were erected to bar access to the street where the meeting hall was located. Burly police officers, dressed in their buffalo coats, escorted me safely to the hall so that I could address the massive crowd. Having received word of threats on my life, I also received a police escort to the city limits after the meeting. I wondered, with some amusement, what would have happened if an attack had taken place just outside the chief's jurisdiction, as I travelled unguarded to my home in Selkirk. I appreciated the chief's concern, yet I couldn't help but wonder whether the city's finest were playing to the daily unfolding drama.

Incidentally, Joe Borowski, the colourful MLA from Thompson, capped events that day by piling coals on the already burning fire, accusing the Winnipeg Chamber of Commerce of acting as streetwalkers for the insurance companies. Borowski, Minister of Highways in Schreyer's first term, was a populist hero in Opposition but by temperament proved unsuitable in a government role. His extreme views on pornography and abortion would persistently result in angry confrontations with his cabinet colleagues, often consuming hours of needless debate in cabinet. Eventually, a public row with his colleagues surfaced over the movies *Joe* and *Last Tango in Paris*, which Borowski considered so obscene that they became pet causes for him. Borowski was eventually to leave the ranks of the NDP government before the end of its first term in office.

At home, Adele received anonymous telephone calls daily. When the Act later came into effect, she kept a rate book handy near the phone so that we could answer potential enquiries about rates charged under the public plan. From the time Bill 56 received first reading in the legislature until it was given

Royal Assent, Adele would receive up to nine of these calls each weekday. A caller would stay on the phone, silent, until she hung up. We were never sure whether these ominous calls were intended to intimidate, and thus weaken my resolve.

The Introduction of Bill 56 for Second Reading

The long-awaited Bill 56 was distributed to the members of the legislature on 6 May 1970. It made clear that the government was planning a universal compulsory scheme in which drivers would be required to carry government-run insurance. Also proposed was a second program to supply additional coverage for motorists wanting more protection than the basic plan. The compulsory scheme would be administered by the Manitoba Public Insurance Corporation. The legislation also provided that the government would later set the rates and classifications through regulation.

The Opposition Leader refused to comment, saying that more time was required to study the complicated scheme. Gordon Johnston, the Liberal House Leader, called for a government meeting with the private auto insurance industry, hoping that an election might be avoided and the Liberals might be able to work out a compromise between industry and government.

Coincidentally, and to our bewilderment, the auto insurance industry did not help its image by making the announcement that rates were being increased. The skillful capitalizing on that announcement by Michael Hicks confirmed the benefit of having a public committee supporting the government position. He pointed out that the average premiums paid by Manitoba auto drivers were 51 percent higher in 1969 than in 1963 and that vehicles and drivers were being reclassified to their detriment.

Walter Weir, who had been slow off the mark in attacking the government's legislation, was attempting to make up for lost time by denouncing the Bill as a blank cheque for dictatorial powers. He assured his supporters that the PCs would fight all the way down the line. Asked if he was prepared to go to the people on the issue, he responded: "I am prepared to go to the people any time the premier wants to. We are going to stand up 22 strong."

The *Winnipeg Tribune*, the bitter foe of government auto insurance, attacked "the pseudo-mystery surrounding the Citizens for Public Auto Insurance Committee." The paper accused me of starting the organization (which was partly true) by my comments urging action to counteract the insurance industry's campaign. It was the beginning of an attempt by the

Opposition to diminish our credibility. If they could succeed in this effort, they would be able to cast doubt on the auto insurance proposals, thus swinging public opinion to their side and enhancing their chances in the event of any early election triggered by the defeat of the government.

Harry Enns, a leading Opposition spokesperson, accused both the government and the Citizens Committee of deceit because canvassers had been sent out with instructions not to introduce themselves as members of the NDP. "It is deception of the rankest order," he shouted in the legislature. The government, he said, was denying that it was socialist and pretending to be nice guys. Reducing this deceit to an easily appreciated conjugal analogy, he said: "When I go to bed at night, I say Good Night, Dear; I am a Progressive Conservative but when he [Howard Pawley] goes to bed, he says, Good Night, Dear, then whispers, I am a Socialist but don't let anyone know."[14]

On 12 May 1970, I introduced the second reading of Bill 56. I did not shy from striking back at the ideological campaign of the Opposition. I pointed out that certain segments in society who had vested interests had always fought every progressive measure, including Medicare, Canada Pension Plan, and hospital insurance. I demonstrated that their predictions of gloom and doom had always proved to be exaggerated. And I reiterated the long, long litany of their dubious claims: political bureaucracy would become rampant if public funds were to be utilized; governments should concern themselves only with coverage for the needy, because creating or sustaining of such coverage for all classes is beyond the power of government; auto insurance should be left to private enterprise, since public coverage would destroy initiative, individual enterprise, ambition, and competition; a premium for comparative idleness would be taken out of the pockets of the laborious and the conscientious; standards would be lowered; there is no confidence in compulsory equalization; requiring people to pay under universal coverage is dangerous; a scheme of individual coverage by the state is socialism.

I showed how the claims advocated by our opponents originated from the debates in the United States in 1830, against tax-supported education for all children. Most of the great public institutions were criticized bitterly when they were first introduced and were called "socialism" as if the word itself was an argument against reform.

I demonstrated to the legislature that the advantages of a public plan included a return of 85 percent of the premiums collected from motorists in claim benefits, representing a savings of one-half of the administrative costs presently incurred under private plans. Earnings from the investments would be used to reduce premiums or to increase benefits. There would be uniformity in coverage and administration for all Manitoba motorists by the creation of one public agency, which would be sensitive to the public needs. I explained that a compulsory auto insurance plan was comparable to a public utility, and that claim service centres throughout the province would facilitate economical and efficient claim-adjusting services. This plan would provide reasonable limits on basic protection for all Manitobans, with the right of motorists to obtain additional supplementary coverage. The Crown corporation could also provide the supplementary insurance on a competitive basis. Moreover, I explained, provincial insurance corporations have every political reason to reduce accidents and claims by insisting on safer driving conditions for their motorists. No discrimination in rates based on age or sex would be assessed to the motorists. Bad drivers would be surcharged additional dollars on their drivers' permits, because that is the fairest way.

On that day, I assured all agents—even those who had vehemently opposed the plan—that they would be given first refusal for all jobs connected with the Crown corporation, and I indicated that there would be some form of compensation to those adversely affected by the institution of the plan. Unfortunately, this early attempt to diminish the opposition of agents failed to ease their concerns, in part because of its lack of specifics and the rather low profile given to the announcement. The major reason for their opposition, however, remained the expectation that the bill, as well as the government, could be defeated and the prospects for public auto insurance in Manitoba killed.

In responding to my introduction of the auto insurance legislation, PC Opposition leader Weir launched an emotional, vigorous, and mainly ideological denunciation of our proposals, describing the bill as the product of a kangaroo court. Weir criticized the bill as giving the government dictatorial powers because the regulatory section of the Act was to be legislated by the cabinet in a secret session, and in his view this wantonly and needlessly converted the insurance scheme into a callous assault on the basic principles of responsible government. He decried the fact that the cabinet would be able to dictate what damages, what losses, what injuries, what deaths, and what risks would be covered in the plan. The bill, he declared, represented an invasion of privacy, a means by which booby traps and mines would prevent access to the benefits. Clearly the strategy pursued by the critics of the auto insurance plan was based on an appeal to an anti-socialist, free enterprise ideology—and, more importantly, was an attempt to arouse public opinion through a fear campaign.

The Desjardins Factor

Only one member spelled the difference between those MLAs lining up on the government side and those in the ranks of the combined opposition. With this almost even division, several difficult decisions confronted the government. Would the bill go to the Law Amendments or the Public Utilities Committee for the usual clause-by-clause study after presentations were received from the public? If it went to the Law Amendments Committee, the government members would lack a majority and the auto insurance legislation could die. The government caucus therefore decided to forward the bill to the Public Utilities Committee, which consisted of twenty-five members with the government having a 13–12 majority. Another perceived advantage of that committee was that the chairperson was Larry Desjardins.

Desjardins was something of a maverick. In the '60s, as a Liberal member, Larry had passionately rejected any policy that appeared even mildly left-wing. The NDP members in the legislature had frequently been the targets of his biting sarcasm. Once, he railed, "they even have a resolution now to put government in the baby-sitting agency, minimum wages, pensions and everything."[15] With the election of the NDP government, however, Desjardins had begun to show some sympathy for the NDP. He had not joined the NDP, and he had repeatedly made it clear that he was a liberal-democrat rather than a social democrat. But he had been attending the NDP caucus meetings. Consequently, Desjardins was bombarded with letters, telephone calls, and telegrams. Personal confrontations occurred constantly.

Another reason for Desjardins' support for the government was his personal friendship with Premier Schreyer. He may have wondered what would occur if this rapport was ruptured (as indeed happened later with Jean Allard, another former Liberal who, although running under the NDP label, later defected from the NDP over sharp policy disagreements).

If there were reasons to think Desjardins would support the bill, there were also reasons to doubt his support. The explosive issue of government aid to schools run by religious organizations was on the legislative agenda. Desjardins, a devout Roman Catholic, made it clear that measures like that were important to him. On the other hand, many NDP members were just as steadfastly opposed to such aid. The outcome of this issue would surely test the government's continued unity.

The PCs recognized not only the government's vulnerability but also Desjardins' sensitivity to his newly formed relationship with the NDP. The agents and the insurance industry were later to exploit this in an effort to shake Desjardins loose from his alliance with his new socialist friends.

At the time, giving the Public Utilities Committee chair to Desjardins was seen as an astute move. Later, it proved not to be. It is true that, as chairperson, he would be unlikely to vote, because his vote would be required only in the event of a tie; yet if his vote was required, Desjardins had already given plenty of signals of his unhappiness with the proposed legislation. Would his newly founded and tentative allegiance to the government survive his fundamental difficulty with legislation that conflicted with his personal principles? Would he promote his own position by forcing concessions from the government?

Larry Desjardins was to cause a great deal of unpredictability as well as melodrama when he entered the debate following my introduction on the second reading. He warned that he would support the plan only if provisions were made for the compensation of agents who were harmed by it. He further stipulated that he would not commit himself to support until he saw the specific details of a compensation plan. (Because Desjardins had earlier acknowledged differences between himself and the NDP caucus, Harry Enns had prophesied that Desjardins would be engaging in soap opera–quality oratory. Desjardins had described those differences as sincere and above board, like those found in a happy family. Enns countered that the liberal democrat was playing a power game and that sooner or later he would be in a position to threaten the government's hold on power. Enns was subsequently to be proven right.)

The debate that raged on second reading was mainly sound and fury, with an overabundance of repetition by all sides of the Assembly. However, three important aspects characterized the debate. First, the Desjardins factor; secondly, the ideological tone of the discussion; and thirdly, the repositioning by both Government and Opposition in the concluding three days of the debate.

Early in the debate, Desjardins warned that the attitude of some of his colleagues was disturbing him, alleging that while they posed as humanitarians, they showed little concern for the agents or for anyone who has made a success of a business. He warned that if the government wanted to stay in power and keep him onside it must be representative of all the people. He concluded that while he would prefer a compulsory, privately owned insurance system, he could nevertheless compromise on this, as it was not an issue of conscience.

Another pivotal vote in the closely divided legislature was that of a former PC, Gordon Beard, now sitting as an Independent, and representing the northern constituency of Churchill. He urged that the government pass all the legislation it had planned for the session except for the auto insurance bill and then take it to the voters in an election. To pass such a wide-ranging bill by a vote of one or two, he cautioned, should not be considered adequate. Another member, Donald Craik, Progressive Conservative member for Riel, called upon the government to break the impasse by holding a referendum.

Ideologically, the PCs attempted to polarize even further an already sharply divided province. The spectre of a future takeover of the life insurance industry was raised in questions to Premier Schreyer. The premier's reply—ruling out life insurance for now, but adding that such a policy might not stand indefinitely—was less than reassuring to the industry.

Backbench government members accused the Opposition of spouting doctrinaire free enterprise philosophy. Wally Johanneson, MLA for St. Matthews, referred them to the words of W.L. Morton and Donald Creighton and George Grant, all Tories of a sort, who had concluded that Canada might have to nationalize all her major industries to retain her national identity in the face of creeping continentalism. Johanneson then facetiously suggested that this government was a mere piker, wishing to establish only one piddling Crown corporation.

On 16 June 1970, Opposition leader Walter Weir introduced an alternative auto insurance proposal. It called for the retention of private ownership in the industry. It advocated compulsory third-party liability and accident benefit coverage, with collision coverage on the insured's vehicle being voluntary. Under this plan, the first $300 of damage to a vehicle in an accident would be covered regardless of fault. A rating review board would look at annual insurance rates, and a preferred good driving rate would be established for young drivers after a period of good driving.

The Government immediately dismissed the Weir plan, which had been developed in close collaboration with the insurance industry. This alternative plan was devised when the Opposition, late in the debate on the second reading, realized that its credibility was weakened because they were seen as excessively negative without having offered anything of a positive nature to counter the public plan. It was an attempt to regain momentum.

During the debate on the second reading, the PC opposition had used the legislative rules skillfully by introducing an amendment urging a six-month delay in considering the bill. This had permitted them to slow the debate to a crawl, and was intended to provide them with the opportunity to gain extra time to build resistance to the Government's legislation. With each MLA permitted to speak again, the expectation was that the combined pressure by the industry and the media, along with the fear of a potential election, might compel the Government to back down or at least compromise.

Speaker Ben Hanuschak was forced to cast a tie-breaking vote, as the motion by the PCs for a six-month delay in second reading went down to defeat. All fifty-six MLAs were in the chamber as the vote was called. Supporting the motion were twenty-two PCs, four Liberals, one Social Credit, and an Independent. Opposed to the motion were twenty-seven New Democrats and Larry Desjardins. The Speaker's tie-breaking vote, the first since the early 1960s, was cast against the motion to delay. Applause broke out both on the Government benches and in the public gallery, in contrast to the reaction there only two months earlier, on the occasion of the protest rally. It was immediately announced that the bill would now move to the legislature's Public Utilities Committee at 9:30 a.m. on the next Friday, and that the committee would take the unusual step of sitting on Saturday with its chair, Desjardins, to hear representations. This committee, unlike the Law Amendments Committee, contained a majority for the Government, as there would be thirteen NDP opposing eight PCs, two Liberals, one Independent, and one Social Credit, for a total of twelve.

The hearings of the Public Utility Committee continued until the end of July. Committee members heard well over 100 briefs, mainly from opponents of the legislation. The agents' association established an efficient system to monitor the proceedings and to ensure that their supporters would appear promptly to present their briefs, regardless of the hour. The sessions commenced on 27 June 1970, in a stuffy committee room in the legislature, in near-record high temperatures. On one occasion, the chair threatened to clear the room and resign after disruptions disturbed the hearings. It was even necessary to recruit three uniformed security officers to keep an eye on the proceedings in an effort to maintain decorum. There was hostility on all sides. Tempers often flared.

In one instance, a disturbance occurred when a pro-Government presenter discovered that his very bad driving record was being passed about among the committee members. Though undoubtedly the industry had been zealous in discrediting the bill's supporters, I was amazed that my own driving record, with several speeding violations, was not also revealed. Indeed, at the very time the opposition and the industry were attacking this unknown citizen presenter, I had an official letter stuffed in my inside suit coat pocket commanding me to appear for an upcoming "Just Cause Hearing" to justify why my own licence ought not to be suspended. I feared my letter would surely hit the front pages. Shortly thereafter, I decided to reveal it myself on an open-line program. I pointed out that drivers like me, with several speeding convictions, would be assessed with a surcharge on their driver's licence. I was pleasantly surprised that my revelation did not create any comment from Opposition members. Politics can be unpredictable! A lesson can be learned here by all politicians: make sure you pre-empt the leaking of any embarrassing news. Better to do this yourself than have it done by your opposition.

In his submission to the committee, Vannan set the tone for the industry in his introductory remarks, branding the legislation a licence to steal being perpetrated on the people of Manitoba. A major industry witness, G.C. Trites, managing director of Wawanesa, said that the board of directors of his company would move its head office to Quebec if the legislation were passed.

Although there were some pro-Government briefs, we decided not to encourage them. We had determined that it would be wise to avoid prolonging the hearings. In this we were only partially effective, as some hostile briefs took anywhere from one to six hours. To attempt to impose a time limit on presentations or close down submissions because they were repetitious was not a viable option in Manitoba because of its populist traditions. As it was, we already faced a constant effort to portray the government as arbitrary and dictatorial. We did not want to add fuel to that fire. Better to wait them out.

While the briefs conveyed different themes, few made constructive proposals for reform. The vast majority pressed for preservation of the status quo. There was little acknowledgment of the grave defects inherent in the industry. In general, members of the industry portrayed themselves as good guys, the champions of free enterprise fighting the evil world of socialists. There were few suggestions for improvement. One brief would attempt an appeal to flattery—e.g., the premier should be a man and withdraw the bill. Another would appeal to sympathy—don't force me to leave the province, or don't cause an economic upheaval. Then there were the religious arguments: the Bible forbids stealing, or the hastily revised and facetiously delivered prayer, "Our government who art in office, socialist be thy name. . . . Give us this day our daily bread and tomorrow take it away from us. Lead us not into democracy but deliver us from the hands of dictatorship." Other briefs described civil servants as "People who occupy space and wait for monthly pay cheques." A constant theme was that the government could not operate an insurance corporation. Although ineffective in persuading government members, such remarks were obviously aimed at, and had the potential to influence, the public in anticipation of an election.

An effort to portray the government's plan as being tantamount to the Nazi extermination program in the Second World War failed to impress the government's four Jewish members. In fact, such extremism, which was so pervasive in the briefs, served to undermine the anti-public insurance case.

The Manitoba Bar Association presented a six-hour brief that threatened the government with legal action if it continued to proceed with the legislation. The Bar warned that the law would be unconstitutional.[16] While all the bluster and threats were to fail, there was one strategy that would succeed, the one that focused on Larry Desjardins, who, as the member entrusted with chairing the crucial committee hearings, was pivotal but highly vulnerable. The message was for Desjardins to look out for his seat.

Some sought to gain his sympathy by comparing the plight of insurance agents to that of Desjardins' former business in the funeral home industry. Would funeral homes be next, they inquired? Others reminded him that he had expressed concern about former premier Duff Roblin's plan to enact compulsory medicare in the province. One agent urged the passage of legislation that would make it illegal for a candidate, once elected, to change ideology or political affiliation. These pleas ultimately succeeded with Desjardins and compelled him later to turn against his own government.

Before the NDP government had completed its deliberations on the premier's proposals for compensation, Desjardins would once again steal the limelight, with a moving speech in which he once more shocked the province. He described the hearings as the legislative system at its worst, a system in which two opposing groups bitterly faced each other with their minds made up, going through a futile exercise and having the gall to do so in the name of democracy. He warned, "If you passed this Bill now, what you have united on culture and language, you will be dividing by class." He denounced the

Resources Minister, Sidney Green, as a frantic fanatic. He criticized the Pawley Committee as being politically biased and conducting improper hearings. He announced that he could not, in good conscience, support a bill implying "Socialism for socialism's sake." [17] Finally, he demanded reconsideration of the legislation and warned that, although he was not unalterably opposed to the government monopoly insurance plan, he would be left with no alternative but to vote against it if there was no reconsideration. A packed public gallery ignored the Speaker's admonition and broke into loud applause, having wrongly interpreted Desjardins to say that he would definitely not vote for the bill.

As I sat through Desjardins' fiery speech, I feared the public auto insurance legislation was doomed and that a provincial election was likely, for without Desjardins' support, there would be no way the auto insurance scheme could muster enough support in the legislature.

Premier Schreyer, who carried the full weight of the government on his shoulders, handled the crisis calmly. At the completion of Desjardins' address, he replied that the speech deserved consideration. He said he was moved by the speech. It had set before him a difficult political course, because without Desjardins' vote, the government would fall, the legislature would be dissolved, and an election would have to be called. The premier indicated that he would take time to ponder the situation. Outside the House, he indicated that he was surprised by Desjardins' action (although he added ambiguously "but not completely").

The agents felt that they had won. In the town of Wawanesa, there were premature shouts of joy and dancing in the streets over the weekend. In the meantime Schreyer held a meeting with Desjardins and Gordon Beard. Beard had announced that he might be able to vote for the legislation under some circumstances.

The following Monday, 3 August 1970, the premier, while attending a premiers' conference on the government-owned ship the *Lord Selkirk*, stated that he did not foresee an early provincial election. He announced that amendments would be introduced to Bill 56 that would deal with the delivery of auto insurance, permitting agents to be involved in selling the compulsory government insurance scheme. He did, however, reconfirm his intention not to allow competition, as that would undermine what the government was trying to achieve. Unfortunately, although the premier had been intending to deliver this announcement prior to Desjardins' ultimatum, it now ran the risk of appearing to be a capitulation to Desjardins' demands. Indeed, government members had foreseen what would occur at the time of the Desjardins address, as they knew that a last-moment effort would be made to achieve a saleable compromise. The Opposition was delirious in its glee that the government had been exposed.

However, in the NDP caucus there was substantial support for an early election, as there was strong support for Bill 56, and only a few voices were advocating its withdrawal or its modification to allow the private sector any increased role. Joe Borowski was one who assumed a hawkish stance: "If they want to force the issue . . . we will be only too happy to oblige them." At one point during a question period in which the Opposition were sharply grilling me, Joe, who was seated next to me, whispered that he would "take the heat off me." Then in answer to questions about some irregularities in his department, he advised that he had fired several departmental employees, laid charges against a contractor, and had a helicopter out looking for a road that was paid for but not found. He alleged that Opposition leader Walter Weir, as the former Minister of Highways, must have known about this and thus should be suspended from the legislature. All hell broke loose in the legislature. Weir angrily tossed the rulebook onto the floor of the legislature and demanded both a retraction and an apology. Joe first refused and then was suspended by the Speaker from the legislative chamber. The following day, however, he reluctantly apologized. Tension was sharply bumped up from what was an already high level. Despite such resistance, there was also sympathy for increased participation by the agents themselves. This was an accommodation caucus could live with.

Vannan demanded a further study that would include fair terms of reference, an unbiased chair, and representatives of the agents and the industry. He proposed that the new task force include no members of previous committees and make no reference to other provincial jurisdictions. He said it was inconceivable that the majority of agents would ever sell insurance for the government. Vannan was obviously motivated by the self-interest of the IBC to continue driving a wedge between the agents and the government. His ultimatums were not intended to be constructive. They were geared to further inflame the atmosphere and possibly to provoke an early election, at which time the industry could heavily finance the PCs. After all, the NDP win in 1969 was seen as an aberration that could easily be reversed by the electorate.

In tandem with Vannan, Weir held a press conference, at which he trembled with tension and condemned the government, denouncing it as a "mud slinging, socialist gang. They must go soon if Manitoba is to be a place where we are proud to work, to invest, to play and to live." On Wednesday, 5 August 1970, Premier Schreyer outlined, in a two-and-one-half-hour address to the legislature, the changes he had proposed, with caucus support. The changes included compensation benefits to agents. Agents desiring to sell insurance would be given a fee of 10 percent for selling the basic government plan, in addition to being able to offer supplementary coverage available from the Manitoba Public Insurance Corporation. Agents who held 25 percent of their insurance portfolio in auto insurance would qualify. It was understood, however, that the public could exercise the option, if they so desired, of acquiring their insurance and licence directly from the government's Motor Vehicle Branches.

While the agents rejected the plan, their president, George Tatlock, did acknowledge that it was a small improvement on the original proposal. Then everyone was shocked by a statement from Sylvan Leipsic, the executive vice-president and general manager of Aronovitch and Leipsic (the largest locally owned insurance brokerage in Winnipeg), a leader in the campaign to stop Bill 56, and a speaker at the April anti-government rally. He announced that while the government plan was hard on the insurance industry, it would be a positive gain to automobile drivers.

Schreyer's speech permitted the government to regain the momentum. There was, however, to be no improvement in the atmosphere in the legislature when the Friday session adjourned early on 7 August 1970, without considering Bill 56. The temperature was high both inside and outside. The scene was one of tension, anger, bared nerves and emotions, outbursts, and political surprises. Gordon Beard privately indicated that he believed the industry had investigated him and some friends to find some issue in their past that could be used to force him to oppose Bill 56.[18]

On 10 August, the legislature moved into Committee of the Whole House for clause-by-clause consideration of the bill. The government announced its intention to introduce amendments, and Larry Desjardins and Gordon Beard voted with the government to defeat Opposition amendments, thereby signalling that both of them were more supportive now that the government was appearing to move on the compensation issue. Gordon Beard said, "I do not feel that at the time it is necessary to have an election . . . [T]ime wasted in fighting an election will bring the Manitoba economy to a halt for almost a year." He did not mention that public automobile insurance was highly popular in his huge northern riding.[19]

On 12 August, I introduced amendments to the Committee of the Whole to establish a transitional assistance board and an advisory board. By evening, Desjardins had announced his intention to support the government bill, and an opposition attempt to send it back to the Public Utilities Committee was defeated in a 28–28 tie vote—with the Speaker, Ben Hanuschak, casting the deciding vote.

In the tense atmosphere of the legislature, the Speaker inadvertently voted against the government, creating a stunned silence.

When the meaning of his action sank in, there were excited cries of "You mean negative!" from the government benches, which were nearly drowned out by the Opposition's desk-thumping. The Speaker apologized to the House and said, "I meant to vote in the negative." Desjardins voted with the government, declaring that he couldn't stomach the thought of going back into the Public Utilities Committee. "I'd like to get the hell out of that committee," he said. "I don't want to go back into that room."

On Thursday morning, 14 August 1970, Bill 56 finally received third and final reading in the Manitoba Legislature, making the province the second in Canada to have a universal, compulsory automobile insurance plan. Royal assent was given the same day. A brand new Crown corporation was born; it would be a lasting legacy for motorists, unquestionably providing them with one of the best public auto insurance programs in Canada. Desjardins continued to cast doubts on the solidity of the government's majority when he suddenly announced his intention to resign his seat at the end of the session. He told a stunned House that his family had received filthy calls and threats. Members from both sides of the House expressed sadness that the business of the legislature could come to this, and they urged Desjardins to continue.

Although Desjardins didn't resign, two by-elections took place the following year, in two opposition ridings that had been vacated—rural St. Rose and urban St. Vital. The NDP won both, strengthening its position in the legislature. These by-election wins were seen as a public endorsement of the Schreyer government's handling of public auto insurance. In Winnipeg, the establishment of one large city (or Unicity) was also a major issue. St. Vital, a suburb, had not been enthusiastic about being included in Winnipeg. Although legislation constituting the public plan had already been enacted, the plan had not been implemented; launching was scheduled for 1 November 1971. Clearly, our triumph in both constituencies was crucial to ensure continued political legitimacy in the period leading up to the plan's inauguration. Although I had canvassed for only an evening or two in St.Vital, I spent at least two weeks campaigning in St. Rose. During this heated campaign I spoke at small meetings in various villages, sometimes accompanied by the candidate Peter Adam; usually we canvassed in whichever cafe or service station people were assembling. A *Toronto Star* news editor wrote that Pawley would "drive his battered Chevy from farm to farm and wade through slush to talk to people who had never met a cabinet minister. He would figure out the insurance rates for everyone's car and show how they were going to save money."[20] Victory was beyond our expectations; but both Jim Walding and Adam won with substantial majorities. The phrase from the song "When the Saints Come Marching In" came true that Election Day, and jubilant New Democrats celebrated late into the night.

Through the difficult and early stages of the building of the corporation, I was appointed by cabinet to assume the responsibility of being the first chair of the first board of directors. This became one of the most meaningful jobs in my political career. I enjoyed every moment of the challenge I was granted, relishing the opportunity to be on the ground floor in the construction of the new Crown corporation.

In the 1973 election, the Schreyer government was re-elected. Like any candidate who canvassed door-to-door in that campaign, I can verify that a substantial reason for the NDP's re-election was the public's clear support for what was then an efficiently operating public automobile insurance scheme.

The battle demonstrates that sometimes the biggest struggles, including those with the most conflict, can in the long term be the most lasting and rewarding politically. Too often, governments, including social democratic ones, retreat rather than fulfilling their commitments to the public. For me, the enactment of public auto insurance would be the primary signature issue influencing my political career in the years ahead.

In its renewal process in the 21st century, the NDP could learn much from this valuable experience on how policymaking, whether in government or opposition, can be strengthened by taking issues directly to the people. Numerous NDP constituency meetings were held to debate the auto insurance plan. For example, Cy Gonick, the MLA for Crescentwood, sponsored a forum that 500 people attended. Present were representatives of the Liberal Party, the Winnipeg Labour Council, Mr. Vannan, and me. The PCs did not attend because they feared the NDP participants would have inside information. Later it became evident that the PCs were reluctant only because they were attempting to formulate, with the help of the insurance industry, an alternative plan to offer to the public.

What was important in the competition for public support was the unusual fact that the government party, more than the opposition, had a plan of action and was able to provide enthusiasm, energy, and a forum to bolster the government in its critical time. The Opposition strategy was to engage in an intense ideological fear campaign, raising the issue of free enterprise versus socialism, with constant references to Cuba, the Soviet Union, and Maoist China; they focused on negative charges and the negative results they assumed would follow a public auto insurance plan. By contrast, the government attempted to deflect the ideological emphasis and direct attention to their proposals, focusing on the positive alternative to private insurance.

CHAPTER 3

A New Role

Attorney General

THE ELECTION OF 1973 was tough and disappointing. Although we were re-elected by a slim majority, we lost two cabinet ministers: Attorney General Al Mackling was defeated in the riding of St. James, as was Health Minister Larry Desjardins in St. Boniface. Both were victims of the intense animosity that lingered in some parts of Winnipeg from the bitter debate over the Unicity legislation, which amalgamated the thirteen municipalities surrounding Winnipeg into one city. The narrow defeat in St. Boniface was later reversed, however, with Desjardins winning a by-election. Together with by-election wins in St. Rose and St. Vital in the spring of 1971, this produced a net gain of two seats. The NDP had a majority.

Our win was achieved despite the actions of the Group for Good Government, a coalition put together by the province's most powerful and influential citizens, with the participation of the Liberal and Progressive Conservative parties. They made sure a single non-NDP candidate would run in certain targeted constituencies. In Selkirk, one of the ridings targeted, the sole opposition candidate was PC John Linney, a well-respected businessman from West St. Paul. Although he was expected to receive the majority of Liberal votes, this turned out not to be the case. I had a distinct advantage in the town of Selkirk, which was the more heavily populated part of the constituency, and many Liberals in the northern part of the riding also voted NDP, giving me a substantial majority.

Although the NDP experienced setbacks, the PCs, led by Sid Spivak, and the Liberals, led by Izzy Asper, had even more reason for unhappiness. At times, the campaign had been bitter. Spivak, a red Tory, urban, and Jewish, had replaced the more conservative, rural, Anglo-Saxon, and Protestant Walter Weir; Spivak was a tough and relentless campaigner.

Representing a right-wing version of the Liberal party, Asper repeated the error of the former leader, Bobby Bend, when he competed with the PCs in 1969 for the province's more right-wing votes. In addition, Asper lost credibility by making exaggerated claims about the purpose of the NDP government's provincial land-lease program, initiated to help young farmers remain on the farmland; Asper warned, though, that an NDP government would embark on a program of nationalizing farmlands. Another advantage we enjoyed was that both Opposition leaders appealed mainly to the well-heeled urban electorate and failed to garner much enthusiasm in rural Manitoba. Neither were the less affluent urban dwellers, including the province's working class, impressed. Without question, Ed Schreyer was far more popular than his opponents. In the final result, Manitoba demonstrated again how progressive and tolerant it is, electing its first Catholic premier and two opposition leaders who were both Jewish.

Until 1973, I had acted as Minister of Municipal Affairs and as minister and chair of both the Manitoba Public Insurance Corporation and the Manitoba Housing Corporation. I relished these responsibilities, especially for the Manitoba Public Insurance Corporation, which put me on the ground floor in launching the newly legislated public auto insurance system. Though controversial, this initiative had been so successful that public satisfaction with it facilitated our re-election. Municipal Affairs, on the other hand, placed me daily in contact with people I was comfortable with, namely the folks on the farms, in the villages and small towns of the province—ironically, areas where the NDP had previously been the least successful politically. Finally, as the Minister of Housing and chair of the Manitoba Housing and Renewal Corporation, I was responsible for all public housing. The NDP considered housing a right, not a privilege, and we had enthusiastically tapped into the plentiful Canada Mortgage and Housing Corporation money available from the federal government to meet the needs of a province expanding (on a per capita basis) more rapidly than any other. Unlike in subsequent decades, the poor had greater access to decent and affordable shelter. My success in these posts would, in the future, assist me in ascending the political ladder.

However, the election results forced a change in my responsibilities. I assumed the role of defeated Attorney General Al Mackling, whose term had been an exemplary one. Mackling enacted progressive legislation, including a human rights code, a comprehensive legal aid system, a law reform commission, and a criminal injuries commission. He also initiated the Consumer

Protection Act and the Landlord and Tenant Act and created the position of Ombudsman for Manitoba. Although my cabinet colleagues Saul Cherniack and Sid Green were also lawyers, I was given responsibility for the administration of justice in Manitoba.

Normally someone else would have assumed responsibility for the politically important Municipal Affairs portfolio. However, several anxious rural municipal people lobbied Premier Schreyer at the last moment, and as a result, I kept it while being relieved of responsibilities for public auto insurance and housing. My connection with the province's reeves and councillors was so strong that, on occasion, Opposition critics of Municipal Affairs would good-naturedly complain in the legislature about the goodwill I received from them. During a debate on 18 May 1976, Lorne Watt, the Progressive Conservative member for Arthur and the Municipal Affairs critic, complained, "I would like to quarrel with the Minister himself, but unfortunately I'm not really in the position to do it because I can't find any of the Reeves or Councillors throughout the municipalities that have any particular disagreement with this particular Minister."[1] I recall at the time some honourable members shouting at him to be careful about what he said.

I combined the dual responsibilities for Municipal Affairs and Attorney General for three years, until Bill Uruski, the popular MLA from the rural Interlake constituency, was assigned the Municipal Affairs portfolio in 1976. In turn, I assumed responsibility for the Liquor Control Commission, a natural responsibility for the Attorney General.

Certainly my term as Attorney General exposed me to the good, the bad, and the ugly in human nature. I had the opportunity to enact legislation which would have a lasting impact on the province—whether reform of the Human rights legislation, the marital property and maintenance reforms, or the introduction of Aboriginal self-policing. Both the high and the low points of those four years gave me indispensable experience and a degree of status that would later help me become the leader of the New Democratic Party, leader of Her Majesty's Loyal Opposition in the legislature, and eventually, the first minister.

I owed much of my success to a strong and well-informed staff. A number of officials could be counted on to provide me with excellent advice. Gordon Pilkey, the Deputy Attorney General, was well respected both within and outside the department. Gil Goodman, later elevated to the Court of Queen's Bench, was always very measured and generous with his assistance.

The career of Murray Sinclair, who began as my executive assistant, has been particularly rewarding to observe. A resident of Selkirk and of Aboriginal descent, Sinclair was always very candid and clever in his advice. His interest in the law gradually increased until, eventually, he decided to attend law school while working with me. He was totally committed to the Aboriginal community and to reforms in the law. He would later be appointed to the provincial court, move up to be the associate Chief Provincial Judge, and then become a Judge of the Court of Queen's Bench and later chair of the Truth and Reconciliation Commission of Canada. Jack Montgomery, known affectionately as "Broadway Jack," was the Director of Criminal Prosecutions. His flamboyant style was fuelled by a great passion for the law and for justice, as well as by his compassion for the victims of crimes. I was fortunate to head a department staffed by such talented individuals, and my success as Attorney General prepared me for what was to follow.

The Office of the Attorney General was unquestionably intriguing and challenging. Each day brought a different problem, and of course, the media loved the juicy news associated with the administration of justice. However, they missed two incidents that caused me some alarm and made me reconsider my future as the province's chief law enforcement officer.

One of these incidents may appear foolish in hindsight. At the time, though, I felt I had been placed in a hypocritical position. Long a proponent of abolishing the appointment of Queen's Counsel, I had tried as Attorney General to persuade cabinet to agree with my view that such appointments represented elitism and political patronage. (I recall receiving annual phone calls from one particular lawyer lobbying for such an appointment, just before the announcements were to be made. My judgment in rejecting his pleas was vindicated years later when he was suspended from the practice of law.)

However, not only was I unsuccessful in my quest to abolish such appointments, I was warned on several occasions that the Attorney General Act required me to hold the title too. On one occasion when I was out of the province on a cabinet day, meeting Princess Margaret and Lord Snowdon in Minneapolis, prior to their visit to Manitoba, the cabinet rushed through an order-in-council honouring me with a Queen's Counsel appointment. When advised of my appointment on my return, I passed a night uncertain how I should respond to it. In the final analysis, pragmatism prevailed over idealism, and I continued as Attorney General with the letters QC added after my name. Years later, I discovered its benefits when I guaranteed the passport application of Professor Bob Krause, of the University of Windsor. My status as an Officer to the Order of Canada, a Privy Councillor, and a former premier was not acceptable—but being a Queen's Counsel was.

The other incident involved the lengthy and bitter Griffin Steel strike in Transcona. Angry picketers repeatedly blocked the entrance to the plant to prevent replacement workers from crossing the picket line. Police were called in to assist the replacement workers, and as Attorney General, I was compelled to lay charges against the offending strikers, despite my sympathy with them. Never before or after did I suffer such intense migraines. For a while I considered resigning my cabinet post on principle. Cabinet colleagues, sensing my reluctance, scolded me for equivocating on what was "after all my responsibility to uphold the law." Despite the pain in doing so, I finally authorized charges and was greatly relieved when the dispute ended and the charges were dropped.

Like the Minister of Finance, the Attorney General can frequently be harmed politically, sometimes irrevocably, during a term in office. An Attorney General has a special constitutional status, unlike that of any other cabinet members. As the chief administrator of the laws in the province, he/she must advise cabinet and ensure that the laws enacted comply with the Constitution. Politics must be kept out of the job. There must be no political influence in the processes of criminal prosecution and civil litigation. This did not trouble me, though. Only in the case of Griffin Steel did I find it difficult to uphold my responsibilities to enforce the law.

I always made sure that the premier and his office were informed of all major developments. Unpleasant surprises—and there are many in this department—would have quickly soured the rapport between our offices. The support of caucus and cabinet is essential to ensuring policy reforms and the supporting legislation, and in retrospect, I believe an advisory committee of caucus members interested in justice matters would have been a good idea. I did ensure there was a constituency in the field that could provide feedback about the department's effectiveness in fulfilling its objectives. One must not allow one's views to become limited to the bureaucratic and political personnel of the legislature.

As Attorney General, my objective was to improve justice for the province's poor, many of whom were receiving mediocre or no legal representation. My own experience practising law in the 1960s, doing pro bono work in the courts in the Interlake region, had shown me families torn apart because of bitter disputes over custody and maintenance. Too frequently, one or other of the parents was severely damaged by the lack of sound legal representation, with tragic long-term harm to their children. Although much was achieved by Al Mackling, with the beginning of Legal Aid and the enhancement of Human Rights protection, a great deal more remained to be accomplished if we were to give all Manitobans equal access to the law.

The Conservative benches often strenuously opposed these efforts. One of the more memorable members of the Progressive Conservative Party I had to deal with during my years as Attorney General was the MLA for Wolseley, Bob Wilson. He was a feisty right-wing populist, a constant critic of the justice system, and regularly on his feet during the debates on the estimates of the Attorney General's department. Critical of what he perceived to be the coddling of the criminals, he would passionately thunder about "the babying of all these people who are less than fit to be on the outside with some of their behaviour and the contempt they have shown for the bloody system and the punishment directed at them." Wilson denounced the liberalism of the '70s, targeting Legal Aid and charging that "because of liberal laws . . . because of Legal Aid—we have got an overflowing court system." He called instead for additional foot soldiers to combat the problems created by this new era. In the 1976 debate on the estimates of the Attorney General, for instance, Wilson demanded that funds be shifted from other departments to mine, to prevent crime.

The Churchill Forest Industries Fiasco

Efforts to extradite Kasser grew from an ugly episode that gripped Manitobans' attention like no other in the 1970s: the Churchill Forest Industries (CFI). Until my assumption of my responsibilities as Attorney General, I had been isolated from this messy issue. During the tenure of the Progressive Conservative government of Duff Roblin, the Department of Industry made a gross miscalculation that was to inflict enormous costs on Manitobans, and the resulting major legal ramifications haunted my term as Attorney General. In the1960s, the Roblin administration was desperate to attract a pulp and paper industry to northern Manitoba to generate jobs; in their opinion, the North had immense potential for development. To assist in this major effort, the government engaged the prestigious Arthur D. Little Company to act as its trusted consultant; the firm coordinated its efforts with the Manitoba Development Corporation (MDC), a Crown corporation that acted as the province's banker in financing investments within Manitoba. In his 1971 book, *Forced Growth*, author Philip Mathias details the extreme measures taken to attract industry to the less affluent provinces of Canada. All of the companies mentioned in Mathias' book[2] gained extravagant concessions from the provincial governments involved, concessions which permitted them to plunder public funds. Due to political opportunism and gullibility, the case of CFI was one of the most appalling examples Mathias describes. Only now, though, with the wisdom of passing decades, can its negative effects be fully gauged.

Great fanfare accompanied the signing of the 1966 agreement between Premier Roblin and Oskar Reiser in Geneva, Switzerland. Back home in Manitoba, the mainstream press and business community effused over the proposed undertaking. The *Financial Post* and other national newspapers followed the Manitoban lead. Premier Roblin's announcement was seen as delivering a major economic "plum" for the province. As excitement and enthusiasm grew throughout the province, only the left-wing monthly journal *Canadian Dimension* and the university student paper the *Manitoban*, with Garry Enns as the editor, dared to ask the tough questions the mainstream media should have been asking. As a result, the public was mainly left in the dark about the details of the transaction. Though it may be hard to believe today, conditions imposed by the investors kept the identity of the financial backers strictly confidential.

By the 1969 election, however, a dark shadow loomed over this project. The political consequences would be severe, undoubtedly contributing to the defeat of Walter Weir's Tory government. While suspicious of the entire CFI affair, Premier-Elect Schreyer remained optimistic that it could still be made to work. Officials with the MDC and the Arthur D. Little firm had convinced the new government that construction was proceeding smoothly. However, that was not the case.

During the three and a half months immediately following the Schreyer government's victory, payouts of over $30 million flowed from the MDC, which administered the loans for the CFI. Regrettably, the MDC officials, charged with protecting the interests of Manitobans, were instead engaged in a series of irregular manoeuvres binding the government to this massive project. The government was left in the dark about these dealings. This may have been, in part, due to the shock felt by the civil service that an NDP government had been elected and an inclination to "end-run" the new government.

Consequently, the money paid by MDC was siphoned off to secret bank accounts in Switzerland and would prove impossible to retrieve when an attempt was made to do so. Sub-contractors were unpaid, and numerous liens were filed against the properties in The Pas. All this eventually left the Schreyer government with no alternative but to assume ownership of the controversial project and attempt to operate it as a Crown corporation. It would continue as a Crown corporation until the late 1980s.

A commission of inquiry, composed of eminent citizens and headed by the former Chief Justice C. Rhodes Smith, was established to investigate what went wrong and to make recommendations to rectify the wrongs inflicted on the province. Eventually this commission criticized all the actors involved in the CFI affair, and it was left to me as Attorney General to seek to recover the monies lost. Lawyers in Winnipeg were appointed to undertake legal action. The commission established that Dr. Kasser, who had clearly been the mastermind behind the whole affair, had taken away $33 million, $26 million of it in excess fees, virtually all tax-free. Kasser resisted our efforts to extradite him to stand trial on criminal charges. To my horror and disgust, the Austrian government informed the governments of Canada and Manitoba that it considered Kasser's actions to be at most a civil fraud, rather than criminal in nature, and it refused pleas for his extradition.

As Attorney General, I rejected initial efforts to settle the province's claims. I was not disposed to settling claims as opposed to pursuing criminal prosecution. It was not until I was premier that I was compelled reluctantly to accept the reality that we had no alternative but to settle the civil claims—at a fraction of the approximate $30 million to which the province was entitled. We were never successful in extraditing Kasser and his associates to Manitoba to stand trial. This whole affair reinforced my firmly held belief that there was one law for the rich and powerful and another for the rest of us.

Human Rights Amendments

Al Mackling had been a leader among Canada's Attorney Generals in pioneering progressive human rights legislation. It was up to me to carry on that tradition. During my term as Attorney General, I put in place a number of amendments to the Human Rights Act. The first was an amendment prohibiting discrimination in employment based on "political belief." My wife, Adele, had suffered such discrimination shortly after our marriage when she had served as secretary of the Winnipeg St. James CCF Association. I

certainly needed no convincing that political belief should be added as a prohibited ground within the Human Rights Act. We also amended the Act to
include prohibition of discrimination on the grounds of disability. A further
amendment was controversial, involving as it did a provision which existed
nowhere else in Canada at the time except for Quebec: it made a mandatory
retirement age grounds for a claim of discrimination. Mel Myers, the energetic and committed chair of the Human Rights Board, and I agreed that
such discrimination was contrary to one's rights.

Another achievement during my term as Attorney General was the establishment of one of Canada's first models of Aboriginal self-government
and of Aboriginal self-policing by the Dakota-Ojibway Tribal Council. I was
personally involved with my department and the Royal Canadian Mounted
Police in creating this model of self-policing by the nation's First People, one
that was designed by the tribal council. My sympathy with Aboriginal people
was further reflected in 1973 when I instructed the department not to lay
charges for violations under the Migratory Birds Convention. In 1978 in the
Catagas decision,[3] Chief Justice of Manitoba Samuel Freedman struck down
our decision not to prosecute, this despite a 1968 Supreme Court holding
that the convention (an international treaty to which Canada was a party)
prevailed over any domestic law. In this instance, although some condemned
it, my stand was appreciated by the Aboriginal people.

The Struggle for Equality

The most important reform instituted during my term as Attorney General
was the passage of the Marital Property Act, providing for the equal division of assets between husband and wife upon the break-up of a marriage.
The legislation grew out of the national indignation at a terrible decision
rendered by the Supreme Court of Canada in 1975.[4] Irene Murdoch, during
her twenty-five years of marriage to Alexander Murdoch, had made contributions that Mr. Justice Laskin described as "extraordinary." Mrs. Murdoch
vaccinated, dehorned, and branded cattle; took them back and forth to the
ranch; mowed, swathed, and raked hay. The money the Murdochs had earned
together went toward the purchase of the ranch, matched by funds from Mrs.
Murdoch's father. Other land had been acquired using money from a bank
account belonging to Mrs. Murdoch.

In 1958, when Mr. Murdoch purchased three quarter-sections of
land and some farm machinery, a purchase financed from the sale of land,

Mrs. Murdoch filed a caveat to protect her interest and refused a demand by Mr. Murdoch in 1968 to vacate it. In the argument and physical altercation that followed, Mrs. Murdoch's jaw was broken and she required hospitalization while it was being rewired. Returning from the hospital, she found herself locked out of the house and her credit cancelled at local businesses. Her only assets were the clothes she wore on her back, and she was saddled with a sizeable medical bill for treatment of the injuries inflicted by her husband. Her young son chose to go with his father. Left with no alternative, Mrs. Murdoch turned to the judicial system for redress. She claimed that she and her husband were equal partners and that Mr. Murdoch was trustee of her one-half interest.

The Court refused to find a partnership relationship between the spouses. The land was in the name of the husband; income taxes had always been filed in his name; no declaration of partnership had ever been filed under the Partnership Act. The trial judge ruled that Mrs. Murdoch's activities were only what would be expected from a wife on the farm, apparently basing his findings on a statement by Mr. Murdoch that his wife's activities around the ranch were "just about what the ordinary wife does." In the Supreme Court decision, Justice Martland, writing for the majority, wrote, "it cannot be said that there was any common intention that the beneficial interest in the property in issue was not to belong solely to the respondent with whom the legal estate was vested." Irene Murdoch's appeal was dismissed with costs. The tragic consequence was that her labours over twenty-five years were not considered to entitle her to share assets jointly accumulated over the period of the marriage.

The Murdoch decision—and a similar decision in the Rathwell case involving a Saskatchewan woman and decided shortly afterwards—seemed to confirm that the legislature needed to intervene to remedy what was clearly an unjust situation. Manitoba women immediately organized in a manner not seen since they had successfully fought to become, in 1916, the first women in Canada to gain the right to vote. Their goal was to develop a strategy that would compel politicians to reform the province's laws and avert the injustices commonly experienced by women in similar situations. Activists in the feminist movement realized that such change would not occur easily. Even with the NDP in government, there were many, including a number of cabinet members, who were either negative or unenthusiastic about supporting any changes in the provincial family law.

The Royal Commission on the Status of Women, which reported to the federal government in 1970, had recommended sweeping changes to family law, but members of Parliament had given short shrift to these proposals. Canadian women soon realized that governments would not implement the commission's proposals without an aggressive campaign.

The Murdoch case, among the leading political issues of the day, proved to be the catalyst. Women from all parties became interested in changing the law. My work within the NDP had convinced me of the organizational power of women, and I realized that they were very capable of effecting change. Once a few women were persuaded of the need for reform, they were successful in inspiring other women and some men to take up their cause.

Activist women who understood the injustices of the current laws formed the Manitoba Action Committee on the Status of Women (MACSW) to work for family law reforms. They were surprised at the resistance they encountered. In one instance, they were refused permission to use an auditorium routinely provided by the Monarch Life Assurance Company for voluntary groups; the insurance company considered the Manitoba group's views too radical. The women also complained about the lack of support from provincial politicians. Before the Murdoch decision, some of our caucus members had vigorously argued with women presenting briefs, insisting that they should not worry about unfair treatment at the hands of the courts. Such intransigence by politicians, many of whom the women had expected to be sympathetic, led MACSW to launch an educational program, its members travelling the province and holding conferences and teach-ins with whatever modest resources were available. During these years, a small core of women provided leadership to the campaign for change.

I realized early on that the issue would be my biggest challenge as the provincial Attorney General. The opposition Conservatives, with their Justice critic, Harry Graham, were likely to be unsympathetic. Many of their members were rural-based, and their views reflected the uneasiness of many farmers who feared their property rights would be jeopardized by liberalization of the province's family laws. Moreover, public awareness of the injustice reflected in the Murdoch decision remained low. Few men or women had paid much attention. Although Nellie McClung and her intrepid band of women had unseated the Sir Rodmond Roblin government in 1915, the subsequent Norris government giving women the right to vote the next year—a Canadian first—Manitoba nevertheless had the reputation of being generally socially conservative.

Recognizing the obstacles that lay ahead, I developed a plan to gradually heighten awareness of the issue. My first move was to refer the matter in 1974 to the Manitoba Law Reform Commission, led by its chair, Frank Muldoon (later a Federal Court judge). In doing so, I was sensitive to the fact that the commission was likely to be sympathetic to reform. Moreover, it was critical that the finest minds in the legal community be compelled to address the need for changes in the law. Finally, this referral would provide an opportunity for women's groups to intensify their lobbying with both the general public and with members of the legislature. The subsequent public hearings that the Law Reform Commission held throughout the province were attended by women presenting briefs in numbers beyond our expectations.

Women activists in the NDP realized that they could not depend solely on those supporting reform in the caucus and cabinet to carry the day. Although they had my ear and that of Saul Cherniack, the highly articulate and respected former finance minister, they knew that others in caucus—perhaps a majority—would need to be won over. Many government members were cool to "messing around" with such a delicate political issue in our second term, so close to our bid for re-election. Some caucus members felt that other issues were more important in our effort to gain a third term in office.

One of the most effective strategies to build caucus support that I have ever seen before or since was developed under the leadership of Muriel Smith (the NDP's past president and future deputy premier in my government), Mary Jo Quarry (the party's newspaper editor), Ruth Pear, Maxine Prystupa, and others. These women knew their target audience, and developed a strategy to reach it. It did not involve noisy, ill-timed confrontation, but rather the systematic organization by individual women of the NDP, who arranged appointments with their MLAs and presented them with carefully developed reasons why the law should be changed. They concentrated strategically on those who were either opposed or unenthusiastic about family law reform. Generally, the women visiting these MLAs had been active in the preceding election campaign within the member's constituency. This plan would prove especially effective where a member had been elected from a marginal constituency and knew that the sacrifice, hard work, and competency of female campaign organizers would be essential to his/her re-election. Women within the party were not content to simply pass resolutions at annual conventions. In addition to lobbying MLAs personally, they flooded the province with pamphlets containing mail-in tear-offs to send MLAs, with pleas for immediate action.

Women's organizations far beyond the NDP grouping flooded the airways and radio call-in shows with calls for action on the issue. They prepared a long list of speakers available to speak to any group that was remotely interested in family law. Critical to their efforts was the need to increase public consciousness of the problem. The Murdoch case provided the raw material for a three-person skit entitled "The Balloon Lady," in which three farm wives—one of them Mrs. Murdoch—were seen chatting over coffee, lamenting the unjust decision of the Supreme Court of Canada. It had awarded a pittance of maintenance for a lifetime spent labouring at every job imaginable on the family farm. In between their outbursts of anger and frustration, the three women (played by June Menzies, Jean Carson, and Muriel Arpin) reviewed the five pieces of legislation, both federal and provincial, that supposedly protected the rights of married women. Finally, each of the pieces of legislation, represented by a balloon, was pricked, preventing the married woman from sailing away. Instead, she ended up a tumbled heap on the ground without her illusory supports and living at subsistence level. The message was clear: a married woman, dependent upon one man's good will, was one step away from welfare. Performed around the province to audiences both rural and urban, the play would become more powerful than many speeches in convincing the public of the necessity of legislation.

By the pre-election session of 1977, an increasing number of NDP caucus members had gradually warmed to the idea of supporting family law reform. Rather than seeing such legislation as an impediment to the government's re-election, an increasing number of New Democrats saw a legislative session highlighted by such reforms as a tonic for an administration that had lost steam and ideas and needed a fresh cause to have any chance of re-election.

It was a proud moment when I finally received approval from caucus and cabinet to push ahead with the legislation. The Manitoba legislature would have the opportunity to show leadership on behalf of all Canadians by correcting the egregious wrongs that had been inflicted by the Murdoch decision. The effective educational campaign by feminist groups had demonstrated that family law reform would be especially popular among women. That gain would offset any political downside. The Tories, a "house divided," would be in trouble on this issue.

The legislation was introduced in the spring of 1977. It would make Manitoba the first province in Canada to provide for the equal and immediate sharing of assets designated as assets acquired during the marriage (except those acquired for commercial, business and investment, or profit-making purposes), upon the separation of a married couple. The sharing of commercial assets was deferred until the marriage was dissolved. The division of family from commercial assets represented a compromise for many women's groups, who wanted immediate sharing of all assets. Other distinctions were also made. The marital home, whether purchased in contemplation of marriage or during the marriage, was to be immediately shared. Certain assets, such as inheritances, damage awards, gifts, or trusts paid to one spouse only, would not be shared.

Some Tories angrily opposed the legislation, accusing us of "meddling in the affairs of families as a socialist government." Frank Johnson, MLA for Sturgeon Creek, protested, "We right here are now starting to legislate how people are going to live and what they're going to do when they're living together, and we don't have that right. Mr. Speaker, when I said we don't have that right, we really don't. We may have the legislative right but this is just straight meddling—meddling—in the house."[5] Although no polls were taken at the time, I had little doubt that Frank Johnson, with his dinosaur-like views, did reflect the feelings of many Manitobans who considered the NDP's actions too intrusive.

As minister, I received considerable feedback, most of it favourable. However, one did not have to travel far to discover animosity. One letter from a farmer's wife in rural Manitoba fiercely attacked the legislation:

> As a rule I believe you make very good decisions; however do not let those women's libbers have 50% of property rights. Shame! Women will never be equal to men, cause when they have children they must stay home to take little Johnny to the dentist or he's sick etc. several days before menstruation they're miserable and bitchy, after a long session of this we have a menopausal bout so no way can a woman do equal work.... Do you mean to tell me women who are driving off to work each day should get equal shares after the husband has made his own meals and helped clean the house? If these pay cheques were being used for farm payments, illnesses etc, I could see the point but the working wife's I know are only putting on a big show, taking holidays in posh places and frittering away time and money.

The writer ended, "I have only two boys and believe me I hope they never marry when I see what the province has to offer. Please do not have a 50–50 split." It was signed with her name and the postscript "happily married for twenty five years."[6] Clearly, opinion was divided along generational lines as well as between urban and rural populations. Among the older generation, it was usual for the husband to have the bank accounts and the property in his name only. The wife would leave all the business decisions to her husband. Among younger people this was less often the norm.[7]

It would be unfair to leave the impression that the opposition was solidly against the reforms. Extensive legislative hearings, one prior to first reading and the other prior to third reading of the bill, revealed deep divisions in the Progressive Conservative ranks, too. Bud Sherman, later the health minister in the Lyon administration, described his experience with the resulting legislation as being one of "the most rewarding experiences of [his] political life." In the final vote, he and several other Winnipeg Conservatives broke ranks with rural and more right-wing colleagues.

The hearings on family law received many briefs and had numerous sittings in a spirit of cooperation. In one submission, well-known Winnipeg lawyer Ken Houston accused the government of proceeding with "undue haste" (despite nearly two years of opportunity for input) and delivered the sharpest criticism of the legislation. Accusing some of the women of "taking cheap shots at judges"[8] and claiming the Murdoch decision had been misquoted and misrepresented, Houston asserted that "if the ladies want equity, if they want justice, the judges haven't let them down."[9]

During the hearings, Saul Cherniack, I, and others spared no effort to expose the fallacies in the representations of those who were presenting briefs against reform. However, Houston would not be without support in my own department. Mysteriously, draft amendments prepared for the Marital Act legislation were leaked to Houston, and he was thus able to comment on them before I had seen them. Moreover, many of the province's largest law firms looked to Houston to articulate their own adamant opposition to the reforms, speculating about difficulties that would be suffered by commercial partnerships with members involved in marital disputes. Of course, we all knew that removing discretion from the purview of the Court would mean less work for lawyers.

Opposition also came from an unexpected source. The Liberal leader, Charles Huband, another lawyer and later a Justice on the Court of Appeal, astonished many Liberal women who supported the legislation; unexpectedly, and without consultation, Huband claimed that the legislation was not necessary because the laws of constructive trust could be applied by the courts in such cases. His statement contradicted the strong endorsement of the legislation given by Lloyd Axworthy, the only Liberal MLA in the House, and left the impression that the Liberals did not know where they were going on this vital piece of reform. Women activists in the Liberal party could not help but wonder where their leader had been hiding during the extensive hearings. His reaction may have destroyed Huband's chance to be seen as more liberal than his right-wing predecessor, Izzy Asper, the now-deceased owner of the CanWest Media conglomerate. Huband failed to make political inroads that were there for the taking. Politically, his stand was to prove disastrous for a Liberal party that had expected to pick up support from the NDP in the approaching election. Voters who were disturbed by the NDP's law reforms, regardless of Huband's stance, turned to the Progressive Conservatives and Sterling Lyon as the most dependable foe of the legislation.

In the committee hearings, women presenters vividly described how they had been affected negatively, often at great human cost, by the antiquated family laws. Their stories had a major impact on the committee members. An articulate and passionate plea by Janet Paxton pointed out that a "man who loves his wife will welcome the opportunity of making her a 50–50 partner."[10] It was Paxton's contention that the legislation would improve, not harm, matrimonial relationships. I will always recall her very personal and heart-wrenching account as one of the more persuasive presentations. Her moving words proved to me that, while listeners may be turned off by abstract and distant submissions, a personal and human delivery encourages those listening to identify with the presenter.

Paxton's principal criticism was levelled at the Family Maintenance legislation, which she felt did not go far enough in curbing the judges' discretion in setting such awards. This contentious legislation amended archaic laws that had made separation and maintenance awards dependent on the conduct of the parties. I saw it as, in many ways, the most important aspect of the reform. All women would be affected. Especially ill-served by the previous law, many women lived in poverty, made subject to the determination of usually upper-class male judges about whether or not they should be granted reasonable maintenance awards. This legislation separated those PC politicians who had supported the Marital Property Act from their female supporters who sought further family law reform. Who says class is not a determinant of attitudes in the development of public policy?

While Liberal MLA Lloyd Axworthy supported the passage of the no-fault Family Maintenance Act, all the Tories voted against it. It had been a surprise to me that the more moderate Tories, who voted for our Marital Property legislation, had been unable to support changes to the Maintenance Act changes. The Tories claimed that they were voting against this legislation because it lacked proper enforcement remedies to deal with defaulting spouses. I acknowledged the validity of the argument, but maintained, "If we are going to travel from point A to point B tonight, distance wise, then both a car and a driver are required. We are improving the car here; we are improving the legislation to-night. Let us also improve the qualifications of the driver that is going to operate that vehicle in the period that lies ahead."[11]

While we successfully enacted the Family Law legislation, it would be jeopardized by the 1977 fall victory of Sterling Lyon's Tories, vehement opponents of the reforms. Premier Lyon put a hold on the legislation, and his government established a committee to review once more the law that the women of Manitoba had worked so hard to enact. Ironically, the committee to review our legislative reforms included their arch-opponent, Ken Houston, who had aroused the ire of the women's groups at the legislative committee stage. In the 1977 fall session, during debate on suspension of the legislation, Premier Lyon was to stumble in a way that would haunt him and the Tories during the balance of their single term in office. Responding to accusations by Len Evans, the member for Brandon East, that he was "anti-women," Lyon retorted, "They say we're anti-women but we Tories are good breeders."[12] In the heat of the debate, Lyon didn't anticipate that his off-hand remarks would become headlines in the Winnipeg newspapers the following day.

In the spring of 1978, despite strenuous resistance from the NDP opposition, the new government permitted unilateral opting-out of the provisions of the Marital Property Act in the first six months after the legislation came into effect. However, the legislation enacted by the NDP remained largely intact, except for those whose spouses took advantage of the newly created opting-out provision. Similarly, while the original legislation called for no-fault maintenance, the PCs altered the maintenance law to permit consideration of fault when a party's actions were clearly repugnant to conduct expected in a marriage relationship. Although this controversial legislation would precede our 1977 election defeat and the victory of Sterling Lyon, it was not one of the major issues in the campaign.

In these times of pervasive disillusionment with the political system, the battle over family law reform shows how a small group of highly motivated individuals can move mountains and compel change. It proves that a government, even in the critical months leading up to a bid for re-election, can be pushed to enact legislation that can really make a difference. It demonstrates the need for careful planning to identify community stakeholders and the importance of coalition-building, the crossing of political lines, and effective communication with the public. I am also proud that we were able to follow the leadership of earlier reforms in the province where Manitoba led the nation and to demonstrate that we were still leading the nation.[13]

CHAPTER 4

Recipe for Success

The Opposition Years

DURING THE SECOND TERM of the Schreyer government, the party membership and the public increasingly felt that we had run out of steam. There were concerns that we were failing to generate another issue, like public auto insurance, in order to rejuvenate the party. After the 1977 election defeat, we found ourselves, with only twenty-three members, back in the role of "The Loyal Opposition." The party rank and file were demoralized and disappointed. Party finances, membership, and organization were decimated by the defeat, and most assumed we would be out of power for at least a decade. All this led to speculation about Ed Schreyer's intentions and his future. Despite mean-spirited attempts by the Tories to discredit him, Ed remained a popular politician and still enjoyed widespread goodwill. His door had always been open, and almost everyone agreed that he was one of those rare individuals who, when granted power, refused to permit the prestige of such a position to go to his head.

Moreover, a general perception existed that Ed Schreyer was the government. He was seen as the strong man with no obvious successors. His charisma had been crucial to our party's success, to the party's membership, and perhaps to Manitobans. Many wished he would remain and undertake the rebuilding of the party. It became clear, however, that he was not comfortable in his role as leader of the Opposition. He was one who preferred to build rather than to tear down—the usual role expected of an opposition leader. He made no secret of his distaste at that role.

The job of Opposition leader did nothing for him. His small, austere offices in Room 250, in the southwest corner of the Manitoba legislature, were hidden away and secluded—his gulag. Many would point out that only the downstairs washroom was further from the action. The quarters were a constant reminder of how far we had tumbled from power. One question dominated our minds: how long would he be exiled there?

The party's most serious problem was the emergence of nasty divisions that, from time to time, would erupt at party committee meetings. Some revolved around disagreements over the provincial NDP government's imposition of the Trudeau government's wage and price controls. This was the aftermath of increasing disillusionment with the provincial NDP on the part of its labour affiliates. Other measures pursued by the party or government had created agitation. For instance, as Attorney General, I was aware that some of our members had early reservations about legislative reforms to the Marital Property Act. On the whole, however, I sensed that most of the tension whirled around personal conflicts rather than policy differences.

Some difficulties grew from the personalities of individuals like House Leader Sid Green and former party presidents Max Hoffard and Murdoch MacKay. They frequently engaged in intense quarrels with party staff, labour leaders, and others. They worried about what they saw as an overly cozy relationship with the labour movement. The pros and cons of anti-scab legislation highlighted this debate.

Our defeat in October 1977, moreover, meant that my political colleagues would re-examine their journeys through life and decide whether they wished to continue in politics or seek a career change. The intense personal interest Ed Schreyer had developed in energy conservation, for instance, fuelled speculation that he might be anxious to pursue a new path to incorporate this worthy pursuit. After my re-election, I returned as an associate to the law firm of Walker, Crystal, and Pandya, the practice that I had established prior to my election in 1969 and then sold when I was named to the Schreyer cabinet in July 1969.

However, I had another interest that continued through the years—in foreign affairs and human rights.

In 1978, this interest had been strengthened when I went to Chile to assist Federico Muñoz, an elderly Chilean refugee from Winnipeg, in the search for his missing son and eight others, some of the thousands who simply disappeared as a result of the Pinochet tyranny.[1] Prior to my departure, on what was unquestionably a bit of a risk, I worried that I might find myself in some difficulties in Chile, and advised the Canadian Foreign Affairs Department and the Chilean Embassy in Ottawa of my intentions. In addition, I made certain that my will and a power of attorney were in order. Elderly constituent

Dick Holland came to my home and begged me to call off my trip. He feared that I might leave Adele and my children without a husband and a father. I was, nonetheless, driven to undertake this mission.

Arriving in Santiago, Chile, Federico Muñoz and I were driven around by a brave young man who could not conceal his nervousness whenever we approached police barricades. He would pop a pill in his mouth, saying, "I live in a nightmare that this will be my last." Throughout my trip, it was clear we were being followed by Pinochet's secret police, and my hotel room was definitely searched.

During my visit, a brave young mother tearfully confided to me, "My husband, an architect and a left-wing opponent of Pinochet, disappeared one morning as he was driving to his professional offices, and neither he nor his car were ever seen again." She added, "My young son keeps asking me each night as he prepares for bed, 'Is Daddy dead? Will I see him again?'" She wept, "I don't know how to answer him. Franco in Spain was more humane: he would line his opponents up and at least shoot them. Their mothers could tell their children that their daddies were dead."

We met with the president of the Supreme Court, José Eyzaguirre. When he learned I was being accompanied by a former dissident Chilean, he tried to exclude the Chilean from the interview and only reluctantly consented to his presence. When it was explained that Federico Muñoz was enquiring about his missing son, President Eyzaguirre spoke at length of what he called the exaggerations and distortions of the "western and Communist press" for its portrayal of conditions under General Pinochet, who was a much-maligned and misunderstood man. As for the missing Chileans, he went on to explain, they were armed terrorists resisting the restoration of law and order by the military. "Those were times of violence," he explained. "This was a national emergency that required the immediate destruction of a Marxist regime that had ruined the Chilean economy." Such rationalizations continued ad infinitum.

Ignoring my statement that the 1973 coup had illegally overthrown a democratically elected government, the president went on to say that in any case, many of the persons missing had gone to other countries or had gone underground. He claimed that it was not the government's business to track down every volunteer exile or malcontent who chose to go into hiding. When Federico Muñoz asked about his missing son, he was referred to the Minister of Justice.

When we later met with Minister of Justice Monica Madariaga Gutierrez, she chose a different tack, saying, "I know that during that terrible time many injustices occurred, that many wrongs must be made right, at least so far is it is possible. But the Government is doing its best to make things right and to heal old wounds." She then said she would personally make every effort to locate the missing nine individuals. She embraced Muñoz, kissing him on the cheek and reassuring him, "Trust in God and me."

When her official letter replying to my concerns arrived, it conspicuously lacked any reference to missing persons in general, or to Federico Muñoz's son in particular, in spite of her promise of a detailed reply. We could only assume that her concern for the missing persons was as insincere as was her kiss. We later learned from an eyewitness report that guards in a prison had killed his son.

I interviewed some of the victims of torture as they were being treated in a downtown Santiago medical clinic that provided psychological help. Some of the unfortunate and brave individuals had their fingernails ripped off; others had electrodes attached to their testicles; and still others had spent weeks suffering from other forms of horrendous and unimaginable punishment. One woman, pregnant and left in a dark room for days, subsequently suffered a miscarriage and became blind.

A priest who had come from the United States confided to me, "After what I have seen here, I have become a Marxist." In the shantytown he worked in, I witnessed long lineups of impoverished women with bowls waiting for soup served by Catholic Church workers. Never have I been as impressed with the work of the Catholic Church, which reflected the liberation theology, as I was in Chile and other parts of Latin America. Even the comings and goings at the Archbishop's residence were documented by police surveillance, I learned on a drive to the residence.

At least 3000 Chileans were kidnapped, summarily killed, or disappeared. A half million Chileans were forced into exile. The mission to Chile left a deep and lasting impression on me, as well as a legacy of anger toward the Nixon regime, which had connived with General Pinochet to overthrow Salvador Allende, the president of a democratically elected government. After my visit, I attended a conference in Madrid, Spain, with a cross-section of the Pinochet regime's opponents. This was the only time during my political career I seriously considered leaving politics and going into the world's humanitarian service. Might I do something for human rights on an international level, I wondered?

Any thoughts I had about a new journey in life, though, were brought to a sudden halt with unexpected developments arising in Manitoba.

An Interim Leader

Ed Schreyer's address to the annual 1978 NDP convention was one of the best I had ever heard him give, increasing my desire that he stay on as Opposition leader. Emotional and extremely articulate, he superbly outlined to the delegates the Manitoba NDP's opposition to the right-wing direction of the newly elected government of Sterling Lyon. It was only weeks after that convention, however, that I was stunned by the bombshell announcement that Prime Minister Trudeau had appointed Ed the new Governor-General of Canada. The announcement astonished the entire nation. Now the party would decide who would take on the leadership and fill the enormous shoes left empty by Ed's departure, a decision that would have personal implications for me. Ron McBryde, MLA for The Pas, telephoned when the announcement was made, urging me to run for the leadership and advising me that I had considerable support in the caucus.

The Manitoba NDP first had to appoint an interim leader to serve until the next party convention in 1979. Some of the party establishment—the party staff and some key executive members—supported the notion of an interim leader who would not be a candidate for the permanent leadership. This was seen as the best method to produce a real race for the leadership, and thus contribute to the rebuilding of the party. Saul Cherniack was the obvious choice for such a position: one of the most powerful and respected cabinet ministers in the Schreyer government, he would be able to block a leadership bid by Sid Green, it was reasoned, serving as a stalking horse and holding the leadership until a clear choice for the leadership became available. Immediately, an angry Sid Green slammed the proposed Cherniack candidacy as a manipulative strategy that focused on the leadership image at the expense of policy development.

My first reaction had been to go along with an interim leadership bid by Cherniack. However, it soon become evident that many caucus members opposed both Green and the party establishment's tactics. Personally, I respected the choice of Cherniack as I believed him to be the most knowledgeable and committed member of the former government. I was also acutely aware of the negative reaction among many in caucus to his assuming the caretaker role. Although impressed by Green's brilliance and oratorical ability, I realized that he would never build a unified party. While some senior party officials expressed support for an interim leader who would not be contesting the leadership at the forthcoming provincial convention, most members in caucus instantly rejected any such ploy. It was incumbent upon caucus to choose the interim leader for recommendation to the party.

Sid Green was the first out of the post in the leadership contest. His entry had been triggered by the party establishment's preference of Saul Cherniack for the interim post. For years there had been unpleasant blood between these two senior cabinet ministers; some speculated that this had originated with Cherniack's refusal to support Sid when he had contested the party leadership against Russ Paulley in 1968, the year before Green ran against Schreyer. At the time, Sid also served as a vice-president of the federal NDP. Many saw him as the most dynamic orator in the legislature, as well as the highest-profile aspirant for the leadership. Sid never shirked his share of cabinet responsibilities, but many saw him as too opinionated and arrogant. His supreme command of the rules and procedures of the legislature served him well. The well-recognized tension between him and the leaders of the Manitoba labour movement was a bonus to several caucus members and others in the party who shared his anxiety about what was perceived as too much labour influence in the party, but a liability to other party members. Green could be trusted to strenuously oppose implementation of any anti-scab law, a measure then prioritized by the leadership of the Manitoba Federation of Labour but opposed by many party members.

I was approached by a number of caucus members asking me to permit my name to stand. Although I had been initially reluctant, I soon realized that, in such tense circumstances, my candidacy might be the best alternative. I was, however, hesitant because like everyone else, I expected the Lyon government would enjoy a second term.

The impression of Sterling Lyon's invincibility had been created when his Progressive Conservatives received the highest popular vote ever captured by any Manitoba party in the twentieth century. Furthermore, no Manitoba government had ever been defeated after only one term in office. Did I wish to spend six or more years on the Opposition benches before having a chance to form the government?

Within caucus, those members who had reservations about either Cherniack or Green preferred me. Some other caucus members were apprehensive about the deepening friction between the so-called Green forces and the Cherniack ones; this endangered the party's prospects for the expected 1981 election. My major reservation about allowing my name to stand as potential leader was fear that I might be saddled with an image as one who would serve only in an interim capacity, and be discounted as the permanent choice for the leadership. Moreover, I was concerned about appearing to be the choice only of the caucus for the leadership. Nevertheless, I decided to go for it because I thought I could better unite the party and put an end to the divisions. Of course, the challenge of seeking the leadership did excite me.

My support tended to be strong among rural and northern party members and in Manitoba's ethnic and cultural communities. When appointed to cabinet in 1969, I was seen as a long shot. My lack of concern for personal appearances would sometimes amuse staff. Sometimes I would become so preoccupied by politics that I would fail to notice my shirt was not tucked in, and either Adele or my staff would need to make sure everything was in place before I made an appearance. On one occasion, at a party fundraising roast attended by several hundred, one my roasters, Murray Sinclair, turned to me on stage and demanded that "the Attorney General take off his shoes and show us holes in his socks." When I did so, there indeed was a hole in my sock; how did he know? Many thought me too bookish and self-deprecating. It was ideas and working with people to achieve them that most moved me. It is true: I hated the electronic ten-second sound bite, but I had never felt comfortable with the news-entertainment format.

Nevertheless, I gradually climbed the rungs of ministerial profile and competence to be considered a leading minister. Among my principal accomplishments were controversial legislative battles including implementing public auto insurance; strengthening the Human Rights Act; legislating a Municipal Planning Act; pioneering the Marital Property and Family Maintenance Acts; and initiating major housing projects for seniors and low-income inhabitants as the minister for the Manitoba Housing and Renewal Corporation. These measures were extremely popular with both the public and the party. My performance as Municipal Affairs Minister had enhanced my standing among rural Manitobans, a constituency normally unsympathetic to the NDP. During the Schreyer terms, my involvement in other contentious issues such as Hydro and MDC had been minimal. Thus any political fallout from them had not rubbed off on me. I was perceived as the boxer who had never been knocked out.

Caucus was the first to express its preference. As we gathered to choose our interim leader, voting procedures required each of us to write down the name of the person we felt should be leader. There were no speeches, and the word "interim" was studiously avoided. Tension mounted as the count was completed and announced: Pawley 10, Green 8, and Cherniack 3. Green was delighted, perhaps because he had achieved his primary objective of handily defeating Cherniack, his chief adversary internally. Green moved that the vote be made unanimous.

Surprisingly, Green's joy about securing five votes more than Cherniack knew no limits. Without waiting for any caucus discussion about how the results should be publicized, he gave notice that he was going to reveal the results to the press. One caucus member (Saul Miller) simply remarked, "He would do what he needed to do." A few days later Sid remarked, "Howard is very capable," and added that "the more he does well the less chance we have for a leadership campaign in the NDP."[2] His comments were a welcome surprise to me, since Sid rarely publicly complimented anyone in the party. They also reflected increasing hesitation on his part about running for the leadership in the fall.

For my part, the caucus vote was a sobering experience. I would have, at most, ten months to consolidate my position as head of the party. This meant not only developing appeal among the membership and public but also increasing the size and role of the party membership—potentially an insurmountable challenge in the aftermath of our 1977 defeat, given the multitude of undercurrents readily visible in the caucus and party. Only by going outside of the legislature and travelling around the province, strengthening the organization of the party, would I be able to affirm my election. The NDP Provincial Council would need to ratify the caucus decision. At the time, I wasn't certain how this body might respond to the caucus vote. I sensed there would be those who would be disappointed that caucus had pre-empted their preference for the appointment of an "interim leader."

I certainly concur with Russell Doern's observations in his book about Green's bitterness toward Cherniack and Miller.[3] However, I believe his loathing of his two cabinet colleagues originated in Green's failed bid to secure their support in 1969, when he ran against Ed Schreyer for the party leadership. It had been evident to most of us in the Schreyer cabinet and the caucus that those wounds had never healed, and perhaps had deepened, menacing the party's unity. An explanation for the apparent support for my leadership was that I was widely seen as a consensus builder, one who might bridge the gulf that was dividing the party.

My reputation was to pay dividends in another respect. In contrast to the eloquent and effective legislative debater Premier Sterling Lyon, I was perceived as a good listener, more interested in eliciting the views of others. Lyon was seen as elitist and somewhat arrogant. Frequently, leadership contests, both within and between parties, seem to involve sharp personality contrasts between the principal actors. One might recall the contrast between the evangelical oratory of John Diefenbaker and the quiet diplomatic style of Lester Pearson. Mulroney and Trudeau, Paul Martin and Jean Chrétien are also studies in contrasts. While these examples are all drawn from Canada's House of Commons and federal politics, the pattern of such contrasts does appear to be part of the political system, evident at the provincial level as well.

The day following the caucus vote, we assembled the Provincial Council, the eighty-five-member body responsible for ratifying the previous day's caucus decision. It came as a surprise to me that the party with all its diverse personalities and perspectives enthusiastically endorsed my election as the interim leader. Green was one of the first to announce his endorsement. Most felt that I was the correct choice to assume the interim leadership and ease the divisions threatening the party. Others probably strategized that I would stumble and free the way for a run by their favoured candidate, whoever he or she might be. The leadership convention was set for 2 to 4 November 1979, in the Winnipeg Convention Centre. Many of the party members left the Provincial Council ratification fearing the party would be incapable of generating the enthusiasm essential for renewal and electoral recovery.

Running for Party Leader

Although I naively believed we would all be ready to pull together as members of one team, it wasn't clear sailing in the 1979 legislative session. I made an early error in judgment. Rather than select as Deputy Leader somebody who would be more acceptable to Sid Green and his supporters, I chose Saul Cherniack. This aggravated the internal tension that lingered in the caucus. Green continued as House Leader, but I soon realized the extent of the continuing jealousy. Once an argument arose over who would lead off in question period during my absence, and I sensed that Green was not happy when I decided that Cherniack as Deputy Leader would fill in for me. He was also displeased by my friendship with caucus colleagues Jay Cowan, Len

Evans, Ron McBryde, and others whom he considered too cozy with both the labour and the feminist movements. I preferred to deal with all the caucus members on an equal and amicable basis, but this was not a practice that led to Sid's good favour.

In the interval between my election as interim leader and the leadership convention, a number of factors contributed to consolidating my position. Some were fortuitous, including the by-election victory of Vic Schroeder in the provincial riding of Rossmere, a riding previously represented by Ed Schreyer. Schroeder's win, in what was seen as a marginal riding, gave the party an enormous boost in confidence, demonstrating that an election victory could be achieved without Schreyer as leader. And despite gains in 1979 throughout Canada by Joe Clark and the Tories, the addition of three NDP MPs from Manitoba added to the sense of our emerging momentum.

I invited these newly elected federal parliamentarians to the legislature: a sense of pride overwhelmed me as I rose to introduce them. An obviously uneasy Premier Lyon, along with other members of his caucus, grudgingly greeted the new MPs. The event sent the message that although the Tories and Joe Clark had made gains nationally, it was the NDP that had gained in Manitoba.

Much of this could be attributed to an early backlash against the Lyon government. It was becoming increasingly apparent during 1979 that Lyon and his administration were pursuing an extreme ideological direction. Polarization was deepening on the political scene. The Lyon government represented the economic and social elite of the province, and appeared to have less in common with most Manitobans all the time. This only served to benefit the political left. The former Schreyer government now looked pretty good to some of those who had voted the NDP out. Maybe this time it would not take the traditional two terms to boot the incumbent government from office.

Cautious optimism developed in party ranks when the results of a province-wide survey by the *Winnipeg Tribune* revealed a 6 percent drop in public support for the Tories since 1977 and confirmed "dissatisfaction with the economic performance of the Lyon government."[4] However, Lyon detected some positive aspects in the results. He pointed out that a party in power is bound to lose support at the midway point of its term, and noted that the Tories hadn't slipped behind the NDP. To him, that was encouraging.

It also helped that the more optimistic public mood made it easier to build the party. During the Schreyer era, the party had not developed organizationally, relying perhaps too much on the magic of the leader's appeal. My experience with the CCF and the NDP had persuaded me of the importance of a large and active membership if we were to regain power. Recruitment became my primary objective in the months leading to the convention, as it did in the period before the election in 1981. There remained other obvious leadership contenders, first among them Sid Green. However, during his term as a principal spokesman for the government, Green alienated many key segments of the party. In debate, his style sometimes got the better of him, and he would take his arguments to excesses.

Sam Uskiw was another potential contender. At one time, Sam and I had been good friends, sharing as we did a pro-active stance on agricultural and rural issues. Sam became increasingly sympathetic to arguments about labour's becoming too powerful within the party. Two other potential contenders—affable and popular Bill Uruski and Willie Parasiuk, recently elected and a former Rhodes Scholar—never declared. Without doubt, the candidacy of either of them would have made it a closer race for me.

I was pleasantly surprised at how little hostility there was to my candidacy from the labour hierarchy. In the early seventies, I had run afoul of the United Steelworkers at a national leadership convention. I supported Ed Broadbent on the first ballot, but when he was eliminated, I switched my support half-heartedly to James Laxer, who was associated with the Waffle, the party's left wing. A senior United Steelworker union officer confronted me about my wearing a pin that indicated my endorsement of Laxer rather than David Lewis, the leadership candidate preferred by the United Steelworkers. He starkly warned, "I will discuss this with your Steelworker Local in Selkirk." Amazed by such intimidation, I immediately made my local Steelworker delegates aware of this incident; they laughed it off and that was the last I heard of it.

It was no secret within the party that I had long distrusted labour's exercise of official slates to thrust its favourites into executive positions. These slates, put together by the labour establishment, proposed certain handpicked candidates for party office. It seemed to me that this made it much harder for those outside the inner circle to make the cut. A few years earlier, the ingenious and youthful Michael Decter (later to become Cabinet Clerk and then chair of the National Health Council) circulated his own anti-establishment slate to convention delegates. It was the same colour and size as the paper bearing the names of the official slate. What a scene Michael's clever move would generate! As a long-time foe of party officialdom, I was delighted.

Thus, it was not surprising that I experienced some pangs of discomfort when Dick Martin, head of the Manitoba Federation of Labour, cautiously approached me in the period leading to the leadership convention and inquired, perhaps tongue-in-cheek, "Howard, we would like to include you on our slate as party leader. We know how you hate slates; do we have your permission?" "That will be OK," I reluctantly agreed.

The first to enter the race was a former party president, Muriel Smith. Muriel enjoyed significant support in South Winnipeg. Many women activists and others associated with the left of the party identified with her. To her credit, she set out the most detailed and substantive program for a future NDP government, a program that demonstrated a coherent understanding of the economic and social challenges facing us. However, the fact that Muriel was not a sitting MLA proved a major obstacle to her campaign.

A later entrant in the race was the veteran MLA for Elmwood, Russ Doern. Russ, a public works minister in the Schreyer government, was an articulate debater in the legislature and had held many party posts. Seen as being closer to the party's right wing, he was, however, not a credible candidate. His judgment on many occasions had not been seen as sound, and one event would overshadow whatever positive accomplishments he had achieved. During his term as Minister of Government Services, he had infuriated populist Steve Juba, the mayor of Winnipeg, by constructing restrooms in Memorial Park. Many resented the location of those restrooms, in the park just opposite the legislature. This issue so provoked the mayor that he appeared at the legislature and attempted to speak from the visitors' lounge reserved for former members, of whom he was one. He was accompanied by a media contingent, which dutifully recorded his display of temper directed at Russ Doern. Doern's support tended to be concentrated around his own constituency of Elmwood and among those in the party who may have considered him to be the best bet to block my candidacy. Neither Green nor Uskiw contested the leadership when they discovered too little support to give either of them a fighting chance.

The three remaining leadership contestants participated in approximately a dozen debates throughout the province. In general, these were good-spirited, and we frequently travelled together in the same vehicle. My best showings were in the rural areas, where my support was overwhelming. On one occasion, however, I got into trouble with Muriel Smith when I related a story that I found funny but she did not. I explained how as a young boy I had become curious about what went on behind the high fence surrounding the barn on our family farm, where the bull serviced the neighbour's cows. To the audience, I confided, "When I peered through a crack in the fence I observed what Sterling Lyon is now doing to the people of Manitoba." Although the audience was delighted, Muriel was not amused and pointed her finger at me; she condemned me for using sexist humour. In the future, I steered clear of repeating that story.

The convention began on Friday night, 2 November, with a leadership bear pit session; it provided an opportunity for the three of us to answer questions from the delegates. Modest policy differences were evident. Many of the delegates' questions appeared to be aimed at the role of caucus members. Smith warned that there was no place for "protecting incumbent MLAs in their constituencies." Doern complained that some of Lyon's cabinet ministers were receiving a free ride from Opposition caucus critics. I warned the delegates against "too much pessimism and cynicism." I also warned that incumbent MLAs—from the leader down—should never take their renominations for granted. A widespread view prevailed within the party that some incumbents were not pulling their weight and that members wanted them to become more involved.

On Friday night, the Smith followers appeared to be in the majority, but with over 800 delegates arriving by Sunday, the day for electing a new leader, much could change, and the tide was turning in my favour. The only doubt my key supporters and I shared was the size of the majority that I would eventually obtain. My nomination was moved by Vic Schroeder, Ed Schreyer's successor in Rossmere and immediate past president of the party, and seconded by Maude Lelond, a rural farm delegate from Elkhorn and a widely respected party pioneer. At 1:00 p.m. the balloting started, and by 2:00 p.m. the count was announced: Pawley had 467, Smith 217, and Doern 53. The results were posted on a giant scoreboard and enthusiastic applause erupted. An animated Bob Mayer, the convention chair, grasped the microphone and declared, "Howard Pawley, the winner and the next premier of Canada...er... premier of Manitoba!"

Asking my two competitors to come forward, I paid an emotional tribute to their contribution to the leadership campaign. I then delivered my acceptance speech with a call for the party membership to meet the challenges of building the party, confronting the power of the social and economic elite, and restoring democratic socialism to power in Manitoba. Adele and our two

Chosen for Best-Looking Baby at the Cooksville
Fair in Ontario, for 1935 and 1936.

Parents T. Russell and Velma (née Medill) Pawley, 1928.

Howard and Adele on their wedding day, 26 November 1960.

With George Stubbs, swearing oath for barrister and solicitor, January 1962.

Selkirk-Interlake constituency event during the 1965 provincial election. Candidate Howard Pawley, NDP leader Tommy Douglas, and campaign worker Eugene Laye.

Leaving Selkirk Hospital during the 1969 provincial election campaign.

Anti-Autopac protestors at the Manitoba legislature. Despite intense industry opposition, public auto insurance became a reality in Manitoba in 1971.

Speaking with a constituent in front of Selkirk constituency
office in the early 1970s.

At the opening of the first Manitoba Public Insurance Corporation Claims Centre in Winnipeg, with J.O. Dutton, general manager, 1972.

Addressing a group of protestors calling for long-term funding for the Osborne House Women's Centre, Manitoba legislature, 11 March 1979.

Howard Pawley, with his wife Adele, celebrating victory after winning the NDP leadership in 1979.

children had not hesitated in their support of my climb to the leadership, and they were with me on the platform. Also acknowledging the applause were my parents, who were introduced to the delegates.

As a party we were now entering a new era. The Schreyer government was behind us. With their usual cynicism, the media by and large missed the significance of this turning point and its relevance to the upcoming election. Some columnists were kind-hearted in a way that may have been intended to damn me with faint praise. Columnist Frances Russell wrote: "Mr. Pawley was so low key, in fact, that many of his most telling denunciations came through almost apologetically. . . . The 44 year old Selkirk lawyer is considered by some to lack the toughness and the instinct for the political jugular necessary for successful political leadership." Alice Krueger, a *Winnipeg Free Press* reporter, warned: "decency, honesty and compassion—all are recognized as admirable human qualities, but they don't necessarily make a good opposition leader. In short Pawley may be too nice for the job." Arlene Billinkoff, the *Free Press* legislative columnist, said, "Despite his assertion that he would be more aggressive, he continued a moderate, quiet-spoken approach while the more attention-getting and penetrating opposition comments were heard from seatmates."[5] Bob Preston from the CBC grilled me about whether I had a reputation for being too honest, while still others wondered whether I would be exciting enough.

What the commentators succeeded in doing was to underestimate me. That would prove to be an advantage in the years to come. Indeed, some NDP delegates worried that I was not sufficiently like Sterling Lyon and that, unless I toughened up, my term would be limited to one year. The implication was that, while some delegates were griping about Lyon's personality, they preferred a leader like him. However, a vast majority of delegates were searching for a contrast with Lyon rather than a politician with the same style.

Several other issues deeply divided the convention delegates. As usual, abortion topped the list of divisive issues. The Wolseley and Crecentwood riding associations proposed the establishment of facilities to meet "the need for comprehensive and preventative reproductive health services." They mentioned the rise in teenage pregnancies and the doubling of venereal disease, and pointed out that in 1978, 1200 women had to leave the province to get safe therapeutic abortions. The newly emerging women's movement firmly championed this resolution. However, the opposing side was well represented. Magnus Eliason pointed out that abortion was an emotional issue the Tories wouldn't touch with "a ten-foot pole." Larry Desjardins, who had been the health minister in the Schreyer government, warned that a pro-choice policy would compel him to renounce his church in order to remain in the party. Compromise was finally reached by a resolution committing the party to support only such facilities as offered "legally acceptable treatment."

Besides abortion, a resolution endorsing anti-scab legislation caused discord. On the convention floor, Sid Green led the Opposition to a resolution calling for a ban on the use of replacement workers in the event of either a strike or lockout; he was delighted when over one-third of the delegates supported his argument against such legislation. However, the resolution was passed. The issue evoked memories of many strikes during the Schreyer years that were either broken or prolonged by strike-breakers.

Troubles Surface

High on the party agenda at the convention was the need to improve party finances. In August, just prior to the leadership convention, the party had been confronted with a mammoth $275,000 debt and had failed to meet its staff payroll. This, along with lagging memberships and continued internal strife, preoccupied the party in the months leading up to the leadership and policy convention.

This strife had become public with the departure of former party president Frank Syms, who had served as the rather controversial chief of the Liquor Control Commission during the Schreyer years. Following his defeat in the Winnipeg mayoralty campaign by Bill Norrie, Syms alleged that the party had been taken over by radicals and communist sympathizers. His anger was fuelled by the fact that several high-profile New Democrats had given their support to Joe Zuken, the veteran and widely respected Communist Party city councillor. Although he was also defeated, he drew considerably more votes than Syms.

Frank Syms disclosed to well-known CJOB radio talk show host Peter Warren that he was terminating his membership in the New Democratic Party. He gave two reasons for his decision. First, he alleged that the "Manitoba New Democratic Party machinery is rife with apologists for Communism and Communists." He complained that in the recent mayoralty election "many high profile New Democrats . . . found it more ideologically compatible to support a member of the Communist Party for mayor than to support Social Democrat or a small 'L' liberal mayoralty candidate." He griped about "too many high profile New Democrats who find nothing good in our system but who entertained no criticism of Communism." His second reason was a protest at what he described as "the takeover of the Manitoba New Democratic Party machinery by a coalition of militant, radical groups and individuals. They include the more militant supporters of the status of women advocates, anarchists, revolutionary workers, party adherents and sympathizers, Trotskyites, etc. whose narrow priorities are their priorities in their NDP activities." These individuals "will be among the candidates in the next provincial election and/or will fill positions of importance should the NDP assume power again."[6] Most Manitobans dismissed Syms' allegations as sour grapes after the severe trouncing he had received in his mayoralty campaign. Nevertheless, Syms' departure was evidence of continuing intra-party strains, which were about to become even more stretched.

Within weeks of the leadership convention, Sid Green lost his position as the Manitoba vice-president of the federal NDP. He was defeated twenty-seven to nine in the Manitoba party caucus vote at the convention in Toronto. Ironically, I cast one of the nine votes in his favour, at the time considering his intellectual input valuable for the federal party. During the meeting of Manitoba delegates, I was sitting near Sid when his defeat was announced. Obviously shaken, he unwisely requested the vote tally, and when it was announced, his face turned white, visible evidence of his resentment at the party's rejection.

Within days, Green declared his resignation as a New Democrat Party member and notified the legislature that he would henceforth sit as an independent New Democrat. He blamed his departure on a group of trade unionists who had hounded him and tried to stifle his influence in the party. Sid felt labour groups had put a price on his head. He thought if he did not run for the leadership, labour would have been satisfied. Instead, in his view the situation only got worse when the same people succeeded in replacing him as a national vice-president.

In Green's memoirs, he appears to blame his departure on several individuals, including Jay Cowan, whom he fingers as lobbying delegates to vote for his competitor, newly elected MP Rod Murphy. Sid does not acknowledge in his memoirs that his style of representation had wearied many delegates, and not just those from so-called labour, including feminist sectors of the party. Green omits mentioning that much of the hostility directed at him had originated in the North, especially from our Aboriginal supporters who had steadily become more disillusioned with Green's antagonism to their anxiety about the level of flooding at South Indian Lake due to hydro construction. Not surprisingly, Green singled out MFL president Dick Martin and Steelworker members Len Stevens and Wilf Hudson for his sharpest attacks. (It was ironic, however, that Stevens was blamed, because ten years previously he had nominated Green when he ran against Ed Schreyer for the leadership.)

I was appalled that Green lacked the courtesy to forewarn our caucus about his intentions. He had served for twelve years in caucus and had enjoyed significant support for the party's interim leadership. Needless to say, most if not all of the caucus members felt that this was an ambush.

Some members, however, did share Green's concerns: Sam Uskiw warned us to watch out for the size of the MFL bloc in the NDP and went public with his criticism of the party's direction during an address to New Democrats in Roblin; his comments, published in the Roblin paper, were gleefully quoted by Wally McKenzie, Progressive Conservative member for that riding.[7] Russ Doern urged that an effort be immediately undertaken to repair the rift between Green and the party. Larry Desjardins proposed that an effort be made, "over a cup of coffee, to heal the wounds." (This was rather ironic, given the level of hostility between Green and Desjardins, and given the fact that Desjardins was in the NDP doghouse at the time for having supported the Liberals in the 1979 federal election.) Several other members complained that some from the labour movement had threatened to challenge Green's re-nomination at the Inkster nomination meeting, expected sometime in 1980. However, Wilson Parasiuk more accurately reflected the mood of MLAs when he "attributed the move to a bruised ego." For my part, I considered the resignation final on Green's part, and I had no intention of attempting to woo him back. Although I admired his intellect, I had in the past been dismayed by Green's behaving as though he were superior to everyone else. For instance, I still recall one occasion when I was meeting with Premier Schreyer on what was a matter of considerable importance to me, when Green barged into the office and immediately monopolized the discussion about his particular issue. He appeared unaware that his rude interruption of my meeting might warrant an apology on his part.

Interestingly, Green decided to break ranks at the same time that the Tory-appointed Burns Commission, composed of insurance and corporate members, recommended that the government transform public auto insurance, our proudest achievement during the Schreyer government term, into a Mutual Insurance Company. Only a few days before the Manitoba Motor League had released a poll showing that 66 percent of Manitobans favoured leaving the Autopac monopoly intact. Only 12.7 percent wanted unrestricted competition from private companies.[8] The upshot was that Green's resignation was overshadowed by this controversial report, which received top front-page coverage while Green's resignation surprisingly garnered a mere two-column headline.

That Green's exodus coincided with the release of the Burns report was politically fortuitous for us. Not only was his resignation overshadowed, but more importantly, the threat to the public insurance corporation had given the New Democrats a new cause to rally around. With the whole-hearted support of our party activists, we explicitly warned the Tories that if they adopted the recommendations of the Burns report, we would, when re-elected, return auto insurance to the public realm. The "highway to Toronto's Bay Street also leads back to Manitoba," I shouted. Neither the Lyon government, nor any potential insurance investors who might wish to return to do business in the province, could misinterpret the local risk they would face. It didn't take long for the Progressive Conservative government, recognizing the political danger of fiddling with the system, to back off this issue. This victory boosted the morale of party activists at a critical time.

There were some advantages to Green's departure. Team play replaced the constant bickering that had plagued party decision making. It was much easier to pursue a positive and focused plan of action, leading to our eventual success in the 1981 election. Moreover, Lyon made the serious error of assuming that the NDP had been irreparably harmed. In the legislature, he gloated about the apparent division in our ranks, joking about "two kissing socialist cousins" now seated. Even the seating the Tories arranged—with Green continuing to occupy a front seat on the opposition side—was designed to highlight the division. This led to overconfidence on the part of the PCs.

A senior Progressive Conservative member for Lakeside and fiery orator, Harry Enns, declared confidentially, "You are not to have the capable mind and eloquent debating style of the Honourable member for Inkster on your side.... It has a certain soothing reassurances for us too, to be assembled again; to be able to look at our enemy at close quarters and see the difficulties that they are in, and that gives us a great deal of encouragement to carry on knowing that we have to do so responsibly because we will be the next government for the next four or five years." This member, who was also the House Leader and a legislative veteran, predicted, "the truth of the matter is that they have conceded the next election to us."[9]

Perhaps the most serious charge, and potentially the most damaging, was one levelled by Warner Jorgenson, the Minister of Corporate and Consumer Affairs and Member for Morris, who condemned my participation in the Throne Speech by craftily associating me with the prime minister, then decidedly unpopular in western Canada: "I am going to offer my most severe criticism of the Leader of the Opposition because I am going to say that it reminded me so much of a Trudeau Liberal. That in my opinion is the worst condemnation that I can make of anyone in this Chamber."[10]

However, this continuous abuse from government members during the final year of our term in opposition only bolstered my confidence. I was reminded of a story Tommy Douglas would often tell: "When you throw a stone into a pack of dogs and you hear some barking, then you know that indeed you have managed to strike your target." The ferocity and persistence of their attacks hardened my resolve to prove them dead wrong.

However, policy differences within the Opposition continued and presented problems as we geared up to fight the next election. Ben Hanuschak, the MLA for Burrows, rose in the legislature on 26 February 1981 to announce his resignation. Bud Boyce also resigned. His defection was especially sad to me as he, unlike Green and Hanuschak, paid me the courtesy of personally forewarning me about his intentions. These three former Schreyer cabinet ministers established the Progressive Party, a development widely seen as being highly destructive to a unified opposition to the Lyon administration.

It was not long before Jim Walding, as NDP Hydro critic, had difficulty living with the party's policy decision to support the export of hydro power, as opposed to limiting its production for domestic use as provided for in the Manitoba Hydro Act. Even after the caucus reaffirmed the party's policy, Walding persisted with his complaints and frequently expressed his dissatisfaction with this aspect of the party's policy. His alienation continued to intensify until, later in the 1980s, it reached the point of no return. It was evident that he had felt progressively more isolated with the departures of Sid Green, Ben Hanuschak, and Bud Boyce. Their departures were a psychological blow to some members of the party and caucus.

The Road to the Premiership and Government

I had to concern myself with the road that lay ahead. How could we turn the party's fortunes around? Too many within the party were half-hearted, rather than fully committed to winning the next election. Many saw the party as tired and indecisive about whether it wished to form the next government. If we were to succeed in the next election, it was essential to convey not only the impression but also the reality of "new blood and new ideas." But I soon realized that a return to governing Manitoba would not result from image polishing. It would only be secured by strengthening the will of the party's membership—not an easy task.

It would have been a serious mistake to underestimate Premier Sterling Lyon, a spirited Conservative, eloquent, and extremely effective in the House. His major weakness was his inability to avoid pomposity and rhetorical excesses. In the 1980 Throne Speech debate, for instance, he provoked much commotion when he charged that "the NDP had forgotten they were in the legislature to help the public interest,"[11] and added, with his usual red-baiting style, "They are not here as advocates of Karl Marx or Engels." Lyon went on: "someone said that socialism is a disease. It's not a political philosophy. It's a disease and it tends to spread. And my honourable friends, I suppose[,] are luxuriating in the fact that they have maybe implanted some of these cells in the corporate body of Manitoba and they hope that they're going to spread . . . my honourable friends opposite haven't made up their minds yet whether they want to be purer Marxists and destroy the system or whether they want to be reasonable people." He even claimed that his government had to clean up a "rat infested nest" left by the NDP.

According to columnist Frances Russell of the *Free Press*, the Lyon government had taken to power "like a whirlpool, implementing its election promises in all directions at once. Civil servants were dismissed, a hiring freeze imposed, a task force on government organization and economy was appointed . . . Controversial though many of those measures were, the Tories knew where they were going and went with all due speed and decisiveness."[12]

The Conservative path at that time represented the dominant temper in North America. To many, newly elected President Reagan of the United States and Great Britain's Margaret Thatcher were seen as representing the future. In Manitoba, Prime Minister Trudeau, with his message about a more active state and a just society, was past history. There was a general disenchantment with government, any government. The times reflected uncertainty, a desire to return to what was deemed to be "old values," however those values might be defined. A strategy had to be devised to ensure the NDP would not be the victim of this mood, represented by Lyon's fire-breathing negativism about government. It was crucial that the Opposition focus on a few issues where the PCs appeared vulnerable; in that way, we could develop credibility as the alternative government-in-waiting.

It was not long before we found that vulnerability. Lyon's economic record was poor. He had been elected on the promise of "fiscal responsibility" but had clearly failed on this key commitment by continuing to run deficits while appearing to disregard economic and social concerns. An exodus of professionals and skilled workers, trained at taxpayer expense, was taking place. This provided us with the ammunition for our attack. Job creation would play the decisive role in our overall strategy for the next election. Len Evans, MLA for Brandon East and an economist, was especially talented in statistical analysis; his expertise proved indispensable in giving this strategy credibility. We were able to demonstrate effectively that Manitoba ranked lower than the Canadian average in real domestic product, retail sales growth, employment increases, average wages, and private investment.

Frequently, we tossed back at the Lyon administration the term they had coined—"acute protracted restraint"—as we disparaged the contradictions in the actions of this first truly neo-conservative government of Canada. Contrary to Lyon's pledges and predictions, the private sector and the market place failed to move into the vacuum created by his withdrawal of government from an active role in the economy. Moreover, mismanagement of the civil service was rampant, with senior positions frequently left vacant for months. Our speeches became crammed with examples of the daily impact on Manitobans, the very real human cost of the Lyon government, its total disregard of those citizens in need of vital programs.

In the 1980 Throne Speech debate I was on the attack, arguing that "acute protracted restraint has become protracted disaster and those have indeed become the hallmarks of this government; hallmarks indeed that have become broken promises, economic decline, secrecy, arrogance, and bottomless hypocrisy. Their own policies have brought Manitoba to its knees."[13] We used very human terms to demonstrate that the government's statistical games would "not fool Manitobans who have seen friends leave the province to find jobs, or who have watched industries folding up or leaving Manitoba."

One incident when I stopped for gas after a party committee meeting has stayed with me. A customer at the station was complaining that no politician could be trusted, that they are all awful. Then he saw me and walked over to apologize. Twenty-one years before, at age seventeen, he had started his own drywall business. Now, age thirty-eight, he realized that he earned less than he was earning five years before. He was fed up with Manitoba and was moving to British Columbia. I had no doubt that this man had voted Conservative in 1977.

The PCs had promised jobs for the young, security for the old, prosperity for everyone. Instead the Lyon government delivered "acute, protracted restraint," and the economy was so shattered that the province had become next to last nationally in growth, investment, and new jobs.

Throughout his term, Lyon failed to achieve his goal of balanced budgets. Instead, a record of mounting deficits was accompanied by reduced public services.[14] Moreover, as one of the most eloquent and high-profile opponents of Prime Minister Trudeau on the subject of the Charter of Rights and Freedoms, Lyon was seen as too wrapped up in the endless constitutional battles between the premiers and the prime minister, rather than with governing Manitoba. Approaching the latter part of his term, Lyon was more prone to frequent flip-flops in budgeting.

Later in the Lyon government's term, we were able to expose some idiotic behavior by senior Hydro executives—the destruction of several thousand copies of Manitoba Hydro's annual report. The report had contained a complimentary farewell message to the former chair of Manitoba Hydro, Mr. Bateman, a civil servant with nearly forty years of service who had been fired by the Lyon government in a controversial dismissal. We managed to stretch out debate over this story for several days. It was revealed that the minister himself had demanded the destruction of the Hydro reports. During the uproar over what the media called "Hydro Gate," an angry Premier Lyon confronted me outside the legislative chamber, chastising me for "making a mountain out of a mole hill." Their error was to prolong the debate for days when they could have minimized the damage by simply apologizing for their foolishness.

Bad luck would strike the Lyon government in a startling way. As members of a party which enjoyed a strong focus on "law and order" as one of its major strengths, Progressive Conservatives liked to contrast themselves to the NDP, which they persistently portrayed as too soft on law-and-order issues.

Thus, the Robert Wilson incident rocked the Lyon government more than any other single occurrence could have. In September 1979, Manitobans were appalled when Wilson, with whom I had tangled as Attorney General, was charged with and later convicted of conspiring to import and traffic in marijuana.

A serious railway spillage of toxic chemicals near McGregor, Manitoba, also provided us an opportunity for an emergency debate permitted by the Speaker, despite government opposition. We used the opportunity to denounce the complete lack of provincial environmental protection to prevent what could be serious human damage after this spill. Jay Cowan, our environmental critic, led this debate effectively. A few years later, this environmental hazard would play a major role in ensuring the legislative enactment of protection in such circumstances.

Building a Successful Opposition

Under the capable leadership of newly elected party president Bill Regehr, sometimes affectionately nicknamed Flipchart Bill, a series of workshops were held throughout the province. Organizational manuals were developed, and dialogue revolved around a variety of topics designed to appeal to the membership: policy, organizational techniques, and the desire simply to build greater rapport and solidarity among activists. The goal was to encourage candidate development in several areas, including public speaking. These meetings were attended by either the leader or designated caucus members. Regional workshops established expectations and goals for the party. When debate on various policy alternatives reached gridlock, meetings of the candidates, caucus, Provincial Council, and MFL executive, aided by a facilitator, were held to reach consensus on the upcoming election platform. Either the leader or the party president circled the items of agreement on the flip chart. To our amazement, often what appeared to be gridlock was broken, allowing other committees (publicity, election planning, etc.) to press ahead with an improved platform and with the support of the membership.

Although this proved one of the most successful initiatives during the run up to the successful 1981 election campaign, there were the caucus dissenters. These included those who later exited the party: Uskiw, Walding, and Doern. Their defection resulted from a general dissatisfaction which mounted sharply during our days in opposition.

I recall one occasion when Bill Regehr, a former teacher, high school principal, and school division superintendent, entered the room and began his presentation. Russ Doern, busy with his own scrapbook, was obviously not interested in what Bill was saying. Finally, in frustration, Bill shouted at him, "Russ, either you're in or out. This is a working session, this is not a peanut gallery, and we're all working together." Russ reluctantly put aside his scrapbook.

We established new committees representing the priorities of different sectors within the party: youth, women, ethnic groups, Aboriginals, the handicapped, labour, and agriculture. These groups participated in policy making, played an active role at party conventions, and served as influential voices in the development of party policy. The key was to ensure that each member felt indispensable to the process.

Breakfast meetings were often held in the legislative building prior to council meetings, where, as leader, I would call upon each constituency president for a "Show and Tell" presentation. The presidents were prepped ahead of time and urged to update us about their successes in membership drives, fundraising, planning, and public action. These gatherings fostered an optimistic mood for the crucial council meeting presentations that followed.

The nomination process required that each constituency was to meet two conditions. First a thorough candidate search had to be conducted, and second, all potential prospects were to be encouraged to seek the nomination. Importantly, this rule also included incumbent ridings. It may have been responsible for the resignations of a few caucus members, but that was a risk we were prepared to take. It was made clear that all incumbents would be expected to earn their re-nominations. There would be no exceptions or private fiefdoms. For incumbents, it meant that attention to constituency matters would be crucial and no shirking of responsibilities would be permitted. We had heard at the leadership convention complaints that some elected members were neglecting their grassroots work at the constituency level. I hoped that my attention to constituency concerns would provide an example. I was proud to have opened up one of the first constituency offices in the province, before any public funding was made available, to deal with the real problems and concerns of constituents. Those coming to the office were often those who had little voice. Assisting them promoted a healthier attitude toward the political process. I believe my active and helpful constituency office was responsible for two achievements in which I took pride: not only did I receive huge majorities in the election polls from those with lower-than-average incomes, but such constituents, contrary to what is normally the case, frequently voted in higher numbers than other parts of the riding.

Membership increases were considered paramount if we were to win in 1981. The goal was to sign up as members 10 percent of the vote received by the party in a constituency in the last election. For my own constituency of Selkirk, where the NDP vote in 1977 exceeded 5400, this would mean that at least 540 memberships were to be recruited out of a total population of approximately 20,000. These provisions ensured that constituency associations would become pivotal to revitalizing the overall party organization.

These changes created some of the most hotly contested nominations in the party's history. New faces became involved. Membership soared to over 25,000. In the Dauphin riding alone, 1300 were signed up. Over 1000 attended a contested nomination meeting in the Emerson constituency. Hard-fought nominating conventions took place in Springfield, Gimli, Inkster, and Logan; hundreds showed up where previously a mere handful would have done so.

Sometimes, though, unfortunate downsides occurred. Nearly 1000 attended contentious nomination battles in both St. Johns and Burrows. In each, some blood was spilled. In Burrows, I was horrified to find delegates split along ethnic lines rather than over philosophical or policy disagreements. Nor did the discord relate to the respective qualities of the candidates, Conrad Santos, Mike Dziewit, and Bill Chornopyski. The fault line was painfully evident as I addressed the over 500 delegates assembled. Those of Filipino descent gathered on one section of the hall, those of Ukrainian descent on the other side. When Santos triumphed, many supporting the defeated candidates left in protest. I was appalled at the situation, and I'm sure my speech that night showed it.

At another convention for the St. Johns constituency, attended by nearly 1000 delegates, a closely fought battle took place between Father Don Malinowski, a Polish National Priest and "a champion of the poor," and Roland Penner, a well-respected law professor and son of a long-time Communist alderman, Jacob Penner. In his nomination speech, Father Malinowski spoke partly in Polish, and, although I did not know it at the time, warned the non-English-speaking party members that "Anyone voting for a communist would spend an eternity in Hell."[15] Although Malinowski garnered the most votes, the constituency executive accused him of paying for memberships and busing in members who no longer lived in the riding, charges of which he was subsequently cleared in a controversial decision by the provincial executive. Penner went on to win the nomination and the election in the Fort Rouge constituency. Both candidates were eventually awarded the Order of Canada.

Another unusual nominating convention occurred in the vast northern constituency of Rupertsland, where a young Chief Elijah Harper, born in a tent on 5 March 1949, had signalled his desire to seek election as an NDP candidate. I travelled to Red Sucker Lake, a tranquil and self-sufficient community of approximately 300 Aboriginal residents only two miles from the Ontario-Manitoba boundary in northern Manitoba. Red Sucker was remote: it was without running water, and the only year-round access is by air. Upon my arrival, Chief Harper warned me that his community operated on "Indian time" and that I should not be impatient if the nomination meeting started late. Three hours later, people packed the community hall—the delay due to a popular John Wayne movie transmitted from Detroit on the recently installed satellite TV. Elijah would go on to be a most effective northern affairs minister and, of course, to play a central role in the defeat of Meech Lake in 1990. He later become a federal Liberal MP for Churchill.

Although we encountered bumps along the road, encouraging wide-open nomination contests was highly effective in building party membership. It was not, as Jim Walding once snidely commented to me, "a rush to sell tickets." The benefits of wide-open contests included not only increased membership but also the recruitment of first-rank candidates who would go on to contribute to our 1981 provincial win. These included Maureen Hemphill, former president of the Manitoba School Trustees Association; Andy Anstett, a highly talented former deputy clerk of the Manitoba legislature; Don Scott, a very competent accountant; Myrna Phillips, a social activist; John Bucklaschuck, a skillful party organizer; Muriel Smith, highly respected former party president; and Eugene Kostyra, Manitoba's CUPE leader. All of these candidates won contested nominations and went on to make valuable contributions in our government. With Myrna Phillips, Muriel Smith, Maureen Hemphill, Mary Beth Dolin, and Doreen Dodick, moreover, we succeeded in putting forth a number of first-rank female candidates in winnable ridings for the forthcoming election.

Preparing to Govern

We developed another strategy to encourage communication with the Manitoba public. MLAs and candidates were enlisted to assist in a province-wide effort to seek public input into policy development. The idea was born out of a three-hour discussion I had with Tommy Douglas as I drove him to Winnipeg from a speaking engagement in Brandon. I asked him what advice he could offer concerning the internal bickering that caused the exodus of three caucus members. His words were, "keep your caucus members busy with the public. There is no better garden than one well tended." He added, "It enriches their purpose and they are thus able to contribute while at the same time demonstrating to the public an opposition party that is prepared to listen to those whom it wishes to govern." The more I thought about his message, the more I realized how relevant Tommy's wisdom was to the circumstances then dominating Manitoba's political scene.

Such activity reinforced the message that Pawley, the new NDP leader, was getting about the province and meeting Manitobans. Doing so played to my strength, interacting with ordinary Manitobans. I preferred this to "becoming a prisoner of the legislature," and our approach contrasted positively with the developing impression of the Lyon government as arrogant and elitist, not much concerned with the views of Manitobans as it barged ahead with its own narrow dogmatic legislative agenda. I also gained the reputation of usually being the last to leave any meeting, taking great delight in not just talking to people but also listening to the difficulties they faced in their diverse communities.

A number of party committees were established, including the northern and small-business task forces, and others focused on farming and the economic survival of the family. Aimed primarily at marginal constituencies, these committees toured the province, eliciting the diverse opinions of Manitobans. They turned out to be a tremendous success. Not only MLAs but nominated candidates too were encouraged to participate. Although they involved protracted hours and required enormous patience, these committees were useful in developing policies in tune with the thinking of Manitobans and also enlivened activity in those communities we targeted. Everyone became involved in the task at hand. Within the party, positive attitudes replaced negativity as we drew nearer to the 1981 election. These task forces provided us with a good idea of what issues could be exploited once the election was called. It was the sort of discreet preparation I most relished.

One of the committees, which included Jay Cowan (MLA for Churchill) and MP Rod Murphy, dealt with concerns shared by northern Manitobans: the rising cost of living, inadequate housing, and Aboriginal rights, among others. In one instance, a committee hearing at the mining town of Lynn Lake was scheduled to finish by 5:00 p.m. but instead lasted until nearly midnight, as we listened to all the local presenters. Only a few hours could be spared for sleep before we rushed off by car the following morning at 5:00 a.m. to reach Split Lake for a session scheduled to begin at 10:00 a.m.

Later during the tour, while driving to Norway House, I insisted that Jay Cowan turn the steering wheel over to me because I thought he was driving too fast. Moments later, I succeeded in smashing the vehicle's oil pan. We arrived at our destination late after hitchhiking the rest of the way. Jay—good-naturedly, of course—never allowed me to forget my misjudgment.

At Oxford House, after several hours of presentations, the local elders forcefully told us that they were weary of politicians who flew in and did not hang around long enough to get a proper sense of the community's needs. Alerted to these sentiments, we discovered a method to extend our stay. Such sensitivity is imperative in politics whether in government or opposition.

The party, of course, had no budget for this community outreach. Indeed facilities at the legislative building were limited, consisting of three undersized offices, one secretary (the able Shirley Manson), and innovative assistants Pat Moses and Laverne Lewycky. There was only a modest budget to accommodate the hefty expenses that would normally be incurred by travel to all parts of the province. Such trips often meant staying overnight at members' homes and eating at their tables. This odyssey received valuable media attention, but its primary function was organizational. I always sent follow-up letters to the party members, thanking them for the warmth and generosity of their hospitality. Such personal contact succeeds in creating an enormous bond between the leader and the membership, and is central to the development of a large cadre of committed members. For each member to feel indispensable to the process, it is crucial to acknowledge the contributions made by all.

Such sensitivity is also paramount when it comes to the relationship with caucus members. I always seized every possible opportunity to congratulate them for worthy contributions or acts, not only verbally but also, at the end of each legislative session, with a letter conveying gratitude for the specific service that member had performed. This practice also provided an opportunity for constructive criticism when that was deserved.

We concluded that in the past, NDP pre-election activity had not been directed toward individual community leaders, but toward partisan audiences and general community visits. We recognized that community leaders are an important "target group" as they tend to be more aware than other community members of how severe an impact the actions of the ruling administration may have on their local economies. Community leaders, small business people, labour, and the heads of municipal farm organizations are tuned in to problems in their area.

To achieve the communication we desired, interest groups and others friendly to the NDP in the community compiled lists of community leaders and checked addresses, with obvious political opponents deleted. Letters went to these community leaders, with invitations to meet the leader or committee members at luncheons or coffee parties. These letters were in addition to general invitations sent to the public to "meet the leader." This reinforced the perception of concern, improved the development of future party contacts, and enhanced the perception that the Tories were on the way out and the NDP on the way in. It was critically important to do this before we were caught up in the rush of a general election. Riding by riding, village by village, town by town, we courted every group the Tories had alienated—students, women, renters, small business, workers, Metis, and First Nations peoples.

By establishing rapport with these local leaders, I had the opportunity to contrast my approach with that of Premier Lyon, perceived as leading an uncaring government and responsible for many of the economic ills plaguing the province. It was critical preparation prior to the 1981 campaign, which would give us only thirty-five days, too brief a time to "reach" community leaders in any significant way.

It soon become obvious that to win an election after only one term in opposition, we would need to focus on a few prime issues, relating to the poor economic performance of the Lyon administration. Economic expectations aroused by Sterling Lyon had once been high; these, however, were largely unfulfilled, generating widespread disillusionment about what should have been the Conservatives' strong suit. Leading up to the 1981 election, all our pronouncements, both in and out of the House, included some reference to the increasingly precarious state of the province's economy. We rejected the advice of those, including professional pollsters and other party professionals, who counselled that the NDP could not succeed if it beat the campaign drums too strongly on economic issues. Sometimes, to its detriment, the Left neglects this most critical issue, as there are those who claim that it cannot run a peanut stand.

When we discussed social issues, they were generally linked to the benefits garnered from innovative job creation programs. We always sought to illustrate the clear linkage between social justice and economic improvement. For instance, surely a tax break for low-income families would do more to drive the economy forward than would tax concessions at high-income levels. We pointed out the contrast between the economic advantages to the province of policies favouring families who spend their spare pennies on groceries and clothes locally, and the impact of policies that enrich the economic elite who would use newfound gains in discretionary spending for overseas travel or offshore investing. Surely the Manitoba small-business community would be better off if modest income families were given more income to spend on their basic needs.

I had also learned that I would have to choose between a socialist party leading public opinion and being more pragmatic. Not everything we seek can be achieved in the short term. Compromises may sometimes be essential; otherwise, one plays into the hand of one's more right-wing opponents. This does not, however, mean betraying one's ultimate objective—a more equitable society. Making substantial progress to this goal is what propelled me to become actively involved in politics. In my opinion, Tony Blair, as prime minister of Great Britain, and Bob Rae, as the NDP premier in Ontario, were examples of social democratic first ministers who, decades later, strayed far from the objectives they had once set for themselves. I was determined not to do this. In other words, although I was forced to accept pragmatism, it would not be at any price. One must, after all, live with oneself.

If we were to win and govern effectively, I saw that we needed to improve our relationship with our allies in the labour movement. The party and the Manitoba Federation of Labour are natural allies; it is essential that both organizations accept the difficult reality that they will occasionally find themselves in conflict. A substantial reason for our defeat in 1977 was the bitter fallout with many activists in the labour movement over our endorsement of the Trudeau-initiated wage and price controls. What could we learn from history to help us avoid future unnecessary conflicts? How could we ensure a more amicable relationship in the future? The purpose of such a discussion was not to find fault or to point fingers, but rather, to avoid the mistakes of the past. Although the relationship may sometimes be thorny, we were convinced that open communication would guarantee progress.

As in most marriages, there may be unhappiness from time to time. However, it is crucial that both parties understand and appreciate the importance of their mutually beneficial relationship. The NDP must be accountable to the larger community; the labour movement must primarily safeguard the interests of its membership. Although this will sometimes result in disagreement, it will more likely produce only a difference of emphasis on various issues. Although there is clearly more pressure when the NDP is in government, skirmishes also surface when the party is in opposition. When we decided not to commit ourselves to the anti-scab legislation proposed at party conventions, it was only natural that some tensions would again mount, but it was generally agreed by both labour and NDP that with an election approaching it was imperative that neither partner veer off the issues we had agreed to focus on. We also realized that it was crucial for the leadership in both organizations to do a better job of informing their respective memberships about the inevitability of occasional differences.

My relationship with the labour movement had evolved positively since the stormy days leading to the formation of the NDP. Dick Martin, president of the Manitoba Federation of Labour, deserves much of the credit for this. The bond of trust which grew between us became a prime example of how such an understanding could work in practice. Trust is indispensable, and it must be reinforced by a process that aims at minimizing conflict. Every effort must be taken to sort out differences and avoid a public debate in what is normally a hostile press. An example of this was the decision we reached about our most divisive internal issue, anti-scab legislation. It would not form a part of our platform in the forthcoming election. Instead, we targeted those matters where we had a consensus.

We had confidence that the NDP and the labour movement could explore new ideas, propose new legislation, and undertake the necessary follow-up. There were many instances of successful public policy campaigns and demonstrations where the party and labour worked well together, including nurses, health care demonstrations, and marches on the legislature.

We developed a process for the party leader and the president of the Manitoba Federation of Labour to communicate and discuss differences, thus improving the odds of resolving them. If differences that might provoke public disagreement persisted, we agreed to be candid and avoid ambushing each other. We recognized that discord would normally only benefit our opponents, although occasionally public disputes, if managed properly, could be strategically beneficial to each of us. In other words, we treated each other as family members would.

———⟐———

After our defeat in 1977, many in the party were discouraged. Yet we chose to seek new ideas and new faces for the party, to reach out to ethnic groups, to Franco-Manitobans, to women, to Aboriginals, and to others who traditionally consider themselves New Democrats. We encouraged contests for nominations and succeeded in building constituency organizations that were stronger than ever before, more than tripling our membership.

Our opponents and the media said we would never win after only one term out of government. Then they said we were badly divided and could never form a government again. Sometimes we did become a little discouraged and believed our critics, but we remained true, kept organizing, and proved with good hard work that we would prove them wrong. We built a rank and file organization second to none. We paid off the debt the party owed after its defeat in 1977. We also developed and articulated a vision about how Manitoba and Canada could become a better place to live and work; a place where those who have no voice can be heard, where those with no hope can look forward to the future, where those who work long and hard can have just reward for their labour and some control over their lives. Gradually a spirit of optimism displaced the pessimism that had earlier reigned. Interestingly this expectation of coming electoral success was not picked up by either the Progressive Conservative government or the media. A truly alternative government gradually began to energize itself.

Machiavelli refers to the leader as being subject to two forces: virtue, which is a combination of "skill and courage," and "fortune," which is an element of luck over which one may have no control. Although the general proposition is true, I would probably replace "luck" with "circumstances." A leader must be able to adjust his/her style to meet the circumstances of the day. In some cases it may be advisable to deliberately present a contrast to the leadership style of one's predecessor or one's rival. In my case, even if a consensual approach had not been my natural style, it would still have been a wise choice to counter the rather patrician, uncompromising style of Sterling Lyon. One must identify one's own strengths and weaknesses with regard to the challenges and build a team accordingly. An opposition leader cannot do this alone: he or she must be supported by a group of trusted individuals who are loyal not only to the objectives of the leader but also to the party. I am pleased that I was successful in inspiring people to pursue our objectives; to respond to circumstances; to shape compromise within a specific set of principles; to take a stand that reflects the best aspirations of a society, despite opposition; and to bring out the best in the team. It means during difficult times to give people reasons to remain optimistic and to tackle challenges. Leadership is about being honest, about having a vision and the conviction to pursue it through both the good and bad times. In this way we had many successful instances in the period between 1978 and late 1981 of joint public policy campaigns and demonstrations, etc., where the party and labour worked well together. These were essential to our being successful in regaining government after only three years.

CHAPTER 5

Assuming the Reins of Governance and Power

THE ANNOUNCEMENT CAME from an excited political aide, who had hurried into a meeting with a small gathering of Carrot River farmers near The Pas, in northern Manitoba: "Sterling Lyon has called the election." The election date was 17 November 1981. I experienced mixed emotions because so much was at stake. Many of us had put in a lot of time—doing membership drives, carrying out provincial tours, organizing nominating conventions, working on policy development, raising funds to reduce the party's debt, and most importantly, energizing the membership. Could we really win this time around? Many people in the party believed that we couldn't. Lyon had been elected in 1977 with the largest popular vote (49 percent) for a premier in Manitoba's recent history. The Tories had promised to reduce the debt, balance the budget, cut government spending, and generally remove "the dead hand of government," restoring the province to economic health. To his supporters, he had delivered the goods.

Sterling Lyon had developed a reputation as an eloquent (if sometimes bombastic) spokesperson for Canadian premiers, chairing their annual first ministers' meetings in their two-year constitutional battle with Trudeau. His adversarial relationship with Trudeau endeared him to many Manitobans, who, like others in western Canada, disliked the prime minister. There had been speculation that Lyon was waiting for the Supreme Court decision on Trudeau's constitutional package. If the decision came down on the side of the premiers, Lyon could run against the Liberals in Ottawa, who were unpopular at that time.

As the Opposition leader, I enjoyed far less public recognition and was unknown to many. Nevertheless, our party's polling showed that I had received high marks for being "honest, fair and willing to listen."

We frequently noticed during this period that the neo-conservatives in Manitoba were exhilarated by the election of Ronald Reagan to the U.S. presidency. On one occasion, I saw some of Lyon's political assistants at the Middlechurch Home in my riding showing off their colourful Reagan ties, souvenirs from a recent Republican Party convention in Detroit. They were the eager shock troops of "the new truth" for those who were beginning to dominate politics during the 1980s.

Some of our supporters had also been discouraged by the formation of the Progressive Party, led by former Schreyer cabinet minister Sidney Green and two other former cabinet ministers, Ben Hanuschak and Bud Boyce. With more than twenty candidates in the upcoming election, they could undoubtedly be a factor in some close races. It was naturally accepted that Green and his cronies would siphon votes from the NDP. In a *Winnipeg Free Press* article, right-wing columnist Fred Cleverley[1] permitted his optimism to get the better of him, forecasting that "No one should be surprised if Green's new party has enough seats [four] in the Legislature to earn a leader's salary from the public treasury and possibly enough to negotiate a few deals with the Conservatives." Others, he claimed, are "willing to put money down that Sid Green will come within a whisker of being the leader of the Official Opposition." Cleverley then proceeded to launch a personal attack against me, advising that "Some are convinced that Howard Pawley will be the first NDP leader in history to begin an election with a full rather than an empty, party treasury and manage to fudge his way into a defeat." He revealed that Manitoba Federation of Labour president Dick Martin was the real leader of the Manitoba NDP: "Pawley has his Martin-phone that tells him when to refill the paper clip box on his desk." Cleverley's one correct claim was that Green's position was, "in many matters of government and fiscal policy . . . far closer to that of Sterling Lyon than it is to that of Howard Pawley."

Unlike Cleverley, I was always confident that the new party under the leadership of Green would be irrelevant in the pending campaign.

It could not be ignored that the Tories enjoyed an electoral advantage. There were at least twenty constituencies in southern and western rural Manitoba where it was commonly known that a yellow dog who ran as a PC candidate would be sure to win. University of Manitoba history professor Michael Kinnear projected that the PCs could win two additional seats, due to redistribution.[2] Kinnear disclosed that in the past election, four ridings had been won by margins of less than 125 votes, and that with a slight shift in popular vote, the New Democrats could have won all four. In Kinnear's view, however, with redistribution only Osborne could be counted on by the NDP. In addition, of course, it is always easier to ensure that the more affluent Progressive Conservative electorate fully participates in the electoral process; rallying the poor is much tougher. The Liberal Party, under its newly elected leader Doug Lauchlan, was not expected to be much of a factor; it was assumed, wrongly, that this would also benefit the Tories.

Sterling Lyon was expected to benefit from two other facts: he had, at the end of his term in government, loosened the purse strings of the provincial treasury and (to a tiny degree) softened his image. As a result, he was seen less as a mean-spirited scrooge trampling on the weak and voiceless in society than as the province's generous benefactor. Indeed, spending had risen by 15 percent in 1981. As Progressive Conservative Party sources confided to reporters, the election call in the fall of 1981 was attributable to the reality that Lyon's personal image had improved.

The Brighter Side

Still, optimism prevailed within the NDP. Membership had soared. Highly competitive nomination meetings drew large crowds and excellent contestants. Tory meetings, by contrast, were sparsely attended. Our polling showed that Lyon's PCs were much less credible on the job creation front than the NDP, perhaps because we were in the midst of a very serious recession. Economic indicators revealed that the Manitoba economy was performing among the poorest of the ten provinces and that Manitoba was actually losing population. The promises Lyon had made during the 1977 campaign were being left unfulfilled. Notwithstanding his leadership at the premiers' meetings, Lyon's image created grave problems for him. Given to excessive rhetoric, he appeared intolerant of other opinions. A perception developed that he was extremely right wing and arrogant.

On the eve of the election we were disadvantaged by the launching of an expensive, tax-funded Progressive Conservative government radio and newspaper advertising program, which urged Manitoba businesses and workers to contribute their talents to the government's mega-projects. The ad campaign cost $150,000. In addition, Lyon appeared twice weekly on prime-time television, in three-minute commercials extolling the achievements of his party; but it was the *government* that paid for the commercials.

The television ads were most effective. As Richard Cleroux wrote in the *Globe and Mail*, "The Tory television ads feature a brand-new Mr. Lyon. He is no longer the vitriolic little street scrapper taking on the mean giant in Ottawa, or the front-line free-enterpriser battling the Socialist hordes. The new image Mr. Lyon is shown seated in a library. He no longer talks like a zealot. He speaks slowly, moderately, soberly, exuding confidence and promising prosperity for the future."[3]

The message underlying this commercial bombardment concerned three proposals, which would allegedly stimulate $3 billion of investment in Manitoba: a potash mine near St. Lazare, proposed by International Minerals and Chemical (Canada); a $500 million Alcan Aluminum Smelter; and an inter-provincial power grid. Great expectations were being aroused that opportunities would cause businesses and workers to flourish. Did it really matter that there was not a single signature to any agreement? The message was clear. Glorious days were ahead if the Tories were re-elected. To elect the socialists would only return us to the distant past.

Even the Tories' strong card, namely putting the fiscal affairs of the province in order, was proving to be a sham. Manitoba's debt had risen from $3.2 billion to more than $4 billion. This was not because of public spending programs to stimulate the economy. The series of deficits under Lyon were the largest in the province at that point in its history. The deficit in 1977–1978 was $191 million; in 1978–1979, $84 million; in 1979–1980, $45 million; and in 1980–1981, it was projected at $100 million. For 1981–1982, it was forecast to come in at $220 million. Although partly the result of a failing economy, these deficits, as the Progressive Conservatives would find, would not necessarily be forgiven, because they themselves had made a big fuss over Schreyer's 1977 deficit.

While it was rumoured that Tory polling was showing them only slightly ahead of the NDP, and in the crucial swing constituencies, the Tories simply claimed that their polling had them ahead. Our own more modest polling verified a tight race between the two parties. However, we thought that the distribution of ridings would tend to favour us, as much of the Conservative vote in southwestern Manitoba was not voter-efficient due to their overwhelming majorities there. Still, even though the closeness of the polling encouraged us, it also told us that we would certainly be in for an uphill battle. A government going into its second term with a high-profile leader is normally expected to have a decided edge.

The Strategy: The Road for a Successful Campaign

We had carefully developed an election campaign strategy well in advance and exercised the discipline to adhere to it. We refused to be sidetracked by other issues. We avoided the temptation of going for any bait that would have resulted in our fighting the election on Lyon's terms. Battling over the mega-projects would have played into his hands. What had a tremendous impact was our competence and earnestness in communicating with people in their own communities about whatever affected them most—lost jobs, rent controls, interest rates, the declining farm economy, etc. We revealed the economic irresponsibility of the Tories.

Contesting the election on our terms meant that our platform did not curry favour with the powerful financial and corporate elite, but rather, addressed the vast majority of Manitobans. Wilson Parasiuk, an economist, a Rhodes Scholar, and a member of Ed Schreyer's Planning and Priorities Committee, along with Eugene Kostyra, CUPE's head in Manitoba and someone respected by both labour and management people for his organizing and negotiating abilities, were co-chairs of the party's election-planning committee. We targeted fifteen constituencies, of which we would have to win six or seven for an election victory. As we saw it, a vote for the Liberal Party would be a vote for Sterling Lyon.

In planning for the election call, we decided that it was imperative to fulfill three fundamental strategies. All statements given, all speeches delivered, all events held, and most importantly, the campaign advertising had to be consistent with those agreed-upon strategies.

The first of these was that the Lyon government would be held accountable for its shoddy economic management. Their promised mega-projects were far from certain; indeed, there was no assurance that they would ever materialize. Essentially, they were desperate attempts to distract attention from the Tory's mismanagement of the economy. Our second strategy was to argue that if by any tiny chance the Tories were able to progress with the mega-projects, they would do so only at a major cost to Manitobans. At stake were some potential giveaways of the province's resources, much like the giveaways of the Roblin government's notorious Churchill Forestry Industries project. Finally, we planned to define the NDP as the alternative party, one unlike the others. Our party would represent those most excluded from society: the workers, the poor, farmers, and small-business owners. We clearly rejected the domination of politics by the moneyed interests and the multinational corporations.

It was essential for us to remember that each election campaign has its own set of dynamics. It is always vital to set the agenda, to avoid distraction, to maintain a sense of momentum, to coordinate the leader's announcements with the overall campaign theme and advertising, and to avoid the appearance of losing momentum by peaking too early.

We did not want to crest too soon. The crescendo should gradually develop, successfully climaxing at the campaign's end. The negative campaign reflecting on the government's policies and record would therefore take place in the first half of the campaign, leaving the last half for a more positive resonance. The same pattern was pursued with the advertising program, which dovetailed with the overall campaign themes. This contrasted with Lyon's campaign, which in the final days showed signs of rising desperation and faltering confidence.

Much credit for our eventual victory must be given to the advertising program perfected by Derek Mazur, contracted by us to create our ads. A competent advertising thrust is crucial to any campaign. Especially innovative were scenes portraying a birthday cake (Manitoba) being carved up and served to various elite partygoers; the message was "Do not permit the province's resources to be given away." These commercials played early in the campaign to set the tone for criticism of Lyon's main platform thrust. Ad jingles and other techniques were important to encourage a sense of momentum. Our choice of "Great people, Great land, and Great future" was much more apt and effective than the negative, defensive tone of Lyon's jingle, "Don't Stop Us Now."

Though we avoided personal attacks against our adversaries and members of the media, we maintained repeated attacks against the Tories as a party, keeping them on the defensive, and avoiding an apologetic or reactive stance. Also, we sustained program announcements that repeatedly put Lyon on the defensive. To his dismay, his own program was not being discussed by many in the public.

Never to be underestimated was the effort of many volunteers at the local level—telephoning, canvassing, fundraising, and doing all types of election work. They were the core of a successful campaign. I recall the effort of so many volunteers in my riding, including Al Scramstad, who raised funds, did publicity, practised law, and at the same time had to deal with his mother's severe heart illness. Labour and the party would run parallel campaigns. A tremendous number of phone banks were organized by the trade union movement, which canvassed their members in their homes and spoke to them one-on-one.

Even now, in this age of TV media and the Internet, I believe that a party cannot hope to accomplish a winning campaign without powerful corporate friends and wealthy patrons unless it has an ample and dynamic membership base to get the message out and guarantee that supporters make their way to the ballot box on election day.

A Rough Start

My campaign didn't start well, which some feared might be a bad omen. Safely arriving at The Pas airport, we started the half-hour drive to town in an older model van. When this vehicle broke down along the way, we anxiously called for assistance. Eventually, we reached the destination of our news conference, to take place inside the massive building that comprised the infamous Churchill Forest Industries project. The overwhelming major-ity of Manitobans were aware of the price tag of this Tory financial fiasco, so the site had been carefully selected to illustrate the catastrophic results that can follow whenever governments build their provincial economy on a mega-project foundation. To our dismay, the uppermost management of the corporation refused us permission to hold the press conference inside, and we had no alternative but to do it outside. Nonetheless, I was allowed to tour inside and meet the workers, who furnished us with a warmer welcome than we had received from the upper management. The inconvenience caused by this displacement really didn't make much difference, but the media placed a negative spin on our early misfortune. Did the NDP campaign lack a good advance person? Was this misstep a hint of what was to come?

By contrast, Lyon enjoyed a good beginning to his campaign. He opened his provincial election tour in the prosperous farming community of Brunkild, just southwest of Winnipeg, where one of his most recent stars, Clayton Manness, had been nominated. In his speech the premier acclaimed the mer-its of his "common sense" and "workmanlike" government. In this staunchly held Tory riding, it was evident that the electors wholeheartedly concurred.

My first campaign announcement was made on Manitoba Crown land just a few hundred metres from the Saskatchewan boundary. There, I pledged that an NDP government would not only establish the Manitoba Oil and

Gas Corporation, a Crown corporation, to explore for oil and gas within the province, but also invest at least $20 million of capital in this undertaking over the next four years. This commitment was fashioned after Saskatchewan's Crown corporation, Sask. Oil, which was enjoying considerable success in developing that province's oil resources. We expected the same to take place in Manitoba.[4] The idea of a new Crown corporation was fiercely set upon by the various executives of the oil industry, as we had anticipated. They asserted that it would be to the public's detriment if the Manitoba government entered into competition with them, pronouncing themselves more experienced at running the oil business. Burdened with high gasoline prices, the public did not necessarily agree. Again, the media and our opponents went ballistic, nicknaming me "Hard-hat Howard." They charged sarcastically that my "glib promises" reminded them of "other adventures in public investment by the previous NDP government." They alleged that if a private industry had made such a promise, it would have been visited by the "securities commission, if not … the fraud squad." Bombastic as ever, Lyon portrayed the announcement of Manitoba Oil as the NDP's "dry-hole policy."

There were those, including some within our party, who privately disputed the wisdom of launching the campaign with a commitment to establish a new Crown corporation. They feared it would only remind the public of some of the insolvent Crown corporations from Schreyer's era. They believed that neither economic development nor government management was perceived as an area of strength for the NDP. However, Lyon's mega-projects possessed the potential to inspire support from the general public, so it was necessary to deliver some distinctive messages that there were alternative techniques for developing the economy and ensuring that all Manitobans would enjoy the benefits of resource development. Undoubtedly, this commitment to Manitoba Oil was a daring, somewhat risky move. But I considered such a move essential at the start of the campaign to command the attention of the public and emphasize the main policy difference between us and the Tories.

One of the key advisers and strategists behind the announcement of Manitoba Oil was Dan O'Connor, a young man who was remarkably able in devising political strategies to keep political opponents on the defensive. Later, in the legislature during the post-election session, Sterling Lyon acknowledged to me that O'Connor's role had been telling. He regretted that O'Connor had not been on his side.

In any event, our campaign gained steady momentum. Meanwhile, the Tories stumbled. In the first day or two of the campaign, Harry Enns, the veteran and colourful but unpredictable Lyon minister, verbally exploded, making derogatory comments about *Free Press* reporter Ingeborg Boyens. His comments were provoked by a Boyens article alleging that Enns's colleague and friend, a senior cabinet minister, had acquired a substantial piece of land near the proposed Alcan Aluminum project.

Enns's ill-conceived over-reaction to the subsequent media story instantly placed the Tories in a negative light with the voting public and succeeded in alienating reporters at the beginning of the campaign. It even produced divisions among Tories themselves; John Robertson, a fellow Progressive Conservative candidate running in St. Vital, expressed shock, complaining that he wept "with shame" that he and Enns wear "the same colours in this election." Enns had the good sense to write a letter of an apology the next day, but the damage had already been done.

A further development was the collapse of negotiations among party representatives over a proposed television leadership debate. We had anticipated that Sterling Lyon would push for such a debate; he enjoyed the debating forum, where he was extremely effective. Imagine our surprise when the discussions broke down because of his party's opposition to the proposed format. Initially, news reports placed the blame fully on the premier's shoulders, and he was forced to deny that he was reluctant to debate. In any event, neither he nor the PCs came out unsullied. I myself was ambivalent about a debate; I would have gone up against Lyon and Sidney Green, both superb orators and both motivated by the goal of making the NDP and me look bad. In any event, it would have separated me from the campaign trail, where I was enjoying success. I deliberately maintained a low-key response to the disruption of these talks; I had no desire to overplay my hand and set off a new round of negotiations. I disagreed with any strategy that would have had me challenging Lyon to a debate or would otherwise have led me to accuse him of being afraid. My time would be better spent on the hustings.

The biggest campaign mishap came when Lyon held a press conference in which he appeared to imply that an agreement had been signed for a proposed power grid with Saskatchewan and Alberta. Premiers Blakeney and Lougheed immediately disputed this; Lyon denied that he had ever claimed an agreement had been signed. As it turned out, all that had been announced was that a prairie energy ministers' draft interim proposal had been in readiness for submission to their respective governments. Nonetheless, some confusion was created. It seemed to many that Lyon was clutching at straws. From our perspective, the possibility of a signature to any of the proposed mega-projects was a ticking time bomb, waiting to go off. If the premier had succeeded in pulling off such an agreement, our campaign would undoubtedly have been made much more difficult. Lyon would have gained credibility from a sceptical public at a key moment. Instead, the questions being asked created more doubt on the part of an already dubious electorate. I cautioned the public about more non-announcements by Lyon before the campaign's end. Maybe the wheels were coming off the PC campaign bus.

I was touring western Manitoba when the supposed announcement about the proposed power grid was made. Upon hearing it, I was disturbed to think that Saskatchewan's NDP premier might have entered into such a deal with Lyon in the middle of our election campaign. Because we were expected to return to Winnipeg by six in the evening, I called an emergency meeting of the election planning committee at the Fort Garry Hotel, and I instructed that a call be put through to Jim Walding, our legislative Hydro critic. I wanted to ensure that we would have the benefit of his expertise. When the campaign bus arrived, we hurriedly made our way to the hotel suite. I did not mask my exasperation and frustration when advised that Walding had answered through his wife, Val, that he would "not interrupt his dinner or his personal canvassing afterwards to attend our meeting." Our discussions progressed without him. (Wilson Parasiuk, the Transcona candidate and a member of the provincial election planning committee, found the time to attend despite his similarly busy schedule.) Following the meeting, I telephoned Saskatchewan Premier Blakeney and received his assurances that no such deal had ever been entered into.

Imagine my frustration again with Walding when he was a no-show the next morning at the canvassing scheduled for the St. Vital Shopping Centre, located in his riding. All our candidates for southeast Winnipeg were expected to accompany me and greet morning shoppers. Unfortunately, Walding's failure to appear then, and the evening before, was a forerunner of his future working relationship with his colleagues and me. In case of victory, it had been my intention to appoint him to cabinet; after all, he was a senior member who had once served as caucus chair. But his lack of cooperation caused me to strike him from the short list for a cabinet position.

The Campaign

In the first week of our campaign, I had a remarkably triumphant tour of northern Manitoba. In Flin Flon, I charged the Progressive Conservative government with conferring the province's share of a local mine on a foreign company; they were, I declared, giving away provincial resources that should instead benefit us all. I committed an NDP government to expand and develop the North's resources through joint ventures involving both the government and the private sector. I greeted miners at the break of dawn, as they arrived for their hard day's work. Later, at the local collegiate, I was sharply questioned about the need for a northern expense allowance to offset the North's high cost of living. Although sympathetic, I carefully avoided any commitment to what would be a costly item, and a local teacher therefore accused me of "sliding around the question." In general, the visit to Flin Flon was a real boost to our top-notch candidate, Jerry Storie, who had replaced Tom Barrow, our former member who had been greatly loved as "a miner and man of the common people."

My next visit was to Thompson, where Steve Ashton, a dynamic young candidate and former president of the University of Manitoba Students' Union, was an obvious up-and-comer in politics. At the beginning of the campaign Steve had been given little chance of defeating Ken MacMaster, the only Tory who had been elected in 1977 from northern Manitoba. MacMaster, a former union officer and Lyon's labour minister, was a particular target in the local campaign. My visit to this northern centre was capped with a visit to striking Inco miners, who were warming themselves around a bonfire in their winter parkas and boots. While I chatted with them about some of the issues they were facing in the strike, one of the miners, Mike Carr, pushed forward to become the first individual in the campaign to call me "Mr. Premier." According to Steve Ashton, my showing at the picket line during this bitter and lengthy strike greatly energized the local campaign.

Later, in Winnipeg, I made a series of announcements in order to ensure that our campaign commanded the attention of not only the media but also the public. Accompanied by Roland Penner, an articulate constitutional lawyer and the Fort Rouge candidate, I listened to about sixty residents at a downtown Winnipeg senior citizens home as they outlined the difficulties confronting seniors. There, I exposed the economic failures of the Lyon government, especially the departure of so many young people from the province to pursue employment elsewhere. Interestingly, many grandparents nodded approval. My visit gained TV coverage in a milieu where I personally felt most comfortable. Assurances were later made in Dauphin to construct more personal care homes and to improve hospital and health facilities. I felt confident, and according to the *Winnipeg Free Press* reports at the time, I was "polished and at ease."

Between these announcements I attended my own nomination convention in Selkirk. About 300 constituents showed up. There, I roasted Premier Lyon for hiding from voters during the election campaign. Manitoba singer Heather Bishop, who unveiled the new NDP jingle, entertained the crowd with the words "Great People, Great Future, Manitoba and the NDP." The words were distributed and the song sung at various times during the evening.

Credibility was added to our campaign when David Sanders announced his resignation from his post as Deputy Minister of Urban Affairs to run as an NDP candidate. The high-profile public servant had joined the government in 1968 when he was an executive assistant to the minister of health during the term of Premier Walter Weir. Sanders accused the Lyon government of losing many good civil servants, including many fired for political reasons. The fact that such an indictment came from a senior rank civil servant—without NDP ties and hired during a former Progressive Conservative term in office—substantially added to our claims that the civil service had been severely weakened during the term of the Lyon government.

Despite a driving snowstorm and slippery roads, I carried my campaign to southeastern Manitoba, speaking to local hog, beef, and dairy farmers. Complaints about high interest rates, gas prices, disgraceful prices for hogs and cattle, and farmers being coerced from their land monopolized all the discussions along the way. Accompanying me was Andy Anstett, the former deputy clerk of the Manitoba legislature. During Anstett's term as deputy clerk, he had become disillusioned by the Lyon government's attempts to jeopardize his impartiality as an officer of the legislature. Anstett was not only a capable campaigner but later proved to be a competent legislator and minister.

During its term, the Lyon government had repealed rent controls enacted during Schreyer's term. They soon discovered the sad consequences of a policy venture that would come home to roost just before the election. Strategically, their policy failure worked out well for us, as concerned tenants tended to live in several marginal constituencies: River East, Riel, Brandon West, and

St. James. Rent control became a priority issue when the tour took us to Brandon. More than 100 angry tenants, including many senior citizens who had encountered rent increases of up to 72 percent, met us. Most of them were far from affluent, and such increases placed them in an extremely precarious situation. As proud people, they wanted to remain independent, but the exorbitant increases were jeopardizing their expectations. I was amazed by both the extent of the anger and the unusually large numbers of protesters. Many who showed up asserted that they had never voted NDP in their lives. As the government opposition, we had resisted the removal of rent controls, and I promised to reintroduce them upon our re-election. In an angry response to this commitment, Lyon charged that I was deceiving tenants by promising that rent controls would not increase shelter costs.

The short-sighted greed of those who had suddenly hiked their rents, knowing an election was pending, was most revealing. If these were Lyon's friends, he surely did not need enemies. A similar turnout of irate tenants would meet with me in the Riel riding, where the ever-hard-working Doreen Dodick was to be victorious against the Tory finance minister Don Craik.

Emphasizing our central message—that the NDP had an economic plan to generate jobs—I flew to Gillam and vowed that, during our first term in office, the Limestone Project would be built with the help of northern residents. We would "reduce the amount of unemployment and the amount of welfare in northern communities by ensuring there are meaningful jobs provided for northerners." The Limestone Station construction, which consisted of parts of the Nelson River Hydro system, had been halted by Lyon in 1977. I stressed that we had all seen, on the Nelson River, the generating station built by Duff Roblin and the generating station built by Ed Schreyer, but no one had seen a generating station built by Sterling Lyon. Contrary to the commitment made by Lyon, I reiterated that an NDP government would certainly not sell to Alcan, or anyone else, any part of the generating station.

Before leaving the North, I flew to Churchill, where I promised that the NDP would not abandon what was indeed an ailing community. We would do all we could to encourage the shipment of goods through the port of Churchill. During my visit there, I was accompanied by Jay Cowan, who had been a member of the legislature since 1977 and one of our most hard-working, conscientious members. A Californian, he had arrived in Manitoba during the early 1970s. Whenever the PCs dared to give him cheap shots about his non-support of the Vietnam War, Jay, an opponent of that senseless conflict, would more than hold his own. He totally ignored them when they dubbed him a draft dodger.

Continuing the momentum in the campaign, an announcement was made in the small town of McCreary that an NDP government would launch "Main Street Manitoba," a program costing $1.5 million annually to encourage downtown revitalization in rural towns. I emphasized the need not just to rejuvenate Manitoba's rural towns but also to create jobs, thus providing hope for young people in many rural areas where few opportunities existed, especially during the recession of the early 1980s.

At Vita, a community of approximately 750 residents, my speech was translated into Ukrainian for the audience. I impugned the PCs for cancelling the Schreyer government's plans to construct a local hospital and personal care home and deplored the general hardship faced by thousands of Manitobans who worked in the health-care sector. I declared that the provincial dental care and pharma-care programs would be expanded under an NDP government to the extent of $2 million. Before leaving Vita, I promised that an NDP government would not provide support for profit-making health-care ventures and that we would encourage religious and non-profit community support groups that entered the health-care field out of love and affection, rather than a desire to make a profit.

The fifth of November 1981 was a monumental day in the campaign. An important message interrupted Premier Lyon when he was attending the constitutional conference in Ottawa. His provincial campaign manager, Nate Nurgitz, warned Lyon that the most recent PC polling revealed that they were in serious political trouble. Nurgitz firmly demanded that Lyon get back to Manitoba. The premier reluctantly complied, but he created an embarrassing situation for himself by quitting before the end of the historic discussions entailing the patriation of the Constitution and the enactment of the Charter of Rights and Freedoms. Lyon's Attorney General, Gerry Mercier, stayed behind to bravely wave Manitoba's flag. It was a clear signal that our campaign, through its daily efforts, was finally acquiring momentum. The overly confident Progressive Conservatives now recognized they were in real trouble and had to go on the offensive to salvage their faltering campaign. Lyon grumbled that the public wanted the campaign to debate issues such as high mortgage rates, high inflation, and high interest rates rather than the Constitution. Though this was what we had been saying from day one, having Lyon agree with us was unusual.

The following day, at a campaign rally in the Gimli constituency, Lyon again lashed out at the previous Schreyer government's record: "If any member of the NDP tries to tell you that Alcan is a giveaway, you ask him about that list of NDP industrial development failures." These were the real giveaways, he added, "the waste of your tax dollars by a bunch of people who didn't know how to run the public affairs of this province."

Premier Lyon then delivered a fiery speech to 450 supporters in Dauphin, where he belittled this "lackluster group of burn-outs who are clinging to 19th Century doctrine [and] really have no place in modern-day society." Moreover, he unrealistically boasted, "they're reduced to less of a group than they were before because three of their former cabinet have left them, loudly declaiming where they are today." The feisty Lyon labelled the NDP "The No Dam Progress Party." This may have persuaded his partisan audience, but it signalled hopelessness to the larger public.

As Lyon was campaigning in Dauphin, I was rallying our supporters in Thompson. Orange NDP banners and thunderous applause (much of it from striking Inco workers) wildly greeted me as I entered the hall. Clearly the town's nine-week strike, affecting 1900 miners, was threatening to defeat the Tory minister, MacMaster. The contrast between my two visits to Thompson and Lyon's total absence from the community during the campaign did not go unnoticed by the local townspeople. Steve Ashton made the difference abundantly clear, saying "Pawley's presence shows that he is not afraid to face the strikers."

The theme of my remarks was to assure the audience that an NDP government would pursue a job policy that placed full-time employment ahead of the welfare economy. Once again, I stressed that the best role for government was working together in joint ventures with mining companies; this would develop the province's resources in ways that ensured jobs and kept the money in Manitoba. I decried Lyon's reliance on a welfare economy in northern Manitoba, in places like Thompson, where the population had plummeted by 4000 people since his victory in 1977.

Lyon was beginning to show some bitterness about what he alleged was biased media reporting. He scoffed at media reports referring to an NDP meeting of twenty or thirty as wildly enthusiastic while his meetings of 600 or 700 were being described as unenthusiastic. He denounced the press for not sufficiently covering a rally in St. James with over 1500 supporters. On still another occasion, he chastised the CBC for its polling practices, which showed the NDP leading.

On Monday, 16 November 1981, Lyon wound up his campaign in Brandon with a rally at the livestock arena, the Keystone Centre, attended by more than 750 of his cheering supporters. The premier attacked what he described as our "Made in Regina Policies." Once again, he condemned the New Democrats for their past record under former Premier Schreyer. He lambasted us for our proposed programs to help farmers and small business, charging that they had been copied from the Saskatchewan NDP government.

In contrast, during the final days of the campaign I was steadily encountering increasing excitement among our supporters, augmenting my conviction that we might indeed be heading for victory. Virtually everywhere I went I was met with enthusiastic clamour about "Premier Pawley." Wherever I came into view at rallies, I was greeted with the familiar thumbs-up gesture that was being promoted by our advertising campaign. Sticking to a standard speech without any new policy pronouncements, I now continually ridiculed Lyon for suddenly embarking on a belated and frantic promise-a-day appeal in the waning days of the campaign. Moreover, although he had made a name for himself by opposing Trudeau's constitutional initiatives and had perhaps been supported by a majority of Manitobans, Lyon had alienated many by appearing to be more obsessed about constitutional battles with Ottawa than with the creation of jobs at home. A favourite refrain of my campaign speeches was that Lyon should be concerned about "patriating the sons and daughters of Manitobans rather than with patriating the Constitution"—a reference to the large numbers of Manitoba's young people forced to leave the province and relocate because of the severe recession punishing the province. I usually received a standing ovation for this line. In fact, as it caught on during the campaign, I began repeating it every chance I got, as it captured what was on most people's minds during the recession of the early 1980s.

In Dauphin, I charged the PCs with desperation, claiming that they "know they have lost the campaign and they know they have lost it badly." Our Dauphin rally was a raucous one. Signs for our candidate, John Plohman, were everywhere; our supporters were wild with enthusiasm, singing and clapping as local songwriter Walter Rutka gave a lively finale to a memorable evening. On the charter plane ride back, carrying all the frontline campaign workers from Dauphin to Winnipeg, a euphoric mood captivated all on board. We were heading to a victory over the Tories and the formation of a new government.

Heading Toward Victory

Speaking to a breakfast pep rally of 250 supporters in Winnipeg the morning before election day, I proclaimed that victory was within sight, emphasizing that it would be one for all Manitobans, not just the NDP. I implored our supporters not to take anything for granted and to guarantee that every potential NDP voter reached the polls.

Having refrained previously from predicting victory, I began to express more public confidence about the promising election result. At one location I discussed a transition committee that would consist of two eminent and respected Schreyer cabinet ministers, Saul Miller and Saul Cherniack. At another location, I predicted we would win from thirty to thirty-five seats (though few shared my optimism). At a final meeting with students at the University of Winnipeg, I jokingly wished Sterling Lyon well on his "farewell tour of Manitoba."

This was dangerous rhetoric on my part, and in some circumstances it could have backfired. Voters can sometimes recoil when this happens. Certainly Stephen Harper of the federal Conservatives discovered this during the 2004 campaign when he wildly predicted a majority Conservative government. It is best, I think, always to speak from the vantage point of being only one vote behind, and while hoping to win it all, to demand an all-out effort until the polls finally close on election day. Gary Doer was very successful in 2007 by repeatedly warning that the party was running one vote behind in each constituency.

In the last days of the campaign, the political pundits were predicting a tight race. Some suggested the weather would make the difference. It was anticipated that in case of rain or cold temperatures, unenthusiastic Conservatives would be more likely to remain home and not vote. From my perspective, we were stimulated by the health of our riding organizations. I knew we could get our vote out.

Personally, I felt good about the tireless campaign I had led. My predecessor, Ed Schreyer, was perceived as more charismatic than I. In fact, a joke had gone the rounds that "Howard's idea of a good time is going to Eaton's on a Friday night and trying on gloves." Many in the party had privately questioned whether I could deliver in a campaign. That had encouraged me to work even harder. When the election was called, few gave this forty-six-year-old "lacklustre leader" much of a chance to upset the clearly flamboyant, fiery, and colourful Lyon. Yet my campaign appeared energetic and confident, and Lyon's sluggish. Often rising by 5:30 a.m, I would be on the road campaigning from an early hour, not retiring until near midnight. Catnaps onboard the campaign bus were revitalizing. Meeting people in shopping malls, main-streeting, or simply plant gating, I had managed to log 11,000 miles and to meet thousands of people during the brief thirty-five-day campaign.

The Results

On election day, I stopped in at both campaign offices in Winnipeg and at polling stations in Selkirk. Wherever I went, there was clearly an upbeat mood of rising expectations. Everywhere, our organization was maximizing voter attendance, drawing more volunteers than ever in the history of the party. Our supporters were buoyant with the expectation of a victory that night. I ran into my old rival from the New Party battles at the time of its birth, Stanley Knowles, who quietly remarked, "You have turned out better than I expected."

That evening, I awaited the first reports at our home near Lockport. Perhaps I was more nervous than at any other time in my life (with the possible exceptions of my wedding and the births of my two children). Before the first polls were counted, the usual media pundits outlined their analysis of the campaign. Paul Thomas, one of Manitoba's most highly regarded political scientists, hinted that I might have hurt my campaign during its final days by my musing to the press that I had expected to win. The announcement of the transition committee, Thomas correctly opined, might be seen as a sign of arrogance. For a brief moment I worried, "maybe he's right." However, as the results poured in, it soon became apparent that we were headed for a sweeping victory. After visiting my own campaign headquarters in Selkirk to express gratitude to constituency workers, whom I had seen infrequently during the campaign and whose arduous work and sacrifice gave me the largest majority I had ever achieved in my home riding, my family and I went to the victory celebrations at the Union Centre in Winnipeg. On the way there, Bill Gillies, my campaign coordinator, turned in the front seat and said, "Let me be the first to congratulate you, Mr. Premier."

We won 47.5 percent of the vote against 43.7 percent for the Progressive Conservatives. In the seat count, we secured thirty-four seats to the

Progressive Conservatives' twenty-three. In the dying days of the campaign, we had begun to anticipate victory, but we never expected such a huge triumph. We were enjoying practically a clean sweep of the so-called marginal constituencies. Electoral gains in Brandon West, Riel, River East, and St. James were especially satisfying. No doubt it measured the extent of the fury against the Lyon government for gutting rent controls. Many talented new members were elected. [5] More women were elected to the Manitoba legislature, the highest number of any province in Canada, and five were from our ranks. [6]

Hundreds of cheering, yelling supporters greeted Adele, Chris, Charysse, and me upon our arrival at the Union Centre. It was a strenuous endeavour to force a path to the platform, and it took many minutes for the campaign workers with their sea of signs to settle down so I could offer my thanks. The words "Pawley for Premier" had already been swapped for "Pawley is the Premier." The campaign workers were enjoying sweet revenge, as was I. Lyon was without a friend in this crowd.

At the end of the evening, accompanied by Bill Regehr, we made our way to the Birchwood Inn, in St. James. There we would spend the night and prepare for the gigantic challenges that would lie ahead.

Assuming the Reins of Government

Our newly elected government was confronted by overwhelming economic problems, including forecasts of a provincial deficit as high as $200 million and threatened cutbacks in federal transfers of as much as $160 million. The question was whether we could succeed in preserving the trust of Manitobans. I was ready to face the inevitable media barbs and criticism directed towards any political leader. There would be the expected antagonism from the predictable adversaries, who were ready to strike as soon as any spectre of socialism reared its head. Fortunately, after undergoing the Autopac debate and serving a term as Attorney General, I had acquired a thick skin.

My leadership of the party and government was based on my firm belief in teamwork. I distrusted too much emphasis on any one man or woman: the cult of personality eventually leads to grave disappointment. I have seen people place their hopes and expectations in so many leaders and have their beliefs shattered. Never did I want to be faced with a situation in which the party leaves all the decision making to the leader. It would also be critically important that we do everything we could to keep in touch with our grassroots. Since teamwork was the goal, a strong cabinet would be the vehicle to achieve what we set out to do. I was fortunate that I had a lot of talent to draw upon. The responsibilities were too great to load on any one person.

This is why the most essential challenge facing me was the appointment of cabinet ministers. To be free of the media and various interest groups, as well as people making representations for themselves or others to be in cabinet, Adele and I, along with some key advisors, drove north from Winnipeg to stay at the lodge on Hecla Island and to put together the first cabinet of my government. The ten days before I announced my cabinet were perhaps the most difficult experience in my political life to that point. Saul Cherniack, who chaired the transition team, wisely advised me to isolate myself from the press, well-wishers, and others. Time would be needed to reflect and to consider the make-up of the cabinet and other key matters. He cautioned, "Those decisions will greatly influence whether you govern for one term, two terms, or longer." Certainly a poor transition can inflict wounds that can undermine a successful term in office.

The night of our victory I telephoned Allan Blakeney. The Saskatchewan premier recommended that it was best to begin the term of a new government with a smaller number in cabinet and then add to this number when others have been sufficiently tested and before the burden becomes too heavy for those already appointed. Also, he advised, the cabinet should balance assorted interests of the party and among elected members. Ensuring competency, above all, was critical to obtaining a balance.

Cabinet-making is a complex task. A bad choice is easily made, yet its consequences can take forever to unravel. Cabinet appointments are often given to elected members who were the critics while in Opposition, but an individual's role as a critic does not automatically make that person suitable for a parallel role in government. There is always much danger in appointing someone who is too much an individualist, and thus wishes to pursue his or her own pet cause. As George Cadbury cautioned, in a memorandum to newly elected Premier Ed Schreyer, "[an] important necessity....[is] the creation of cabinet solidarity and the development of a cabinet personality above individual ministers who, while running their Departments, will be asked as cabinet ministers to create an overall entity with a view above departmental needs? Such an entity can both override and protect ministers when necessary. This will be especially necessary when new ministers from inexperience or over-enthusiasm make inevitable mistakes."[7] The most critical necessity is the formation of a team committed to the objectives of the government, one where individuals will not be derailed by personal agendas.

Retrospectively, I believe I was fortunate with my choice of ministers. Although some later came under vicious attack from media or the Opposition, they generally acquitted themselves well. In my admittedly biased view, a more honest and hard-working group could not be discovered anywhere else.

An omission from a cabinet list can regrettably result in adverse consequences. The best example of this was the eventual desertion by Jim Walding on the critical 1988 budget vote. Walding's conduct in the election campaign, which displayed a lack of teamwork, caused me to cross him off my list for consideration as a cabinet appointment. My appointment of him as the Speaker appeared to be the best choice for this former chair of our caucus. Questions were raised about why I included Larry Desjardins, who had neither supported us in the federal 1979 election nor won friends with his vacillating on the auto insurance issue and his ardent hostility at party conventions to pro-choice resolutions on the abortion issue. I had to weigh both his reputation as a senior elected member who had eventually made it possible for the Schreyer government to survive, and his competence and well-recognized experience.

Shortly after our electoral success I was confronted with an overly ambitious Henry Carroll, the newly elected member for Brandon West, who warned me that unless he was appointed to cabinet he would have no alternative but to sit as an Independent. I wasn't about to be intimidated or bullied into rewarding any member who made such a threat. If that was his attitude, I suggested, he might take up his seat as an Independent earlier rather than later. He obliged—and thus ended his commitment to sit as the NDP member for Brandon West.

Of course consideration must be given to loyalty and seniority. The new cabinet must also take into account social-economic origins, ethnicity, and gender. Some newly elected members would require additional time to gain experience. Elijah Harper, for example, emerged as a highly respected minister of northern affairs and champion of Aboriginal self-government, after several years of internship as a backbencher and as an assistant to Minister of Northern Affairs Jay Cowan. Elijah himself recognized this; he advised my aides, "I am not prepared for it at this time; I'd rather wait and get used to things." Elijah was not interested in grandstanding or being a star. He was interested in gradually working his way up.

The public will scrutinize the cabinet selections. Will women assume traditional female roles in portfolios such as community affairs or social affairs, or will they be involved equally in all cabinet portfolios? I was fortunate to be able to appoint Muriel Smith as minister of economic development as well as deputy premier. In addition, more women were appointed to cabinet than had been the case with any previous Manitoba cabinet; also appointed were Maureen Hemphill in education and Mary Beth Dolin in labour. With the problem of regional balance, however, I was left with the party being overrepresented in certain regions of the province and underrepresented in others.

Sensitivity was encountered when I sought a balance between those representing "the old guard" and "the newcomers," those elected for the first time. I certainly sensed concern from old-timers over the prominence given to some of the newcomers. It was no secret that Walding felt unjustly passed over for the newly elected members.

During cabinet discussions, I found it crucial to defer personal comments until various ministers had offered theirs, so my comments would not prematurely shape the direction of the discussion. To enhance collegiality, I tried various techniques, such as temporarily removing an item from discussion to permit some face-saving if a minister appeared to be losing support. Sometimes an issue would be re-cast or put in a wider context so that the direction would not be seen as a win-lose situation, or the discussion would be deferred and resumed at a later time in order to permit a consensus to form. As I witnessed in the Schreyer years, it is not just the strength of individual members of a cabinet but how they interact with one another that is critical to the competent execution of any government's policies and programs.

Caucus

We made considerable progress in developing some innovative methods to enhance the role of backbench members of the legislature. Real votes were held in the caucus with all caucus members, including its cabinet members, so that all members were on an equal footing. Caucus members attended and participated in cabinet committees and reported back. Detailed briefings of budget estimates and proposed legislation were always shared with the caucus. Caucus approval was required for the legislative process flow chart. Personally, I feel we should also have ensured more rotation of caucus members within cabinet, as I believe most members can benefit from a stint in caucus.

My presence at caucus meetings would always be vital to address the concerns of its members. To assist the caucus, we determined that members should be employed in committees comprised of not only party members but also others with interest and expertise in various portfolios, who in turn could advise cabinet ministers. Some of my ministers were very successful in using such committees. I especially recall the success enjoyed by Eugene Kostyra while he was in cabinet.

In my view, more private members' resolutions and bills should reach a vote. The House should also be given a greater role in approving major appointments. While free votes should be encouraged on some occasions, I would caution against too much enthusiasm on this score. I discovered there is little need for many free votes if a caucus works together as a team. Moreover, free votes may pit one member against another in a public venue and create unnecessary dissension, which is to be avoided; and if there are too many free votes, there is also a greater likelihood that a weak member may buckle from the pressure from powerful lobby groups, break ranks, and face the finger-pointing of other members.

Finally, caucus members must never be taken by surprise by announcements. They must always be kept fully informed, for constituency awareness is critical to a successful MLA's political career. This is especially true in matters concerning the riding. What is most shattering to an MLA is being blind-sided—discovering after the fact that a unilateral announcement affecting his/her constituents has been made without the member's knowing anything about it. Members justifiably see such occasions as lost opportunities to gain a little credit for influencing an accomplishment. I did everything I could to prevent the impression that a member was invisible or ineffective.

Senior Public Servants

Like cabinet appointments, key public service positions may have long-term implications. Moreover, senior appointments in the civil service can have even greater impact than cabinet appointments upon the morale and mood of public servants. Our handling of Derek Bedsen is a case in point. Although widely respected, Bedsen, clerk of the Manitoba Executive Council, had been associated with the Conservative administrations of John Diefenbaker and Premiers Roblin, Weir, and Lyon. When we were elected in 1981, we replaced Bedson with Michael Decter as clerk of the Executive Council. Decter had been planning secretary to cabinet in the final months of the Schreyer administration and was a senior person with the Priorities and Planning Committee of cabinet. Thus, the signal was sent that the public service should identify with the goals of the new government. It was our intent to symbolize a new order and new management in Manitoba. (After Decter left, we were fortunate to recruit George Ford as his replacement.)

The principal secretary's position is not one to be envied. My experience tells me that the secretary usually becomes a lightning rod for resentment when they do the premier's bidding. This official is feared inside government, where their word can make or break careers. Sometimes they are accused of handpicking cabinet ministers' aides or replacing them with handpicked people. The secretary also controls the premier's agenda and decides who gets in to see him for an appointment, and when. In our case, as the NDP and the Progressive Conservatives had shared power for much of the previous twenty-five years, there had been little need for wholesale public service bloodletting. Bill Regehr, a close friend, a former superintendent in the Lord Selkirk School Division, and the architect of our success during both our years in Opposition and our election to Government, assumed the responsibility of becoming my principal secretary. Bill was a tough, resourceful organizer who had an uncanny talent for motivating people to fight for the same cause. He was devoted to my vision of a more open party, and he was the person who ensured that everyone's opinions were heard. His successors during my government's term were two highly competent individuals, John Walsh, the former party secretary who was one of the masterminds of our win, and Ginny Devine (who would later marry Gary Doer), highly regarded for her work with Attorney General Penner and subsequently with me.

Dan O'Connor took on the role of the government's communications and coordination secretary. Dan was the first person to spot weaknesses in the Tory's re-election campaign, and he was our major strategist during the campaign. I was most impressed by his abilities to set a target and then develop the most effective approaches. Prior to his arrival in Manitoba to work in my office when the party was in opposition, he had been the executive assistant to Alexa McDonough, the NDP leader in Nova Scotia. He had a monastic devotion to politics, usually putting in sixteen-hour days. Dan was to be succeeded by Cliff Scotton, a long time CCF-NDP warrior, who added his expertise in advising NDP leaders on communications approaches.

Aims for a New Government

As I progressed along the electoral road to becoming the premier of the province, I was compelled to become more pragmatic than I had been in my earlier days when I had opposed the adoption of the Winnipeg Declaration and, subsequently, the formation of the New Democratic Party. My attitude evolved because I was able to witness the persistent, step-by-step progress toward our aims. For me, political involvement means more than career building; it should represent the journey toward a final destination where a truly democratic socialist society is built. Over my career, I tried to sustain a long-range vision of ensuring a greater equality of incomes and a fairer distribution of power in society.

During my time as premier, the party adopted a statement of aims that illustrated our short- and long-term objectives. A committee chaired by Lawrie Cherniack wrote it. Its words were inscribed on the back of NDP membership cards. To me they clearly portrayed my role as leader of the party, and they provide a useful benchmark for evaluating the performance of an NDP government. I believe my government came off pretty well when assessed in relation to the party principles set out in the statement. It read:

> Our society must change from one based on competition to one of cooperation.
>
> - We wish to create a society where individuals give according to their abilities and receive according to their needs.
>
> - We believe present human endeavours must become environmentally sound in order to ensure that future generations may have access to an abundant and diverse biosphere.
>
> - Our commitment to the electorate is to be forthright about our long-range goals as well as practical about our short-term political activities.
>
> - Our purpose as a movement is to foster social change toward a more cooperative society. Our purpose as a political party is to develop a public mandate for that social change through giving individuals greater control in the economy, their workplaces, and their community.
>
> - Our actions and words must reflect our fundamental faith in the capacity of people to live cooperatively and to work for the betterment of all.

Management of a Provincial Economy

Contrary to the attitude prevalent throughout Canada in the early 1980s, I believed government must be prepared to step up to the plate in difficult economic times. It was my firm conviction that governments must spend more during such times, even if it meant going into a deficit position. Our program reflected a social democratic philosophy aimed at reducing the disparities in the distribution of income and power within society. We supported a much more activist role in minimizing the hardships inflicted by the free enterprise system's imperfections. The primary thrust was job creation, including public and private development. This was to become the centrepiece of my government's time in office. All other initiatives (except for the French-language issue) would pale by comparison.

Of course, our government was restrained by the financial and constitutional limits on any provincial initiatives undertaken by any activist government. Manitoba is a smaller, less prosperous province with much less political influence than larger, more affluent provinces like Alberta, Quebec, British Columbia, and Ontario. Nonetheless, Manitoba, "the Keystone province," did benefit in the early 1980s from having both an advanced political culture and a diversified economy. It was better off than most other provinces during the recession of those years. Unlike Alberta and British Columbia, Manitoba never suffered economic volatility, a problem especially evident in Alberta, where thousands of mortgages were foreclosed upon. Manitoba was characterized by economic stability, albeit at a modest level of growth.

Throughout our time, while other governments were slashing social services, we continued to preserve and improve them. Unfortunately, this did mean increasing taxes; we had no alternative if we were to ensure that the economic woes hitting all Canadians would be minimized for the most vulnerable in Manitoba. Interestingly, although the political right and other powerful interests angrily derided them, these tax increases were generally maintained into the 1990s and even after 2000. Our economic success in the midst of difficult times, compared to that of other provinces, cannot be challenged.

Reflecting on our taxation policies, I can't help but be proud that our NDP government was prepared to proceed with increases. Governments today, fearful of doing so, recklessly disregard the potential long-term damage an unmanageable deficit can inflict.

Economic Policy Launched in 1981

The main priorities of our NDP government would be threefold: to establish an economic base strong enough to encourage job creation and retain youth in the province; to maintain and enhance social services and programs that were feasible, given the financial pressure to which the province was subjected; and to encourage a fairer, more equitable provincial community. Wherever additional benefits were provided, they would go to those in the greatest need.

I saw that success depended on working cooperatively with the other levels of government and encouraging a greater partnership with labour, business communities, and, most importantly, community groups. Throughout our policy-making and program-making process, we integrated social, environmental, and economic goals; rather than looking at policies in isolation for their potential positive or negative influence, the cabinet maintained a steady eye on the goals we had been elected to achieve.

Ideologically, the "politics of polarization" dominated Manitoba, and a fierce debate raged over the best way to minimize the catastrophic economic and social fallout of the early 1980s. The government headed by Premier Sterling Lyon had embraced a market-driven approach in response to the economic turmoil. By contrast, our newly elected government supported a much more activist role in minimizing the hardships inflicted by the system's imperfections. This resulted in the Manitoba Jobs Fund initiative, aimed at creating jobs in all sectors of the provincial economy. It was modeled on the Keynesian approach—spending money in bad times to increase aggregate demand to stimulate the economy.

My government launched the Jobs Fund with a commitment of more than $210 million, on a per capita basis by far the largest amount spent by any province in the 1980s on measures to reduce unemployment. The fund primarily focused on long-term investment that would eventually lead to permanent jobs. Importantly, much of this money was targeted to job and skill training and technological development in essential industries crucial for Manitoba's future. Additional funding, in partnership with the federal government, resulted in $400 million (during a five-year term) that was allocated toward the agricultural, food processing, forestry, mining, rail, and bus transportation industries in an extensive effort to maintain and improve the province's international edge and strength in these critical sectors.

Jobs Fund programs would also be directed toward assisting the province's rural and farm communities, including one launched to make money available for Main Street Manitoba projects to improve downtown business areas in rural towns. This was a high priority in the overall plan of stimulating economic opportunities throughout rural Manitoba, permitting rural people and those in the North to remain in their own communities.

Social Contract

An early challenge confronted us, one that could have destroyed our relationship with our friends in the labour community. Nonetheless, we had no alternative but to obtain their cooperation. During the early 1980s, provincial premiers across Canada, such as Bill Bennett in British Columbia, Grant Devine in Saskatchewan, and even the centralist Bill Davis in Ontario and the more ideologically left-wing René Lévesque, were imposing wage freezes and cutbacks on their public sector. Manitoba could not be an island unto itself; clearly, we also had to slow the escalation of costs. But we were determined to discover a more innovative way to do it. I wanted to put a stop to our rising unemployment rate. Public sector unions could not be spared, but displacing public sector workers would not stop the deteriorating employment numbers. I believed it would only do the opposite.

It was in this atmosphere in 1983 that I decided there was no other choice but to invite the leadership of the Manitoba Government Employees' Association (MGEA), representing 12,000 public employees, to renegotiate their contract, which had been signed in 1982, only a few months before the rate of inflation had plummeted with the deepening of the recession. It was politically critical that we show that the provincial deficit had not increased because of the scheduled wage increase. Moreover, money had to be made available to decrease unemployment. I called Gary Doer, then president of the MGEA, and emphasized to him that neither the government nor his union could live with a 10.5 percent increase in wages. A public backlash would erupt against any union that appeared to be isolated from the impact of a recession that adversely affected so much of the population.

I emphasized that money was urgently needed to reduce unemployment in the province. The first reaction by the MGEA was one of surprise and to say "NO." This mood soon changed as their leadership considered the potential adverse reactions. Over a period of two to three days with the participation of the leadership of the government and the MGEA, we worked out a solution. Eugene Kostyra, formerly with the Canadian Union of Public Employees, Jay Cowan, a former United Steelworkers of America organizer, and Mary

Beth Dolin, our newly appointed minister of labour, would all prove highly influential in their negotiations with the representatives of the MGEA.

We agreed to delay for three months the second yearly increase that they had negotiated in their contract. As a result, the government saved $10 million in the fiscal year ending 31 March 1983. Although the employees would eventually get their negotiated increases, the delay in implementing them amounted to an average contribution of $600 by each MGEA member. Thus $10 million was added to the Jobs Fund. It came about as a result of trust and understanding. A critical and positive force ensuring the success of talks was Dick Martin, who, on behalf of the Manitoba Federation of Labour, saw the efforts in broad rather than narrow terms, insofar as labour would be contributing to a fund committed to reducing joblessness in the province. The ugly experience with the Ontario Accord in 1993 contrasts sharply with our experience with this accord.[8]

The Environment

Any discussion of the economy must interlink with matters pertaining to the environment. Hazardous workplaces have both social and economic impacts, but the latter are frequently overlooked. My government in the 1980s was one of the rare exceptions in this regard. The legislation we put in place definitely signalled that we were embarking on a new era. We were clearly giving the message that we would do in-depth analyses of all environmental impacts and begin to assess cumulative impacts. With that goal in mind, we began to retool the legislative and regulatory mechanisms.

The Dangerous Goods Handling and Transportation Act had gone through an extensive consultation and planning process with both the public and private sectors throughout the province. The proposed legislation was then redrafted to address the concerns raised during this consultation phase. The new Act was intended to give the province the capability and the authority to regulate and react to site-specific problems regarding the manufacturing usage, storage, transportation, handling, and disposal of dangerous goods. It was also intended to accommodate the establishment of hazardous waste disposal facilities in Manitoba. As well, the new legislation required that a cradle-to-grave manifest be put in place for hazardous wastes, so they could be tracked from the generator to final disposal.

Under the legislation, transporters of hazardous waste would have to be licensed, and they would be required to carry adequate third-party liability insurance and adhere to stringent site-specific requirements. The legislation also required that environmental accident response capability be improved. Surely a healthy environmental setting contributes to the economy, as do improved working conditions for those with a low income and few benefits.

Despite our successes, Opposition leader Sterling Lyon fiercely continued to denounce our government as "incompetent" and unable to run a "peanut stand let alone a province." In response, I took my case directly to the people in a series of public meetings and appearances. This ensured access to the news media. I never played down the problems we faced, but made a practice of telling audiences that things were every bit as bad as they thought they were. To a Brandon audience I declared, "I would not like to be a finance minister at this time." To a Winnipeg audience I warned, "These are rotten times, my friends."

Our programs in government reflected a social democratic philosophy, whose objectives were to gradually reduce sharp disparities in income distribution. It is well recognized by economists that severe recessions adversely affect income distribution. It is now also recognized by some that prosperity can, unfortunately, have the same effect without appropriate government policies and programs. Our administration was determined to ensure that Manitoba would make every effort to offset this regressive trend.

CHAPTER 6

Anatomy of a Political Nightmare

The Language Controversy in Manitoba

EARLY IN OUR FIRST TERM we were to be derailed in our attempts to concentrate on economic recovery. No other policy initiative was as detrimental to us as our well-meaning attempt to protect French-language rights and services. The public was overwhelmingly antagonistic. No lengthy intellectual, historical, or legal discourse outlining the solemn covenant that had been entered between Manitoba's English- and French-speaking peoples at the province's entry into Confederation could lessen the intense resistance. Reasoned arguments about the colossal financial cost that would be inflicted on the province if it should defy the upcoming Supreme Court judgment would make not a scintilla of a difference to the outraged public. Our opponents launched massive protest rallies, and our government was powerless in its efforts to lessen the anger aroused. Personally, I was devastated by the bigotry, though it characterized only a fraction of those who opposed the language legislation. But I also was disgusted by the total incoherence that prevailed, provoked by fears deliberately fanned by those who knew better but had only one motive—to advance their ulterior political designs.

Some History of the Dispute

When Manitoba became a province in 1870, half of its population was French speaking. Today, various towns reflect this French presence in their names: Portage la Prairie, Ste. Agathe, The Pas, St. Jean, and Dauphin. The population balance was soon tilted by an influx of English-speaking settlers from Ontario, who the early French-speaking settlers feared would submerge their culture. To allay these fears, language guarantees were inserted in the Manitoba Act, which brought Manitoba into Canada. Section 23 reads as follows:

> Either the English or the French language may be used by any person in the debates of the houses of the legislatures, and both those languages should be used in the respective records and journals of those houses; and either of those languages may be used by any person, or in any pleading or process, or issuing from the court of Canada established under the British North America act 1867, or in or from all the courts of the province. The acts of the Legislature shall be printed and published in both those languages.

These provisions were certainly not radical; indeed, they were identical to those granted to the English-speaking population of Quebec under the British North American Act. These provisions included the right to use either language in the courts and in the legislature, and the requirement that statutes be published in both languages.

The newcomers from Ontario, who were largely Protestant and Anglo-Saxon, brought to the West their deep prejudices against both the French and Catholics. The Manitoba legislature reflected this when it abolished the 1870 language guarantees, replacing them with the Official Languages Act of 1890, which decreed that only the English language could be used in the courts, in the legislature, and in the publication of provincial statutes.

Although there were some minor challenges to this legislation, the laws and practices of the government of Manitoba were determined for decades by an illegal Act of the Legislature. All this ended in 1976, when George Forest, a resident of St. Boniface and a prominent language crusader, was issued a parking ticket and promptly refused to pay the fine because it was written completely in English, contrary to a provision in the City of Winnipeg Act requiring bilingual municipal notices be issued to the residents of St. Boniface. When the provincial court convicted Forest, he turned to the County Court of St. Boniface in an appeal, which he wrote entirely in French, relying upon the provisions of Section 23 of the Manitoba Act.

There, Judge Armand Dureault deemed Manitoba's Official Languages Act unconstitutional. As the province's Attorney General at the time, I advised that the Crown would not consider the ruling as "a binding precedent." Forest was left without any alternative but to seek relief from the Manitoba

Court of Appeal, where he requested that the Official Languages Act be ruled unconstitutional.

To assist him, Forest demanded copies of the relevant statutes, including the Summary Conviction Act, the Winnipeg Act, and the Highway Traffic Acts, must be supplied in French. It was an unprecedented demand. I agreed to provide these relevant statutes but only if Forest paid the sum of $17,000, representing the total cost of translation. Retrospectively, I saw this was a mistake because it was attaching a price to minority language rights. Forest responded by seeking a *mandamus* order from the court, directing that the statutes be provided as requested. The registrar of the court refused to accept his documents on the basis that they were contrary to the provisions of the Official Languages Act.

When the Schreyer government was defeated in 1977, the succeeding Lyon government became responsible for the language issue. The Forest case eventually wound its way to the Supreme Court of Canada in 1979, where the clock was turned back to 1870; the 1890 Act was invalidated, and French was legally restored as an official language in both the courts and the legislature of Manitoba. Shortly after that decision, Manitoba started the process of translation; it was estimated that about 14,000 pages of laws and regulations would need to be translated. Thus, the language rights spelled out in Section 23 were restored to their constitutional status by the Forest case.

With enactment of the so-called remedial legislation in 1979, the new government failed miserably. Its tinkering with Section 23 of the Manitoba Act was worthless in precluding future court challenges to the validity of Manitoba laws, and it did not honour the province's obligations under Section 23. In neither practical nor legal terms did the Lyon government's Bill 2 succeed in addressing the complex questions respecting the validity of those statutes, which had been enacted solely in English. Fortunately for them, the Lyon government was not around much longer and thus escaped the repercussions from their ineffective legislative actions. Lyon's "band-aid" approach simply managed to get him past an election. It was useless in dealing with the fundamental legal issues.

With our victory in 1981, I was once more tossed into the same predicament that had haunted me as Attorney General five years before; the French-language file was again uppermost on the political agenda and demanded immediate attention. Beyond the narrow legal issues, the new government desired to provide provincial services in French to those who belonged to the French-language minority. Indeed, we enthusiastically pressed ahead with the translation of informational documents, including driving licences, marriage licences and birth certificates.

The Société franco-manitobaine (SFM) annual convention took place in St. Boniface within the first few months of 1982. I personally appeared and summarized the initial achievements of my government in beginning the intricate task of providing French-language services. Not being bilingual, I delivered my speech in English, except for a few sentences that had been carefully written in French for me to read to the more than 500 delegates present. I stumbled badly, and my lack of even the most rudimentary French was readily apparent; however, the endeavours from the heart appeared to be warmly welcomed. Referring to my own family heritage, in which my French-speaking unilingual great-grandfather had married my equally unilingual English-speaking grandmother, I explained that neither had understood the other's language but that this had not hindered them from enjoying a loving and wonderful marriage in which they had raised eight children. In the same way, I assured them, my being unilingual would not hinder our having an excellent relationship together.

It did not take long before the precise legal effect of Section 23 was tested. It occurred in the case of *Bilodeau v. the Attorney General of Manitoba*. There, the argument by the plaintiff was that the failure to enact the statutes in both official languages rendered the speeding ticket inoperative. The majority of the Manitoba Court of Appeal rejected this argument, holding that the wording of Section 23 was directory and not mandatory. However, dissenting in part, Mr. Justice Monnin held that whatever may have been the case prior to Forest, the implications of Forest were such that there was, and there had been since 1979, a constitutional requirement that all the provincial statutes be printed and published in both official languages, and since the province had failed to do this, the statutes were therefore inoperative.

We were faced with the worst possible predicament, a probable appeal and a future decision on appeal to the Supreme Court of Canada, which could potentially declare Section 23 mandatory. The potential consequences would be massive and result in the most detrimental ramifications for Manitoba. Undetermined was the status of statutes not translated into both English and French. In 1982, after two years of translating, a meagre nine of 450 statutes had been completed at an outrageous cost of $400,000. It was estimated that the mammoth task of translating ninety years of English-speaking laws would drag on for at least six more years, and cost in excess of $10 to $15 million, with the biggest obstacle being the shortage of appropriate translators, who were in scarce supply because the assignment required not only linguistic skills but also a grasp of complex technical and legal matters.

Worse, an entire century of legislative enactments might be declared null and void by Canada's highest court. According to our legal advisers, that prospect was unlikely; however, it did exist, and Manitoba could be without any laws at all. That would result in what was described as legal chaos, where our laws, whether they pertained to hunting, driving, labour relations, or any other matter, would be unenforceable. We received these legal opinions from Dale Gibson and Kerr Twaddle, two eminent constitutional advisers on the preferred course of action. Whatever action was chosen, it was unpredictable how the higher courts would decide. But while the legal arguments were unclear, there was no doubt from a historical or justice perspective what the proper agreement should be with the minority language community.

Whatever the ultimate legal disposition, we had always intended to translate all the statutes enacted since 1979 into both languages. Also to be included were their regulations, but only if absolutely necessary because of the cost and delay that would be incurred. We were in an extremely precarious situation. While there was admittedly only a minor risk that the Supreme Court would ever declare all our statutes void, a less grave judgment would still produce severe difficulties for us. Without any ideal alternative to select from, Attorney General Roland Penner decided to commence negotiations with the federal government, the SFM, and Bilodeau.

To do so, the Attorney General wanted the cabinet's authorization to initiate negotiations with all the parties to the court action. Around the cabinet table, we seriously underestimated the political reaction that would erupt. After all, we were only rectifying a historic wrong. Naturally, none of us had any sympathy for the kinds of forces responsible for the 1890 legislation or for the current day anti-bilingual voices, which were both vociferous and frequently heard. Moreover, with my government finding itself increasingly cash-strapped in the midst of the severe economic recession of the early 1980s, an agreement might successfully avoid unnecessary outlays. Translating a bunch of dated statutes and regulations dating back to 1890, for example, appeared pure folly. Also, the issue could seriously deflect public attention from what was our central priority: the retention and creation of jobs in the midst of the recession.

We were reassured by the initial signals from Ottawa that they were supportive of a just settlement. Prime Minister Trudeau wished to enhance his own vision of minority language protection throughout all of Canada and would likely allocate substantial resources to this task.

We were unquestionably naive about the potential for a political explosion, which later erupted with a vengeance. We had never given much heed to the language issue previously. Personally, I was instinctively uncomfortable with it; over the previous decade, I had frequently encountered hostility to bilingualism, leaving no leeway for a middle course. Although I warned my colleagues not to be overly naive, none of us imagined that the issue would become as explosive as it did. Regrettably, the alarm bells failed to go off in time to alert us. However, even if they had, I suspect we would still have chosen to do the just thing.

Although difficult, the negotiations ended well, and to our amazement, we reached an agreement requiring only a limited number of statutes to be translated, the most commonly used ones. Furthermore, the federal government would provide financial assistance to municipalities requesting money to facilitate the provision of services in French. In addition, the provincial government would provide French-language services in all census areas within the province where there were sufficient French-speaking residents to warrant them. Moreover, the central offices of Crown corporations, ministries, and departments would have bilingual capacity. All parties included in the negotiations were pleased with the results; it seemed like a win-win situation. However, guarantees to consummate these protections needed to be enshrined in Section 23 of the Manitoba Act.

The first news of the successful completion of the negotiations took the form of an announcement by Prime Minister Trudeau at a local Liberal meeting on 16 May 1983. The news media, especially the CBC, heralded this achievement as a major historical breakthrough in the long-standing language impasse that had confronted Manitoba; it was interpreted as a mark up for official bilingualism. Trudeau's announcement was delivered in French without any warning to us. Regrettably, its nature was such that it set off a firestorm.

Two days later in the Manitoba legislature, Sterling Lyon pounced. The former premier had obviously been hiding in the bushes preparing to ambush us, to borrow Roland Penner's colourful description. The Opposition had been informed of the negotiations and had even been sent a copy of the draft agreement by the Attorney General. No reply to the correspondence was received from Lyon.

Having incorrectly informed the legislature that language rights had been fully restored by the legislation enacted by his government, the former premier charged that the proposed NDP amendment went too far, claiming it would lead to the same "social divisiveness" that was created by Ottawa's bilingualism policies and inflicted by court-ordered school busing in the United States. In a hard-hitting speech on 29 June 1983, he asked why negotiations had taken place behind closed doors, and he demanded public hearings. Manitoba, he said, had "capitulated" to the federal government and set up a "tyranny" of a tiny minority.

Lyon created public anger when he lashed out in fury, shouting:

> Is [the Attorney General] telling us that it is House business that the Dean of Law School and departmental officials of his department constitute some institution or some committee of this house that will go out and propagandize the position of this government on the amendment to section 23 that they are bringing in? Is this his position? Because if that is the case, he should have made a statement to the house at the beginning about what the intention of this government was in its little propaganda venture. This has nothing to do with a committee of this house setting properly and hearing representations from the public. This is a unilateral, authoritarian decision being made by an incompetent government to deal with one of the most fundamental constitutional amendments that this province has seen.[1]

He demanded that further action on the matter be suspended and an inter-sessional legislative committee be organized to hear public representations on the issue.

A few days later, Lyon also demanded an election on the issue. After they obviously failed to obtain our assurance of one, the Opposition moved to adjourn the House. For the first time on the issue, they walked out of the legislative assembly and the division bells were allowed to ring. (The bells that summon members to the House for a standing vote are not turned off and no vote is taken until the party whips advise the speaker that they are ready for one.) The Tories remained out until the end of the day's session. They had declared war.

During the early stages of the debate it was increasingly evident to us that we had seriously miscalculated; public apprehension and the Opposition's determination to obstruct the government's constitutional proposals were growing. On 27 June, under pressure, I announced that legislative committee meetings would be scheduled inter-sessionally. Also, we distributed throughout the province a pamphlet explaining the proposals.

It was clear that the Prime Minister's Office had also given no thought to the potential fury that would emerge from his premature and unilateral announcement. We had failed to prepare either a communications plan or a plan of action. The actions of his office reinforced the perception, advanced by the Progressive Conservatives, that my government was gladly dancing to the prime minister's tune. To Manitobans, we were seen as simply bending to the whims of a zealous Franco-Manitoban minority and, allied with Trudeau, participating in the appeasement of Quebec nationalists and separatists.

The delay in acquiescing to the public hearings was a foolish error on our part. It was seen as an act of an "arrogant and totalitarian government" that did not much care about public opinion. It provided ready ammunition for those that accused both senior governments of "pushing French down the throats of Manitobans." This accusation was given greater credibility by what appeared to be the government's willingness to ignore public opinion, as was subsequently expressed in civic plebiscites. It would have been preferable for us to have been out front and agree to hearings and potential changes from these. In addition, if this course of action had eventually permitted the case to go to court we could have still lived with the consequences. Mulroney, with the Meech Lake Accord, would repeat the same mistake.

Disapproval of our approach came from unexpected quarters. During a crucial 1983 conference on Aboriginal constitutional matters, called by Trudeau, Quebec premier and separatist leader René Lévesque approached me and let me know in no uncertain terms how he viewed "the folly" of our language policy. René mocked Trudeau's "obsession" over bilingualism. "It just will not work," he said; and he warned that I would pay "a high political price" for my efforts. His remarks contrasted sharply with the soothing utterances of support rendered privately to me at the same conference by New Brunswick premier Richard Hatfield, who condemned the actions of his Conservative colleagues in Manitoba.

Another serious setback occurred in June 1983. Russell Doern, the NDP member for Elmwood and a former Schreyer cabinet minister, reported to his colleagues that he intended to poll his constituents to determine their opinions about the extension of French-language services in Manitoba. It was widely known throughout party circles that Doern was deeply angered by not having been appointed to cabinet; he was in a sour mood. At that point Doern was not wildly popular among the public; nevertheless, all that would radically change within a few months. After receiving the results of a rather unscientific poll that showed, perhaps not surprisingly, that a large majority (93 percent of 433 respondents) of his Elmwood constituents were opposed to our language bill, Doern went public on the Peter Warren show on CJOB radio on 22 June 1983, denouncing his government's language initiative.

That morning I had been in the Emerson constituency as part of my regular summer tour, meeting rural Manitobans. I was ambushed by Doern's attacks against the legislation; Doern gave no warning of his intentions to go public. His opposition naturally attracted much media attention. Angered by this, I was left with no alternative but to summon him to my office and to politely advise him that it would be better for him not to attend further caucus meetings until the language issue was resolved. An uproar ensued when Russ later told the media that we were denying him the usual caucus support services. His accusation was patently untrue. The truth had been that he had wanted the government to provide him with a private secretary and other services that were not available to other members of caucus. Doern deeply resented that Peter Adam, the minister of government services, had denied these additional services. When the smoke finally settled, it was seen as just a tempest in a teapot.

On 16 August 1983, I spoke in support of our resolution in the House, which contained an agreement guaranteeing up to three weeks of legislative committee hearings throughout the province during a House recess; moreover, all subsequent bell-ringing would be limited to two weeks' duration. I stressed that our constitution not only reflected Manitoba's history but also had to meet the needs of all Manitobans. I urged the House to accept the reality that "the shaping of a constitution must be an ongoing process. It is the fundamental principle that guides our nation to be truly reflective, the emerging realities of a continually progressive nation. Our constitution must be a living tree, which serves all our people." Referring to the diverse ethnic makeup of Manitoba, I pointed out that

> our beloved Manitoba has become a cultural mosaic blessed by dozens of ethnic groups, which, like a garden of many flowers, holds

greater beauty and greater charm and, like an international family in miniature, provides that all mankind can live in peace and harmony, and can be strengthened and not weakened by our diversity. We have an obligation to look at the question of French language rights in a sympathetic way, yet a realistic way, a way that is reasonable and is sensible. Denying this fundamental point would be a denial of her history, our heritage, and our reality as a country.

Unfortunately, offering sentiments of this nature, given the turmoil of the times, was tantamount to spitting in the wind.

In such a nasty political climate, the all-party legislative committee undertook its hearings. During the course of a month, 305 oral presentations and ninety-nine written briefs were submitted. These meetings were sometimes stormy, and consequently they received considerable media attention. Some briefs were philosophical, some practical, some fiercely bigoted. The Progressive Conservatives were willfully striking matches on the tinderbox of sensitive emotions for political gain. The long and painful journey had bitterly divided the province.

It was evident that the political situation was quickly deteriorating; it became imperative that I meet with Prime Minister Trudeau. At 24 Sussex, we thoroughly discussed the historical and political importance of achieving a satisfactory solution, one that would best serve the interests of Manitobans. The prime minister understood thoroughly the difficulties that the French minority had suffered for nearly a century in being discouraged from communicating in the language of their choice. However, I warned the prime minister of the political danger in Manitoba if a Manitoba solution was portrayed as one being imposed by Ottawa. At the meeting, I complained about his premature announcement and how it got us off to an ugly start. Why had it taken place without any consultation? To succeed, I cautioned, it would be crucial that he and other Ottawa politicians keep their distance; there should be no appearance of interference. "Your bilingual policies are unpopular in Manitoba," I cautioned. The prime minister seemed to acquiesce to my pleas and assured me that he understood the province's sensitivity. From the vantage point of the prime minister's grounds, we gazed over at the Quebec side. The prime minister vigorously stressed the importance of protecting minority language rights, not only in Quebec but also in Manitoba. Clearly, Trudeau was deeply worried about the secessionist threat in Quebec. The message he gave was clear: there was too much at stake for Canada. I always admired the prime minister for his intellectual insight and his ability to analyze and see the larger picture.

On my return, the lunatic fringe, which exists in any society, quickly surfaced. Day after day, whenever I left the premier's office, I was surrounded by a few angry protesters, all warning of the imminent takeover of Canada by "a Francophone conspiracy," of which Trudeau and Serge Joyal, a Trudeau cabinet minister and chief spokesperson for minority language rights, were seen as the ringleaders. According to these protestors, to prevent my getting a swollen head, I had become "their pawn." Vehement telephone calls were relentlessly made to my home at its listed number. Adele was the recipient of much of this abuse, the magnitude of which exceeded the uproar accompanying the auto insurance debate in 1987.

At the municipal level, storm clouds were quickly gathering, encouraged by the activities of these fervent opponents. The Union of Manitoba Municipalities was one of the first organizations to express its opposition; this was especially disappointing, as it was an organization with which I had always enjoyed a good relationship since my time as municipal affairs minister. Although predominantly conservative, its members were straight-talking representatives. Repeatedly, municipalities would let us know of their hostility to the proposals. Demands grew for a referendum; some municipalities advised that they were pushing ahead with their own in conjunction with the approaching municipal elections. Even Winnipeg mayor Bill Norrie apologetically confessed that he felt he had no alternative but to do likewise. Obviously embarrassed by what he was about to do, he expressed his profound support for our language initiative but felt he had to bend to the intense pressure from a vocal citizenry demanding a vote. I was deeply distressed; such a referendum would be bitterly divisive. I urgently telephoned some NDP city council members, attempting to stiffen their spines. Although I thought I had succeeded, when the going got tough, most deserted the ship. Obviously, opportunism surfaced not only among the ranks of the legislative opposition but also among those who reigned in city, town, and municipal offices.

In the fall municipal elections, the unpopularity of our legislation was emphatically demonstrated by the size of the majorities, usually running three or four to one against our proposals. In my own constituency of Selkirk, the language question did not appear on any municipal ballot, to the consternation of some of my own constituents, who had been obviously upset by our initiative. Waiting at my home polling station to cast a vote for municipal candidates,

I was confronted by a neighbour who was not the least bit amused when she discovered no language question on her ballot; she departed in a huff without voting at all. It was clear that a storm had hit the province; the electorate was angry. In the fall of 1983, we had a major political crisis to resolve.

A barrage of telephone calls bombarded all members of caucus and a flood of letters poured in objecting to any amendment that would benefit the francophone minority. Perhaps no other issue during my time in politics brought such an outburst of hostility from the public. Many Manitobans saw language rights for Franco-Manitobans as a threat to themselves.

This nasty mood was only aggravated by a parliamentary resolution passed in the House of Commons declaring support for the Manitoba legislators "to take action as expeditiously as possible in order to fulfil their constitutional obligations and to protect effectively the rights of the French-speaking minority of the province." The federal Progressive Conservatives supported this resolution. Their newly elected leader, Brian Mulroney, pleaded for support, saying, "This resolution is about fairness. It is about decency. It is an invitation for cooperation and understanding. It speaks to the finest qualities in this nation. I say to you on behalf of my entire party, on this or any great issue that affects this nation, that we stand before you, Madame Speaker, united in the sunlight, ready to work for a better Canada." At the time, some incorrectly thought it was a major coup to get such all-party agreement, an event which was extremely rare. But in Manitoba, the official opposition better reflected the prevailing mood; the federal resolution was seen as an effort by national parties under eastern control to dictate language policy to Manitobans. Had he listened to my earlier advice, Trudeau would have sensed the danger in proposing such a resolution. But importantly for Mulroney, with a federal election pending, the opportunity to support the resolution created a highly positive image for him in Quebec.

Our polling verified what we were hearing in results from various municipal referenda, the letters sent to our offices, and the angry telephone calls being made to our homes. We were seen as ramming French-language policy down the public's throats at the behest of Trudeau, who of course was seen as bowing to the Quebec agenda. Opponents saw our government as fixated on an issue irrelevant to most Manitobans and not doing what we should do to prevent the terrible toll exacted by the national economic recession. It showed that the strongest opposition was coming from rural and older residents. Those opposing the legislation had several main objections: its unfairness to other ethnic minorities (29 percent); its cost to taxpayers (23 percent); the issues being forced by government (18 percent); the divisive nature of the issue (14 percent); the lack of need for Manitobans to speak English (17 percent); and, to a small degree, concern over how the legislation would affect employment opportunities (3 percent). No matter how we interpreted the polling results, the public was not getting our message. The irony of this polling was that the largest negative objective was "unfairness to other ethnic minorities." Indeed, the reality was that the leadership of the diverse ethnicities was solidly in support of our efforts. Rod Murphy, MP for Churchill, captured the point beautifully: "If the majority in our nation ever decides that it is going to use its power as some in the province of Manitoba are trying to do ... then no Canadian is safe, no religious minority is safe, no linguistic minority is safe. No individual or group of individuals with different beliefs from the majority is safe in this country."

The reality was, of course, that we were doing well, indeed the best of any province in Canada, with our job fund for stimulating economic activity; however, the general public was not hearing this because of all the noise being generated by the language debate. If there was to be any chance of success, we would need to show more flexibility than we had to this point. It was necessary to undertake changes to restore public confidence.

One of the most challenging decisions I was compelled to make was a shift in the ministerial responsibility for the legislation. Although Attorney General Penner was able, articulate, and brilliant, although he had achieved considerable success in the difficult negotiations, his opponents had successfully personalized the issue; and his detractors saw him as too distant and somewhat intellectually arrogant. Moreover, there was some tension in cabinet and caucus, and this, perhaps unfairly, settled on the Attorney General.

<hr />

My first step in reshaping our image was to appoint Andy Anstett as the new minister responsible for piloting the legislation. Youthful, bright, and articulate, Anstett had gained a reputation as an able orator in the legislature, an exceedingly aggressive campaigner, someone who could maintain his cool under fire. Our second step was to substitute legislative amendments for some of the earlier constitutional amendments involving provincial government services delivered in the French language. Third, just before the House reconvened, a meeting was arranged with the new leader of the Opposition, Gary Filmon, in an attempt to get him on our side. We were convinced that we had met many of the Opposition's concerns about the original proposal. We expected that under a new leader they might prefer to get this divisive issue behind them. By making significant changes in the legislative package, we were, we believed, giving them a face-saving means to do so and claim some victory.

A meeting took place with Gary Filmon in my office on 14 December 1983. Bud Sherman, acting as the new leader's backup, was his witness to whatever discussions would take place. Filmon's demeanour was that of a nervous and insecure young man who had a few days earlier assumed the Tory mantle from Lyon; he listened as Anstett and I slowly and meticulously outlined the changes that we were prepared to make. These removed French-language services from the constitutional amendment and put them in ordinary legislation, capable of being appealed or changed in the normal fashion by the legislature alone. It was obvious that Filmon had been thoroughly coached and warned not to make concessions or signal the slightest hint of his intentions. He was evasive in responding to our questions about his position. Afterwards, we concluded that the good news was that, unlike Lyon, Filmon had no firm position on the fundamental issue itself and, if left alone, would prefer to compromise than fight.

However, it was also our reluctant view that he would be unable to carry his right-wing, anti-bilingual rural caucus with him. On one occasion, invidious comparisons between Filmon and Lyon had been fuelled when he passed up a chance to speak on the language proposal in the legislature. When NDP members hooted and jeered, Filmon stood and seemed about to say something, which under the rules of legislature would have prevented him from speaking on the issue again; that never happened because Lyon's unmistakable voice erupted out from the back row, "Sit down, sit down." Filmon sat down quickly, and the NDP members had a field day mocking his subservience to his former leader.

With expectations fuelled by media reports that the language issue might be coming closer to a settlement, optimism dominated our ranks for a brief time. But unknown to us, the Tory caucus and individual offices and homes of PC MLAs were being barraged by a massive bombardment of telephone calls demanding that the Opposition reject any offers of compromise. This right-wing opposition was making itself felt throughout the province.

The Monday following our meeting, Filmon rejected any chances of a compromise. His caucus was unanimously opposed to our proposals: amending Section 23 of the Manitoba Act was unacceptable to them. They demanded that our proposals be forwarded to the standing committee for privileges and elections; of course, this would have kept the issue on the front burner for some time yet. Filmon even questioned whether our proposals had sufficient approval from the Société franco-manitobaine (SFM) or from Bilodeau, himself. The Progressive Conservatives' strategy was clear. It included emphasizing the personalities and images of the past, making sure the debate raged about old issues, and seizing upon any fresh or old evidence that "behind" the proposals were the hands of the prime minister, the secretary of state, and a small group of "French fanatics." They furthermore alleged that this was a major issue warranting an election call. They raised doubts about the legal opinions in order to create a sense of public uncertainty. They even had the bravado to boast that they were pursuing a unifying course for the province. All this caused Anstett to lash out at them for their "tactics of misinformation and play to the gallery of emotion."

The NDP strategy, on the other hand, was an attempt to persuade the public that we had listened to the submissions at the public hearings and had made changes to produce measures that Manitobans could accept. It was our desire to focus on the economy and job creation, and to look forward and minimize any repetition of the earlier poisonous exchanges. However, all our efforts were futile in limiting public opposition. Death threats were made against the lives of Leo Robert, president of the SFM, Roland Penner, Andy Anstett, and me. At first, my inclination was to dismiss them as not being serious. Our party office staff regularly received similar threats. However, the Winnipeg police convinced me to take them more seriously. A letter containing the threat included certain information that the police suggested could have been known only by the murderer involved in a recent Winnipeg homicide. Security for my family was arranged; Charysse was escorted home from school by the RCMP and still remembers the embarrassment of having an officer coming to her classroom for her. Our property was surveyed for possible security weaknesses; other precautions included regular surveillance. The costs to obtain such ongoing security would have been enormous, and I had no intention of burdening the public with this, so we decided to take our chances. Retroactively, I think this was perhaps reckless on my part, in view of the rage existing. However, we did permit my premier's car to be equipped so that it could be started remotely from my office as I prepared to drive home or elsewhere, because fear had been expressed that somebody might be able to trigger the car to blow up when started. (A side benefit of this was that the car would be heated up for me in the winter months or cooled in the summer ones.)

On 1 February 1984, Anstett was confronted by his angry constituents and others at a Springfield meeting organized by Grassroots Manitoba, an organization made up of people specifically opposed to the proposed legislative changes. The meeting was attended by over 1000 protesting the legislation. When Anstett refused to knuckle under, he was assailed by shouts for his resignation. Even some Franco-Manitoban observers in the audience feared the bitter divisions developing. Anstett's constituency of Springfield was adjacent to some French-speaking communities where the backlash was more intense than in most other parts of the province. Interestingly, Springfield constituency was also the home of many families who were descendants of United Empire Loyalists.

A Grassroots Manitoba representative contacted me on the Friday morning after the Springfield meeting, inviting me to attend a specially organized meeting of his organization in Selkirk on the following Sunday evening. Also in attendance would be renegade NDPers Russell Doern and Herb Schultz, two of the most vehement opponents of bilingualism in the province. I politely refused their invitation but advised that I would hold my own meeting the following Wednesday evening; I billed it as a constituency accountability session. In so doing, I could control this meeting better than one being organized by the zealots for Grassroots Manitoba in Springfield. A number of steps were taken to ensure that there would be some semblance of support present. First, co-chairs Peter Duchek, the highly respected reeve of the Municipality of St. Andrews, and Allan Scramstad, now a young local lawyer, were chosen to preside over the meeting. Second, telephoning was done throughout the constituency to maximize turnout of supporters. Third, informational material was made readily available at the meeting to explain our perspective.

As the meeting was called to order, I gazed out on the overflow, standing-room-only crowd packing the school gymnasium. Not only had our supporters shown up in large numbers, but buses had brought Grassroots Manitoba supporters from various communities outside the constituency. Adele and Charysse insisted on sitting on the platform with me. Because of threats made on my life, the RCMP were in attendance, but undercover, to maintain surveillance. I opened the meeting by outlining the ethical, legal, and historical base for our legislative proposals. When I finished, the co-chairs announced that they would allow questions from the audience. Since our meeting was billed as a constituency-accountability session, questions were limited to residents of the constituency. This, of course, created a noisy commotion from many of the bused-in Grassroots Manitoba supporters. The chairs steadfastly rejected their objections, and the meeting proceeded.

One of the questioners, a youthful Darren Praznik (who a few years later would become a member of the Conservative caucus, as well as health and French-language services minister in the Filmon government) angrily enquired how I justified making French an official language in Manitoba when there were more Ukrainians than French among the province's population. It was a popular question among many who refused to recognize the important legal consequences flowing from the 1870 covenant. Some of the other questions were positive, some negative. Neverthless, we had ensured at least a draw by organizing the meeting. The following day, articles appeared on the front pages of both the local weekly *Selkirk Enterprise* and the *Winnipeg Free Press*, reporting that I had been greeted both by cheers and jeers.

In order to maintain pressure on the government, Grassroots Manitoba organized a massive rally at the legislature. Before the rally, I met with several of its leaders, including Grant Russell and Bobby Bend, a former health minister in the Liberal government of D.L. Campbell. A thick pile of petitions was handed to me demanding that the government withdraw its legislation. At a meeting with the rally leaders, I was unable to correct their many misconceptions. As expected, speakers at the rally spewed the same inaccurate, intemperate, and intolerant misrepresentations that were now common fare. They raged about the Trudeau and the Pawley governments' attempts to impose French on Manitobans. Some even stood outside my second-floor office door, threatening to smash it down and chanting, "We want Pawley." Legislature security staff was compelled to take up posts there.

Organized animosity persistently followed me on my tours outside the legislature. During the heat of the controversy, while I was attempting to tour some Winnipeg constituencies, I began to speak to approximately 100 people at a stop in the River East constituency about job creation and various other policies to improve opportunities for youth, when suddenly a majority of those in attendance refused to permit me to continue. I was compelled to engage them in noisy debate concerning the language issue. Many swarmed around me, and one fanatic cried, "Heil Howard." The most popular comment, repeatedly hollered at me, was "I don't want French shoved down my throat." Angry New Democrats in attendance began to accuse the protesters of fascism and bigotry. The mood grew increasingly tense when somebody in the crowd shouted for a vote on whether the French-language issue should be discussed. The crowd split sixty to forty in favour of those who opposed the language legislation. They formed ranks on one side of the room, calling upon me to speak to them. Bill Blaikie, the NDP MP representing Winnipeg-Transcona, remarked, "It would take the wisdom of Solomon to know how to handle a situation like this." At first I had politely ignored the protesters and their catcalls and slurs, but when this failed to work, I agreed to meet with them but insisted they listen to me. The standoff persisted. A Chilean refugee made the most intelligent comment of all when he warned, "I saw this happen in my country. When people don't listen to each other anymore, it means danger." This confrontation received substantial press coverage the next day, as intended by the local anti-language participants. It highlighted the difficulties we encountered in our attempts to communicate the overall governmental program to Manitobans.

Members of several right-wing groups become actively engaged in the campaign against our proposals. In April 1984, journalist David Roberts revealed that members of the Ku Klux Klan had joined Grassroots Manitoba; Roberts' source was Anne Farmer, the Klan's national director in Vancouver.[2] Raymond Hébert's authoritative account of the French-language crisis outlines the activities by other right-wing groups involved in the Grassroots campaign; these included the extreme right-wing Canadian League of Rights, who had a hall booked for a meeting by the president of the Union of Manitoba Municipalities. The League of Rights representative Conrad Kelly was also a member of the delegation that presented a petition to Lieutenant-Governor Pearl McGonigal. Among the signatories of the petition was Ron Gostick, founder of the Canadian League of Rights and editor of the *Canadian Intelligence Service*, described by leaders of the Association of Rights and Liberties as racist and anti-Semitic. Indeed, it was reported that Gostick had proposed the presentation of the petition to the Lieutenant-Governor.

These pressures, however, did not deter us from proceeding with the language package in the legislature. Much of what we had earlier intended to change by constitutional amendment was now being included in a legislative statute with these important provisions: the provision of bilingual services at the principal offices of Crown corporations, government departments, and the courts; the provision of services in designated districts where warranted by population; and the appointment of a language services ombudsman.

Immediately upon the session's resumption date, Filmon rejected the bill and the Progressive Conservatives initiated their filibuster. The Tories continued to oppose the revised form of the proposed Section 23.1, which stated, "As English and French are the official languages of Manitoba." The Opposition attempted to move the deletion of this section, alleging that the new text still affected matters beyond the court's jurisdiction. The Opposition took this position despite a legal opinion advising otherwise, provided to them by Kerr Twaddle. By 24 January, we were left with no alternative but to move closure, the first time this had been done since 1929. The bill was permitted to make its way to the legislative committee, where fifty-seven public representations were heard. However, a continued Tory filibuster blocked the resolution containing the amendment in the chamber.

During my nineteen years in the Manitoba legislature, I had never before witnessed, nor did I witness after, such uncontrolled emotion and such venom as dominated the legislature during the long days of raucous debate. Members vilified each other—shouting epithets such as "rat," "liar," "bigot," "baboon," "zealot," "fool," and "sleazebag." Sometimes, the name-calling would degenerate into racist comments: Gerard Lecuyer, the member for Radisson and the environment minister, was labelled "Kermit the frog." On another occasion, an individual in the public gallery who screamed "Call an election!" had to be removed by security officers. The legislative debates are replete with extreme utterances. Repeatedly in the Opposition's comments during January and February 1984 was some kind of implication that our government was illegitimate. Harry Enns referred to NDP members as "strangers." He added, "Conservatives understood Manitoba … by virtue of the fact that our roots, by and large, on this side of the House are far deeper than many on that side of the House … the fact of the matter is that we have inordinately large numbers of persons on that side whose roots go back to not more than five or six or ten years in the history of Manitoba, whether it's from Ontario, whether it's from Wisconsin, whether it's from Chicago." Sterling Lyon also called the NDP "strangers" and denounced the government as a "bedraggled collection of . . . individuals who by accident and mistake, some of them, wandered into a seat, got a nomination, were elected here." Wally McKenzie ranted about the "wild eyed socialists running rampant over there." On other occasions, Lyon repeatedly claimed Penner was "a communist," and he once hollered, "At least . . . I've never subverted my country the way you have"— this despite the fact that Penner had bravely served in World War II. Lyon furthermore denounced the Manitoba Association of Rights and Liberties as a "great bunch, funded by the Attorney General, a communist, yeah, great bunch."[3] When Lyon was once suspended from the legislature for three days, he grumbled, "well, now we know the communists are really in charge"; and later yelled on a standing vote on his suspension, "you'll hear the bells for quite a long time, you bloody reds."[4]

At 3:15 p.m. on Thursday, 16 February 1984, Opposition members of the legislative chamber failed to return to their places. The division bells rang until 2:45 p.m. on Monday, 27 February 1984. When the Opposition refused to respond to the division bells calling them for a vote, Speaker Walding refused to force one. Clearly, the official opposition was hell-bent on preventing a vote from occurring. After several weeks in which little was accomplished, Anstett moved that the legislature impose a rule to limit bell-ringing. The Opposition persisted in their refusal to uphold the constitutional principle of responsible government by which a majority of the members support the government and have the ability to assure that it governs. Continuing for days or more, the constant refrain of the bells (actually buzzers), although they were turned on low, was a constant irritation, since they symbolized the helplessness of our situation. Each day our members would show up for the anticipated vote, only to find that the Speaker again refused to call one because the Opposition members had failed to take their seats. Day after day, the national press from one end of Canada to the other applied generous quantities of ink to stories about Manitoba. The uncertainty that consequently prevailed blocked us from getting anything else done. Only the annual NDP convention provided some temporary relief.

At the convention in Brandon on 18 February, I condemned in the strongest possible words the PC MLAs for walking out of the house for "the twelfth time in six weeks." In attacking them for stalling passage of the legislation, I condemned them for preventing the government from dealing with more important matters, such as the economy and jobs. I was delighted with the response from the delegates; they stood solidly behind the government despite the widespread concern that the language battle would surely cost us the next election. During the convention, more bad news reached us when a *Winnipeg Free Press* poll suggested that less than 12 percent of Manitobans would support the NDP if an election were held then. Outside the convention hall approximately thirty opponents of the legislation picketed. More anger emerged when Herb Schultz, brother-in-law of Ed Schreyer, and his assistant while Schreyer was premier, was expelled from the party. Personally, I was not happy that the party decided to do this. I felt we had enough problems outside our control without this battle internally. Emotions were, nonetheless, too intense. His expulsion had to be taken by the delegates.

Upon the parties' returning to the legislature, negotiations to end the deadlock quickly broke down. As a last resort on 21 February, I forwarded a public letter to Walding demanding that he take immediate action to bring the impasse to an end. I warned him that it was unacceptable for the rights of the House and the principle of responsible government to be defied any longer. With all due respect, and in view of the continuing obstruction, I requested that he now notify both party whips within a specified time when the two votes would be conducted to decide the question of privilege before the House. I further advised that members of the government caucus intended to be in the chamber at 2 p.m. that day for these votes. We looked without much hope to the Speaker to force the Tories to return for the vote.

Our expectations that little would be gained from our appeal to Walding did not go unfulfilled; he obviously had different views from ours. Frances Russell claims Walding's wife, Valerie, was herself active in the anti-bilingual Grassroots Manitoba movement.[5] Avoiding any responsibility, the Speaker replied only two hours after the receipt of my letter. He claimed, in a sharply worded rebuff, that "since the House is close to effecting a change in its rules" he was "surprised that I would request that he would contravene the existing rules and procedures at this time." Any unilateral action on his part, he suggested, would only be a betrayal of the impartiality of the chair and would seriously undermine the integrity of the Speakership. In view of the foregoing, he refused to accede to my request. The *Globe and Mail* dismissed the Speaker's actions, noting that "Speakers are frequently called upon to take unilateral action that is, to make a decision which may please one side and displease the other. It goes with the job and has not, so far as we can see, undermined the integrity of the office."[6] The *Winnipeg Free Press* also chastised the Speaker, saying, "surely tradition and precedent demand that the first duty of the Speaker is to ensure that the institution can function."[7] The protection of minority language rights and the maintenance of the British parliamentary tradition were being unfairly placed on the back burner.

If the objective was to slow the legislative and public policy program of my government through the French-language services issue, it was meeting with success. I was disappointed that the new Tory leader appeared to consider this acceptable in a democratic system. Moreover, it was apparent that the Tories did not intend to honour the written agreement of 12 August 1983, which stipulated that bell-ringing would be limited to two weeks. Realizing that they were not about to return to the chamber to vote, and so left with fewer and fewer options, I telephoned Prime Minister Trudeau, advising him that we could do little more to resolve the matter and were left with no alternative but to pull the plug. There was a long silence on the other end of the line; Trudeau was obviously distressed by this unwelcome news. He urged us not to withdraw the legislation, but I could give him no comfort.

Immediately, the federal political parties, including Mulroney and the Conservatives, unanimously passed a multi-party resolution calling upon "the government of Manitoba to persist in its efforts to fulfil its constitutional obligations to effectively protect the rights of its French-speaking minority in a spirit of tolerance civility, amity and generosity." Mulroney articulated the same position he had taken in October when the first Commons resolution was passed. His Manitoba colleagues in Parliament boycotted the vote, but this proved inconsequential; he was a hero in Quebec, standing up against his own party in Manitoba.

Both Liberal MP Lloyd Axworthy and NDP MP Rod Murphy courageously spoke in support of the Commons resolution. Forcibly, Mulroney warned Winnipeg Assiniboine MP Dan McKenzie and any other potentially rebellious MP that they would face expulsion if they persisted in their opposition to bilingualism. Only two weeks earlier McKenzie had wildly denounced our proposed legislation as "a socialist attempt to irreversibly destroy the provincial fabric of peace and harmony." As well, in a radio interview, Mulroney disassociated himself from the provincial party's bell-ringing tactics that were stalling the language measures. Once again, all this made Mulroney unpopular in Manitoba, but it did wonders for his approval rating in Quebec.

Rather than harming Mulroney politically, as had been their intention, Trudeau and those around him had only enhanced the Opposition leader's reputation going into the election expected in 1984. On the other hand, in Manitoba, Filmon's position was obviously popular with those Manitobans who viewed the provincial Tory leader as standing up against not only Trudeau but also his own federal leader. The involvement of the federal government was counterproductive. It created negative rather than positive reaction throughout the province. Indeed, the government actions, incorrectly seen as being Quebec-inspired, had, at the best, a neutral effect and at the worst a quite damaging effect on our efforts to resolve the matter within the Manitoba political process. Neither Mulroney nor Trudeau enjoyed much credibility in Manitoba; they were seen as two federal politicians who pursued a Quebec agenda—the equivalent of swallowing a poison pill in Manitoba and western Canada.

To my amazement and consternation, the false perceptions spread by our opponents continued to dominate debate in the province. About this time the CBC covered a Grassroots rally of 300 in Beausejour, where a local farmer griped that the constitutional proposals would eventually cost him his job. Watching the interview I could not but be convinced that he actually believed it. On another occasion, a farmer told a friend that he was being forced to farm in French. The explanation? Sometimes, the farmer claimed, chemicals spilled on the outside of a can, obliterating the English-language instructions and forcing him to read them in French.

Stories of this sort became commonplace. In the Winnipeg Safeway just over the Osborne Bridge, an elderly lady would go along the aisles several times a week, methodically turning the corn flakes boxes (and all other packaged food) so that only the English-language side would show. The manager warned the clerk, a young man, just to ignore her, not to turn them back again or try to even up the language situation. Clearly, local peer pressure played a major psychological role in forming such opinions. To our government, it was increasingly clear that we had no alternative but to try to minimize the damage being done to us daily. The options—letting the deadlock drag on, or calling an election, or replacing the Speaker—were all abhorrent to us. The Tories, bolstered by public opinion polls and municipal referenda, would have been squarely in the driver's seat if an election had been called. To replace the Speaker was not a feasible alternative because the Tories would only repeat the bell-ringing and prevent the nomination of any new Speaker. Finally, permitting the stalemate to persist would prolong an intolerable obstacle to proper governance.

For instance, the Department of Finance would encounter difficulty in the payment of its accounts. Our funding shortage was in the neighbourhood of $26 million, the result of priorities changing during the fiscal year. A supplementary bill had not been introduced, as it was anticipated that the session would end sooner. Payments to suppliers were already being withheld, and within days the civil service payroll and services for various programs would be without funds. The payment of special warrants was not possible while the legislature was sitting. We were faced not only with a language deadline but also with many other pressing concerns. Moreover, to present a supply bill to the legislature would only provoke further bell-ringing by an opposition tasting blood and attempting to force an early election that would obviously favour them. Clearly, they were prepared to use any means available to them. As maddening as it was, our only alternative was to deal with other items and not allow the entire process of government to be paralyzed by the stalemate over the language proposal.

The only option available to us was to end the session and resume other government activities. Passage of a special warrant ten days after the House rose would permit the appropriate payment of bills. But the problem, along with its potentially disastrous consequences, remained. The Bilodeau case would proceed to the Supreme Court of Canada, where it would be heard in 1984 and likely produce a decision in early 1985; this raised the prospect of the issue being before the Manitoba legislature in 1985. If the Manitoba Court of Appeal ruling were sustained, the public reaction would be that the government had subjected the province to eight months of unnecessary tension and strife, with likely deleterious effects for English language minority rights in Quebec. The opposite extreme would be a decision that rendered Manitoba laws invalid, thus generating legal chaos. Although unlikely, that would necessitate emergency passage of a constitutional resolution to validate our statutes. Our government's earlier stance would be vindicated, but the issue would no doubt remain controversial. The third and most realistic prospect involved a decision finding the Forest decision mandatory but imposing time limits for translating the statutes, similar to those contained in the proposal we had placed before the legislature. If legislation was required, it likely could be postponed until after the next election.

Finally on 27 February 1984 during the twelfth consecutive day of bell-ringing, the Lieutenant-Governor, at my request, prorogued the legislature; the constitutional amendment and the Language Bill were thus both killed. Section 23 of the Manitoba Act remained unchanged. The Opposition had succeeded in hijacking the parliamentary system. For my part, I refused to acknowledge that the government had really lost, declaring, "You don't lose when you are playing, for example, the hockey game and your opponents run into the dressing room after the second period and then refuse to come out of the dressing room for the third period. Your opponents lose." Nonetheless, the Tories celebrated victory. They held a private party in the basement of the legislature; the straight faces they had tried to maintain inside the house turned into broad smiles once they were behind closed doors. Another reason for their joy was their confidence that this issue would result in my government's defeat in the next election. Since the political solution had failed, no alternative remained but to permit the matter to proceed to the Supreme Court of Canada. The federal government initiated such a reference by requesting a ruling as to the validity of all Manitoba statutes.

The Political Fallout

Certainly the anti-bilingual actions of our opponents had been well covered in the Quebec press. Canada's Official Languages Commissioner tabled a scathing indictment of the tactics of Manitoba's three most ornery opponents to bilingualism, pointing to the "uglier sentiments, of which one can only feel ashamed," exemplified by the opponents of the Manitoba government's resolution on French-language rights. Richard Cleroux claimed in the *Globe and Mail* that "the eyes of Canada are on Manitoba this week; the image appearing was that of a racist and bigoted province with a lack of understanding of the basis on which this country came together in the first place."[8] He further charged that the Tories, by refusing to vote, "paralyzed the legislature as surely as if they had put the key in the door." He added that the Tory walk-out tactics were something new in the province: "no political party here had ever before refused to vote, day after day, vote after vote."

Mulroney's support of the French-language resolution in the Manitoba legislature and his subsequent endorsement of the House of Commons resolution did wonders for his support in Quebec. Nor did it hurt him in the East that he had warned his caucus members, as well as aspiring Conservative candidates, that they had best get on board in support of bilingualism; it not only appeared to enhance his support in Quebec but also succeeded in earning him kudos in Ontario and Atlantic Canada. Against this, his support of minority-language rights opened deep wounds within the Manitoba Progressive Conservative Party. Richard Clereoux in the *Globe and Mail* wrote, "Manitoba leader Gary Filmon said federal leader Brian Mulroney is hurting the party by continually talking about the Manitoba language issue. Conservative supporters in Manitoba are ripping up membership cards and refusing to make political contributions to the Tories because of what Mr. Mulroney has been saying publicly about the language issue."[9]

Subsequently, Brian and Mila Mulroney were the recipients of an extremely hostile reception by Manitoba Conservatives at the Winnipeg Convention Centre. This event received the kind of national attention that gave Mulroney an even greater political boost in Quebec, where he most needed it. His successful bid for power in 1984, made possible by record Tory support in Quebec, proved the wisdom of his position. As for the Manitoba Conservatives, they had nothing to lose. At the most there was only one constituency where there were French-speaking majorities. Had there been a dozen, their strategy would have undoubtedly been different. In retrospect, the only downside was that seeds were planted that later gave birth to the Reform Party.

In contrast to Mulroney, the newly elected Liberal leader, John Turner, would seriously stumble on the language issue by appearing uncertain. In interviews with the media, Turner ducked the question by insisting that the language issue should be considered a provincial one. In Quebec this position played into the hands of the Parti Québécois and their zealous efforts to restrict language rights of the English-speaking minority This faux pas by Turner would symbolize the general uncertainty and ineptitude of his campaign and its advisers. And it would cost him dearly in his bid to retain his prime ministership.

On 13 June 1985, the court ruled, just as we had anticipated, that all Manitoba laws passed only in English were indeed invalid. Minimal time was provided to translate them. Although the cost involved would be exorbitant, there was no alternative but to begin the expensive task of translation. The day the Supreme Court made its decision, I rose in the legislature, declaring, "and the Supreme Court decision brings us to the close of a difficult period for many Manitobans. We can, we must, now leave behind those things which might divide us."[10]

In retrospect, it can be argued that we ought to have permitted the language issue to go to the Supreme Court rather than trying to head it off with negotiations; had it not been for our naïveté, we might have known that it was extremely unrealistic to persuade Manitobans to accept such compromise. It should have been obvious that there remained in Manitoba residual resentment toward the imposition of bilingualism by what was seen as the "Ottawa powers." We were fully aware of Trudeau's unpopularity. If we had permitted the matter to go to the Supreme Court and then subsequently dealt with the fallout, it could have been easier to convince Manitobans that the law had spoken, and there was no choice. Such a course of action would certainly have created more credibility than one in which we appeared to be generating unnecessary fear based on legal speculation about the possible outcome of a future court ruling. Having said this, though, I do believe that we had the moral responsibility to attempt to resolve the issue at the provincial level.

Some have suggested that the response may have been better if the constitutional package had been presented by me rather than a minister. However, if I had been constantly in the forefront on this issue—one seen as irrelevant to the lives of most Manitobans—it would have been difficult to make a political recovery in time for the 1986 election. No one can be certain about alternatives that might have been, but I suspect the Tories would have dug their heels in with me as furiously as they had with Anstett.

Some critics dispute our emphasis on the legal and pragmatic reasons for the agreements; some seem to dismiss even the need to use this line of reasoning. I think they are wrong. All government members, on the basis of an historic covenant between two founding nations, presented the agreement, one that had not been honoured and that justice demanded be honoured now. Admittedly, other arguments were also employed, which I believe we correctly viewed as assisting us in selling the agreement to a larger segment of the population. Selling it solely on the basis of the moral high ground would not have spelled the success that some imply. Perhaps debates about whether or not other means should have been employed are counterproductive. It is probable that with the mood of extreme hostility, both to bilingualism and to Trudeau, little could have been done to salvage the package.

During 1992, while teaching at the University of Windsor, I took my public administration students to visit the Manitoba legislature; there they met, among others, Sharon Carstairs, Manitoba Liberal Party leader and later a Liberal leader in the Canadian Senate. She maintained that my government's highest moments occurred when, despite enormous animosity, it sought to protect the rights of the province's French-language minority. Unquestionably, no other issue hurt us as much politically during our time in government. Indeed, we discovered the "politics of language" the harsh way—by being the victims of the mighty and passionate emotions it unleashed.

Nonetheless, Carstairs is right. Despite our errors and even some blundering, this was indeed one of those rare occurrences when a group of courageous politicians were at least trying to do the right thing, even though a huge political price was exacted in the process. It was a turning point in my political career. Until this issue I had never suffered defeat, and in some ways might have been considered as living a charmed life in politics. Clearly, that was no longer the case.

CHAPTER 7

The Challenges Confronting Us

The 1986 Election and After

THE POLITICAL FALLOUT from the turmoil of the French-language issue resulted in our support dipping to a record low of 12 percent. In its aftermath, cabinet convened urgently at the Holiday Inn in downtown Winnipeg to thrash out whether we could recover in time to win the next election. The mood was despondent; the possibility of a second term appeared remote. As with the cabinet, this frame of mind also dominated the caucus and our membership. I retained a gut feeling that if we could properly strategize we might just manage to get ourselves re-elected. It was imperative that we hammer out a plan to rebuild, one that would allow us to serve Manitobans for a second term. We all recognized that discipline was critical for us to have a chance for a comeback. We would need to focus on those issues that would allow the majority of Manitobans to relate to us.

Uppermost on our minds were the bitter French-language debate and the resulting fallout. This issue had aroused some of the meanest, most emotional outpourings that I had ever witnessed. A consistent and focused approach was essential to begin the countdown to the next election. To be re-elected, we devised and subsequently pursued a plan to focus on the economy for the balance of our mandate.

Part of the plan was to minimize any continuation of debate on the language question. Public statements would be limited to a bare minimum, and I would act as the sole spokesperson. Every effort would be undertaken to avoid being drawn into analysis of the language controversy following the court decision, and we would avoid discussing either the process or the substance of the lengthy legislative battle. When the Supreme Court ruled, we would avoid regurgitation of the issue—not to mention gloating and self-justification.

For the remainder of our term, the emphasis in all initiatives had to relate to job creation and improvement of the Manitoba economy. Polling indicated this to be our strong card. With every announcement—be it pertaining to cultural, social, or judicial themes—the central focus would be on the number of jobs preserved or created. Hydro development would be a major part of this strategy. Discipline from all our members would be necessary, as would a careful communications strategy to ensure the central focus on jobs and the economy. New energy was also required to rebuild the party, to heal any wounds that might still exist, and most importantly to renew and recruit new members.

Another emotional and thorny issue for my government was, undoubtedly, abortion and the right of women to free choice. In 1983, Dr. Henry Morgentaler had made a decision to operate a free-standing abortion clinic in Winnipeg, and since then the issue could not be ignored. It was one on which I would find myself regularly at loggerheads with many of our party activists. This especially distressed me because I favoured the free choice position. When I presented my leader's report to both NDP council and executive meetings, there would often be angry criticism of what was perceived as a lack of leadership by my government on this contentious issue. I recall at one federal convention being constantly chastised by a number of delegates from various areas of Canada for what was seen by them as inaction on a critical issue by an NDP government that should surely know better.

My difficulties were both legal and political. First, from the legal perspective, I knew no one in any provincial government had a role to play in this statutory-defined role of law enforcement. As my Attorney General, Roland Penner, aptly explained, the Winnipeg Police Department was not a provincial agency.[1] The Criminal Code cannot operate on the personal beliefs of a provincial Attorney General, a lesson I had learned during my own term in that office.

The political ramifications of our stand on the abortion issue (although legally correct) proved politically costly. Many party activists were extremely frustrated. Under the Criminal Code, we were, by law, required to undertake prosecutions. Attorney General Penner was confronted by several angry demonstrations, reminiscent of those that occurred as he was bravely attempting to enact the French-language changes. Leaving aside the criminal law concerns, I had important political reasons for not pursuing this issue at the provincial level, where such action could not produce any legal result.

Moreover, in my view, private clinics operated for profit were hardly the best route to provide any form of medical services; hospitals were the proper alternative if the law favoured such services.

Politically, this issue would only deepen divisions within our party and among many of our strongest supporters. That there were many within our support base who opposed a pro-choice position was not lost on me, as much as I disliked it. As with the French-language issue, we would have no control over these differences, the consequences of which would be decidedly divisive, inevitably undermining of our political base and thereby impeding our efforts to successfully fulfill the commitments we had made during the 1981 election campaign.[2]

With only months to go before our government's fall in 1988, the Supreme Court ruling came down on the side of Dr. Morgentaler's challenge to the existing abortion laws. Personally, I cheered, as a divisive issue over which we really had no power to control was now, at long last, behind us. Best of all, we could, now operating within the law, proceed to ensure that adequate facilities would be provided to allow an abortion if that was the woman's choice.

A Positive Setting for the 1986 Election

The Manitoba Jobs strategy was one of the success stories in Canadian provincial policy making in the 1980s. This assessment was reached through an analysis of Statistics Canada data not only by adherents of the NDP (such as Ed Broadbent, who pointed repeatedly to Manitoba as a model for federal NDP policy on the economy), but also by two former prime ministers, Turner and Mulroney. In the middle of the 1984 election campaign, former Prime Minister Turner had mistakenly referred to an exodus of Manitobans under the NDP and was compelled to correct his error by giving a generous tribute to the health of the Manitoba economy. Even Prime Minister Mulroney, at the first ministers' conference in 1985, paid tribute to the work of the NDP government of Manitoba: "I looked at the Manitoba results over the past year, record growths of 4.3 percent and unemployment rate down to 8.6, which is remarkable compared with other provinces."[2]

By the mid-1980s, the province was able to boast of the lowest youth unemployment rate in Canada. Other data identified Manitoba as the only province without a significant increase in the numbers of poverty-stricken Canadians during the early and mid-1980s. My government, consistent with its overall philosophy, succeeded in distributing income a little more fairly.

Some of our successful initiatives included an emergency interest relief program for over 3000 farmers, business people, and homeowners to deal with the pressing crisis of high interest rates; the revitalization of the credit union movement; the Homes in Manitoba program, which enabled many Manitobans who could not do so otherwise to purchase a house, and which thus stimulated the construction sector; the Career Start program, which helped many young people to obtain their first jobs through the Jobs in Training program; the restoration of rent control to ensure that rent increases were kept to a reasonable level; the Main Street Manitoba program; the highly successful $210 million Jobs Fund; the establishment of a $23 million emergency mortgage rate relief plan; and various forms of assistance to the small-business community, including interest rate relief, venture capital, export promotion, research and development supports, information technology, one-stop shopping, and a favourable differential tax rate.

Many of these initiatives were greatly supported by a series of multi-pronged, federal-provincial economic development agreements in the sectors of mining, manufacturing, tourism, and small business. These were later terminated in the mid-1980s when the Mulroney government came to power.

Although we did not, contrary to expectation, increase the sales tax immediately after our election, we did institute a 1.5 percent payroll tax, which remains law today. New spending was focussed toward housing, health-care facilities, free dental care for children up to grade 12, partial payment of the cost of eyeglasses for seniors, and an expanded home repair program. These policies—as well as our willingness to travel down an unpopular path, or at least one not well travelled at the time (or indeed subsequently)—speak well for the major successes of my government during its term.

Although the rural areas were not the major bases of political support for the NDP, under the leadership of Agriculture Minister Bill Uruski my government did pursue an extremely pro-active series of programs in support of the province's besieged farmers. Early in its term, my government launched an interest relief program to minimize the devastating consequences of Ottawa's high-interest-rate policies upon family farmers struggling to survive. Many farms would have been lost through foreclosures on their mortgages in the early 1980s if not for this government initiative. Despite opposition from many quarters, my government continued to support orderly marketing of agricultural products. Strong government support was especially required for the hog and turkey marketing boards.

My government also undertook action to prevent severe upward pressure on prices for farmland by enacting the Farm Lands Ownership Act. This legislation increased opportunities for local farmers to acquire farmland in the province of Manitoba. In addition, it aimed at restricting the sale of farmlands to out-of-province investors and corporations more interested in land speculation than in farming. In the same manner, my government undertook steps to discourage urban sprawl in the rural farmland surrounding Winnipeg. Unfortunately, too many municipalities were more interested in obtaining a higher tax assessment through approving subdivision developments than in preserving the rich agricultural farmland. It was disappointing that we did not better establish an urban limit line because the urban sprawl around Winnipeg has continued, with negative consequences to all. Overall, strides were made in promoting land use and watershed planning in rural agricultural areas, but admittedly, much more should have been achieved during our term.

By 1985, my government successfully enacted Canada's first pro-active equal pay equity program for the province's civil service, universities, and health care institutions. The government was able to work with the MGEA to ensure its successful implementation, in a manner that permitted it to be gradually extended to the private sector. Tragically, Mary Beth Dolin, as the minister responsible, would never see the fruits of her labour; she died from cancer before the end of our first term in office.

One of my government's first initiatives (16 April 1982) was to increase the minimum wage. This increase would bring the provincial rate to $4.00 per hour, the second highest in the country. We firmly believed that increasing the incomes of those at the lowest rungs of society made economic sense in a recession. After all, they are the ones most likely to spend the monies in local stores rather than spending it on foreign travel or placing it in offshore accounts, as do those with greater discretionary incomes. The old argument about higher minimum wages chasing away investment was proven wrong.

We also enacted first contract legislation, which provided for compulsory arbitration of first contracts at the request of one of the parties when an agreement could not be reached. Although we did not proceed with anti-scab legislation, we did take action to better balance power between labour and capital. This would contribute to a healthier economic situation in a relatively small province such as Manitoba.

Prior to our government taking office, there was discrimination in the province with respect to the calculation of survivors' pension benefits. The existing policy principally discriminated against women who were predeceased by their husbands. Through the commitment and hard work of our female MLAs, our new legislation would ensure that each survivor would obtain a guaranteed proportion of their spouse's pension. This measure also applied to part-time workers as well as full-time employees.

In 1983, our government, with Jay Cowan as minister, enacted amendments to the Workplace Safety and Health Act. These amendments were aimed to reduce and prevent workplace accidents or occupational illnesses often resulting from substances in the air (chemicals, carcinogens, etc.). The changes to the legislation were designed to assist both employers and employees in their efforts to create and maintain safe and healthy workplaces and working practices. The amendments introduced three basic rights of employees: the right to know, the right to refuse, and the right to participate.

Limestone Is Launched

During our first term, I recognized that a major economic action was necessary to sustain long-term economic stability in the province. The Jobs Fund was obviously only a short-term shot in the arm to an economy severely battered by the recession. A long-term economic thrust was essential. We investigated various alternatives. On several occasions, we met with government, business, and labour leaders to discover whether any consensus existed for potential future initiatives. The one economic initiative that clearly enjoyed the greatest agreement was the restarting of northern hydro generation or what was known as the Limestone Project. The question was, how could we justify such a launch? The credit for this project must be given to my energy minister, Wilson Parasiuk, and Manitoba Hydro board chair Marc Eliesen. They came up with the plan to begin negotiations with some utilities to the south of us in the United States, and their successful efforts eventually led to the Limestone station announcement. To my knowledge, no government, minister, or bureaucrat had made such an attempt in the past.

Like the Jobs Fund, the Limestone Project was crucial to ensuring economic progress in the awfully challenging times facing Canada at the time. It would prove to be most important economic initiative of our term.

The generating station not only fulfilled the additional energy needs of our province but also generated a surplus for major exports of energy to the Twin Cities region of Minneapolis and St. Paul. The high point occurred with the announcement of a contract to supply the Northern States Power Company of

Minnesota with 500 megawatts of firm power for twelve years at a rate higher than that paid by Manitobans. This sale resulted in the earlier start-up of construction of the Limestone generating station, and it was projected to generate more than $3 billion in construction, provided principally by Manitoba employers and workers. This sale represented the single largest sale of power in the province's history and at the time was one of the largest hydro-energy transactions ever undertaken in Canada. The province was expected to net a profit of $1.7 billion. In fact, it is my understanding that in the year ending in 2003, the province received approximately $4 billion in revenues. The original contract ran until 2005, and an agreement was signed to renew the contract in 2005.

The environmental impact of the project was of major importance. Selling hydro-generated power from northern Manitoba displaces thermal generation in North America and therefore diminishes greenhouse gases. Moreover, unlike previous hydro projects, the Limestone Project never resulted in flooding. Environmentalists were pleased with its minimal damage to the environment.

The Tories sometimes mocked the Limestone Project from their opposition benches as "Lemon-stone." Like all our major achievements, it proceeded only after we beat back what was strenuous and sometimes hysterical resistance from the Opposition. Gary Filmon went before the National Energy Board in a vain attempt to dissuade it from approving the venture. As leader of the Opposition, he argued that Manitoba Hydro had not done its homework and that the risks of the sale had not been properly analyzed. In the days that followed, the members of the Opposition acted as if frightened of their own shadows. (I described them as "Chicken Littles.") It was an opposition prepared to do anything possible to prevent economic development through energy development.

Nevertheless, this hydro project would generate thousands of person years of employment, much of which remained within the northern and Aboriginal communities. A carefully designed and massive job-training program was launched to ensure that these communities would receive maximum benefit. One of its legacies was that many workers with newly acquired skills would later choose to remain in the North and contribute their skills to their community's advantage. The fact that this program gave preference to northerners, and especially Aboriginals, became a contentious issue in some quarters. I recall a visit to Thompson, where I was greeted by signs posted along the highway from the airport to the city, angrily declaring, "Pawley is an Indian-lover." However, our northern members—Harry Harapiak, Jay Cowan, Jerry Storie,

Elijah Harper, and Steve Ashton—all did a fantastic job of selling the project to northerners by their continuing communication with their constituents.

It is true that sales to the Twin Cities challenged what had been excellent relations with our neighbours in North Dakota, a major supplier of coal to various U.S. power utilities. On one occasion, then-governor Sinner requested a meeting with me to voice his concerns. Our discussion, a little animated, took place in the back seat of the car driven by intergovernmental specialist James Eldridge. Apparently this avoided the provisions of North Dakota's "sunshine law," which stated that any meeting attended by any elected official must be open to the public, including the media and television cameras. After the meeting, our positive relations with the governor continued, and some credit was given to me for the softening of the North Dakota legislation aimed at thwarting Manitoba by refusing permission to build the Mandan line, which was critical for the transmission of hydro power to the Twin Cities. The sale of hydro power came with a commitment to establish a Heritage Fund that could be utilized to better the lot of future generations.[3]

Limestone was pivotal in providing us with the momentum that would successfully put us back into the running for re-election. The Limestone generating station was officially opened on 5 September 1991. With five of ten units in operation, the station was ahead of schedule and $1 billion below budget. Only 2 percent of such projects worldwide are completed under budget and ahead of schedule. Credit was given to the workers for having no work stoppages and for achieving a better safety record than that of any previous Manitoba Hydro project of this type. Former Manitoba premier Gary Doer was correct when he referred to our hydro project as having been one of our most successful legacies to Manitobans.

Looking Ahead to the Next Election

During the 1985 legislative session, we were successful in steering clear of Opposition attacks. Indeed, the Progressive Conservatives would complain that we had denied them an easy target to fire at. At the conclusion of the session, we had to choose whether to go to the electorate in the fall of 1985 or wait until the spring of 1986. To our delight, the provincial Tories had blown away their huge lead over the NDP in only a few months.

The marked economic improvement sparked a buoyant mood in my caucus. We had achieved substantial gains, successfully reversing much of our loss in popularity arising from the French-language services conflict. However, the polling also showed that we still had considerably more catching-up to do before we could assume victory. A by-election victory in the fall of 1985 by Marty Dolin in the Kildonan riding, so ably represented by Mary Beth Dolin prior to her tragic death, verified this. Many pundits pointed to a decline in support there from the previous election as evidence that we could lose a province-wide vote. The question of whether we should go to the polls in the fall of 1985 or postpone the election to the spring of 1986 was debated at great length.

By 1986, the economy would begin to enjoy an injection from Limestone's construction. This interval before an election would give us opportunities for additional kudos; for example, when I firmly stood up for Manitoba against federal cutbacks at a scheduled first ministers' conference in Halifax. The growing unpopularity of the Mulroney government, with both their cutbacks and decisions rendered in other areas, hurt the Manitoba Progressive Conservative Party. The Mulroney government would have brought down another budget that, we surmised, would be out of favour in Manitoba. The "tuna-gate" scandal hurt the Tories, as did their bailout of some banks in Alberta.

Also successful was our continuing strategy of placing the Progressive Conservatives on the defensive by pushing issues that we knew would contribute to an image of indecisiveness on their part. The pay-equity initiative placed them on the defensive; much of their hard-core base was opposed to this popular policy thrust. The Limestone Project issue obviously created tension too; their deputy leader threatened that a newly elected PC government would go as far as winding back the launch of the project if it had begun, while Filmon attempted to duck this issue.

There would also be increasing fallout from anger over the actions of the federal government. Failure to receive $72 million in equalization from the federal government gave us a big stick with which to hammer away at the provincial Progressive Conservatives. The federal Progressive Conservatives' failed attempt to discontinue indexing of old age pensions caused tension in the provincial party. We forced them to stand in the legislature to back a resolution opposing the Mulroney government's attempt at de-indexing, thereby escalating the tension in the Tory ranks.

Another issue that would cause conflict in the Progressive Conservative Party's constituency arose from a law compelling the province's motorcyclists to wear helmets. Outside of Alberta, Manitoba was the last province in Canada to establish such a mandate. To reduce deaths and injuries on the highway, seat belt legislation was also enacted. Both measures provoked substantial opposition, as evidenced by numerous protest rallies that attempted to pressure the government to back down. We would not. These were preventive health measures that reduced the cost of health care. Both were left in place by the Filmon government.

Finally, the government of Manitoba became the first and only one in Canada to declare its province a nuclear-free zone. During the annual peace walks, a broad representation of the local population participated, including Mayor Bill Norrie of Winnipeg, the premier of Manitoba, and federal cabinet minister Lloyd Axworthy. Although it was an all-party resolution and received unanimous legislative support, Progressive Conservative support appeared reluctant. Nevertheless, they realized the popular support for this resolution precluded them from opposing it.

It was not surprising that divisions in the PC Party surfaced in 1985 at their annual provincial convention in Brandon. Though Filmon pleaded with his delegates to stop openly criticizing him, it was known that important factions and individuals in the party were unhappy with his leadership. The Confederation of Regions Party had been formed, drawing many members from the PC Party's core. We were convinced that the PCs had not yet bottomed out and we had not yet peaked. Consequently, even though the polls showed marked improvement by the fall of 1985, we decided to postpone the election until the spring of 1986.

While different strategies were put in place to overcome our low polling results after the French-language issue, Adele and I spent the summer and fall of 1985 attending fairs and many other public events in the rural and urban areas without a break until the decision was made to stand for re-election in 1986. To help get out the message, we had to get out there and meet with people from various communities.

The 1986 Election

An overall theme of our 1986 campaign was "Standing Up for Manitoba." This focus was especially relevant with the rising unpopularity of the Mulroney government and the measures they had undertaken or were about to announce in their forthcoming budget that were expected to harm Manitobans. I was amused by the Conservatives imitating this theme in their 2006 election with their slogan "Standing Up for Canada." Unlike the Conservatives of 2006, we used the slogan to refer to standing up for Manitobans against powerful forces, including oil companies. Despite rising oil and gas prices in 1986, no other party would aggressively pursue this issue.

The campaign was launched after the weekend of the twenty-fifth annual provincial NDP convention, at which Ed Broadbent was our guest speaker. In his remarks Ed boomed "Go get 'em!" as he tossed a pair of orange running shoes at me. These shoes were meant to symbolically carry us to our second-term victory. The mood had been turned in our favour from a year earlier. The delegates wildly cheered both Broadbent and me.

The following Tuesday at 1:00 p.m., sporting a polka-dotted tie and pin-striped suit with a tiny NDP bronze pin on my lapel, I would end months of speculation by announcing the 18 March election day. Then I strolled down the front steps of the legislature proudly waving my orange running shoes in the chill minus 15°C air and boarded my campaign bus. Much time had lapsed since the cabinet retreat discussion at the Holiday Inn when we feared a tidal wave of voter hostility would surely overwhelm us.

To minimize the harmful consequences of association with the previous Progressive Conservative leadership of Sterling Lyon, Filmon attempted during the campaign to present his party as being more centrist. He also tried to raise fears about the Limestone Project contract, suggesting it was more politics than economics. Although consolidating business support, his opposition to extending pay equity to the private sector was not well received by most women workers in the province. Worried telephone calls by numerous female callers to an open-line debate I participated in with Filmon on the Peter Warren radio program compelled Filmon to waffle on this issue. This would prove to be an election strategy that benefited us, as he was compelled to fight on two policy areas, representing in the public mind the NDP strengths. Moreover, in a desperate bid to attract votes from Manitoba motorists, he promised a 10 percent rebate on auto insurance premiums. In general, to our relief, his party's platform would prove uninspiring. Perhaps political professionals played too central a role!

A grave event occurred during the campaign, one which had an adverse impact on my capacity to campaign as effectively as I would have liked. My attention was divided between the campaign and the deteriorating condition of my father, Russell, who had been rushed to Seven Oaks Hospital. It didn't help that polling released only a week before the vote gave us an inflated percentage of support, thus causing some overconfidence in certain quarters within the party. The death of my political hero, Tommy Douglas, and my taking leave of the campaign to attend his funeral in Ottawa, were emotionally draining. The assassination of Olof Palme, the prime minister of Sweden, was another distressing blow for me; I had met him when he visited Manitoba.

Another challenge I faced during the campaign was the leadership debate. Although uncomfortable with TV formats, I recognized a debate could not be avoided. I was fast off the mark to challenge Filmon to participate in one. However, I realized that one misstep, one mistake, would land my face on the cover of every newspaper in the country. Pundits would have a field day deliberating about where I went amiss. Everyone would know where I went wrong, including friends and family. As premier I had the most to lose. At the very least, it was essential not to come out of this the clear loser!

Two events during the debate would be critical: The first worked to my advantage when the moderator gave Filmon the opportunity to ask me any question he wished. To my delight, Filmon wasted this opportunity to enquire why Manitoba didn't have a pavilion at the Expo '86 in Vancouver. I was astonished at such an unexpected gift. Could this be the toughest question the PCs could hurl at me? It provided me an opening to make political hay. I shot back that Manitoba was more interested in improving health care, education, and job creation than investing in pleasure domes by the sea. I scored well on this one.

The second event worked to the advantage of the Liberal leader. Filmon and I had heatedly exchanged some charges and counter-charges, and unfortunately the debate had disintegrated into a noisy finger-pointing exercise, an exchange of vigorous accusations and denials, as we both sniped at each other. To some charges from Filmon I countered, "not true." The camera showed Sharon Carstairs, the newly elected leader of the Liberal Party, watching all of this unfolding with glee. The strict hand of the teacher was essential, and Sharon seized the opportunity. Scolding both of us, she reminded viewers that this is exactly what we have seen in the legislature for the past four years. Subsequent polling by the *Winnipeg Free Press* showed the results from viewer feedback, confirming that Carstairs and I had both come out ahead. Certainly, I had the most to lose, yet Filmon, my principal opponent, appeared to have trailed in third position. Nevertheless, it is indisputable that the strong showing by Carstairs would benefit her and improve the Liberal Party vote.

My visit to a rally in Swan River was cancelled just a few days before the election. The night before the Swan River event was to occur, I had received an urgent call that my father's health had sharply deteriorated, and his death was imminent. I rushed back from Russell, Manitoba, to be present with my mother, Velma, and my family, as we sat by his hospital bedside during the final difficult hours of his life. Hoping he could hear these words despite his circumstances, I tearfully whispered to him at his bedside, "we are going to be re-elected and I love you." I was reminded of the anguish inflicted on my predecessor Ed Schreyer when his father died during the 1977 election campaign.

The very capable and handsome Leonard Harapiak, sometimes referred to as Manitoba's R.F.K., won the Swan River seat anyway, the first time this rural riding had ever gone NDP. But the election win was a bitter-sweet experience for me; though we did manage to scrape through by a narrow margin, my father had died the day before. I realized it would not be an easy second term in government. Anything could happen, including a premature defeat of our government in the legislature.

Undoubtedly, during the critical lead-up to the election, our focusing on job performance was the primary reason for our victory. We had developed a solid track record on the issue of jobs. Manitobans had trusted and continued to trust us on the maintenance and enhancement of social programs. Contrary to the pervasive forecasts after the angry language debate, the Conservatives failed to take power. Many voters did go to the polls still complaining about our position on the French-language issue, but they reluctantly voted for us because we were trusted on the economic issues. We were criticized by some for seeming to run for cover on the French-language issue, thus permitting the bigots to win the day. But this criticism was neither accurate nor fair. The court had already spoken, and it was more important that we achieve re-election so we could carry on with our progressive programs. Indeed, Grant Russell's lawsuit was postponed by my lawyers. If the trial had taken place during the campaign, one can only imagine how much media attention the case would have generated, awakening memories again of the bitter language dispute.

We won by a narrow margin. We lost constituencies in River East, Riel, Brandon West, Ste. Rose, and Springfield. By gaining Swan River, our net loss was kept to four seats. Another factor that I believe diminished the size of our majority was the publication of polling in the week leading up to the election, which inflated the size of NDP support. I believe these polls led some New Democrats to remain at home on Election Day, as it appeared that the election would not be as close as it turned out to be. Election night was nerve-racking for me. Even though we had won, for which I enjoyed some relief, I had a strong intuition about how hazardous our circumstances were. The departure or death of just one of our members could overthrow us. Little did I know this would occur in the budget vote two years later.

Finally, some additional talent arrived in cabinet: Leonard Harapiak won in Swan River, Gary Doer won Concordia, and Judy Wasylycia-Leis was successful in St. Johns. They would serve with distinction in my cabinet. Later Judy was elected to the House of Commons, and Gary Doer defeated the Filmon government in 1999. Jim Maloway would take Elmwood, defeating Russ Doern. The popular Winnipeg councillor Harvey Smith would take Wellington, and Manitoba's best farmer, Clarence Baker, won in Lac du Bonnet. We all deeply regretted the loss in Springfield of Andy Anstett, who had served so well during the French-language debate and had undoubtedly paid the price for this. Andy lost in a squeaker, by just fifty-five votes, and I believe we erred in not appealing this loss. In addition, two hard-working MLAs, Phil Eyler in River East and Doreen Dodick in Riel, were defeated. Peter Fox (the Speaker during the Schreyer government), Brian Corrin, Don Malinowski, Sam Uskiw, and Pete Adam (a cabinet minister during our first term), had stepped aside in Concordia, Wellington, St. Johns, Lac du Bonnet, and Ste Rose, respectively.

Some unfortunate events also occurred following our re-election in 1986. In general, the controversies were unjustified; they were ignited by the Opposition and the media to serve their own purposes. They played a minor but consequential role in the erosion of our popular support, causing us to be more vulnerable and leading to our eventual defeat. I relate them only to see what can be learned from them.

However, during our second term in government we had to wrestle with instances of serious embarrassment from errors that had taken place on the Crown corporation level. Some of these were costly to taxpayers. In particular, processes ensuring accountability of the Crown corporation to the minister, to the cabinet, to the legislature, and to the public were not robust. Too often, policy decisions reflected the vision of public administrators instead of politicians, and occasionally politicians avoided responsibilities that were clearly theirs to assume.

Costly affairs involving the Manitoba Telephone System (MTS) subsidiary MTX and the Manitoba Public Insurance Corporation (MPIC) highlighted the need to enact legislation that would ensure better accountability to government by the bureaucrats administering our Crown corporations. Prior to our terms in power, previous governments had also encountered difficulties; corrective steps to minimize the opportunities for further such abuses were therefore overdue.

A careful review of the Proceedings of the Legislative Assembly of Manitoba over the years will show that such failures have generated many questions. Ministers were blamed despite potentially exonerating circumstances. The boards of directors failed to understand their proper role, tending to focus more on operations and less on strategic and public policy issues; perhaps their role as directors was not clearly set out in their mandate. Sometimes, corporations like the MPIC and MTS did not sufficiently foresee problems or use suitable crisis management techniques to limit damage. In retrospect, it is clear that we should have enacted reforms in the Crown corporations, which would have tightened up accountability and headed off some of the difficulties we encountered during our final two years in office. By 1986, my administration had been convinced that better processes were essential to keep Crown corporations accountable. The government and the electorate required maximum accountability.

After considering all the factors involved in accountability, control, corporate autonomy, and performance, the government in 1987 enacted legislation known as the Crown Corporation Accountability Act, 1987. This structure was designed to precisely define the responsibilities of all those engaged in the process. An early warning system was required to alert those at the political level of any planned corporate actions. Political accountability meant that the public had the right to know and the government had a duty to disclose intentions, successes, and failures. The Public Investment Corporation of Manitoba (PICM), a cabinet committee, would deal with mandate as well as the long-range plans and capital expenditures of Crown corporations. It would apply "policies relevant to all Crown corporations" and report to cabinet." Unfortunately, the Filmon government later weakened much of this legislation. The PICM, formerly consisting of cabinet ministers, is now a "repository of business talent and expertise for Boards to draw upon for orientation, co-ordination and advisement with matters such as strategic planning, performance measurement, capital expenditure, consideration and financial reporting." Its membership now consists of appointees and not ministers with direct responsibility.

Transparency with rate approvals is also essential. For instance, given the hostile reaction to the auto insurance rates announced by my government in December of 1987 and the resulting lack of public confidence in their fairness or necessity, it was unfortunate that we had not established an independent review of auto insurance rates.

Shifting to a More Progressive Agenda

In 1987, our new government would move to the left. I recall advising Ed Broadbent of our intentions: his response was "Good." Our new agenda would reveal a number of long-awaited reforms. Party activists would cheer the flurry of new initiatives. These included amendments to the Human Rights Act pertaining to sexual orientation, progressive moves dealing with labour relations to assist smaller and weaker bargaining units, and environmental legislation that placed Manitoba as the leader among Canadian provinces. These were all brave political choices, ones we could embrace with enthusiasm. These would be our own doing! They would make Manitoba a more equitable province.

The Battle to Protect Sexual Orientation in the Human Rights Act Amendments

As Attorney General in the 1970s, I had not considered amendments with respect to sexual orientation as a part of a strengthened Human Rights Act. Within the caucus there were, at that time, no proponents of such amendments, and so they never became an internal issue. A decade sped by before momentum surfaced on this issue. After inheriting a very good Human Rights Act from the Schreyer government, we had launched a review in 1982, led by a distinguished Faculty of Law professor, Dale Gibson, newly appointed chair of the Human Rights Commission. His Policy and Legislation Review Committee held hearings throughout Manitoba and in 1984 proposed an entirely new Manitoba Human Rights Code. Its principal recommendation included protection from discrimination based on sexual orientation in the Human Rights Act.

In 1986, Roland Penner, the Attorney General, made this recommendation to caucus. Our political situation was precarious, and many of us, including myself, were apprehensive. Discrimination on the basis of sexual orientation was an issue that would be highly divisive. It reactivated shadows of the French-language issue, perceived as distracting us from our primary obligation, fighting unemployment. Thus, Roland's failure to achieve a majority vote on his first caucus endeavour was hardly unexpected. There were clearly three camps on the issue: a small minority had serious moral reservations; a second group, though some did not necessarily disagree with the need for such legislation, had serious reservations about prioritizing such legislation at that time; and a third group firmly supported the amendment and were enthusiastic about proceeding. Personally, I was associated with the second group.In 1987, Roland succeeded with a second attempt. By this time I was willing to proceed but continued to recognize the pitfalls: some of our members might bolt ranks on this contentious moral issue. One by one, I called these MLAs into my office and discussed with them the basis of their opposition to the amendment. I was anxious to assure myself that the reason for their opposition was not truly moral conscience. I concluded that none, in fact, possessed such a reason for voting against the legislation. How could any member justifiably argue that he or she opposed providing equal rights to all Manitobans, regardless of their sexual orientation? We would advance on the basis that this was a government bill; thus the whip would apply and every member appreciated that defeat would hurl us into another election. I remained apprehensive about this risk until the matter was finally determined.

The Opposition felt they had another hot button issue and could hardly contain their glee. It was evident that many of them thought we had horribly miscalculated and that this legislation would hasten our demise as a government. Opposition members were united and vicious in their attacks. In the provincial community it soon become apparent that there was substantial fear about the volatile nature of this legislation. The challenge facing us was to limit the reaction to manageable levels.

Hostility was surfacing from various religious groups. Church leaders charged that the bill would coerce churches to breach the Bible when hiring pastors, teachers in separate schools, or any part-time workers in any church. Some ministers would argue that the scriptures included homosexuality with drunkenness, murder, immorality, greed, and perjury. One argued that Bill 47 was one step from destruction of the family and society as we know it. Such opponents of the bill would make the legislative committee the focus of their efforts to thwart its passage.

However, the clergy was not of one mind on this issue. Two United Church ministers supported the legislation, stressing that, "in God's eyes, all are created equal, regardless of sexual orientation." "You can go to the Scripture and torture out a few quotations as has been done," Rev. Bob Haverluck said. In total, about 130 briefs were presented to the committee, with opponents heavily outnumbering supporters. Among those urging adoption of the bill was Glen Murray, who was to become a popular mayor of Winnipeg and, later, nationally prominent.

The Opposition cleverly targeted several individual members of our caucus who they assumed were, for one reason or another, most vulnerable on the issue. Obviously they hoped these members might fold and end up voting against us, thus triggering a premature election, which could then be fought on this explosive topic.

An example of the Opposition's attempts to arouse religious fears involved reading quotations from the Bible. The member from Brandon West, James McCrae, led the way with this method of attack. He had done some research on the scriptures and discovered passages that he recited to us. He claimed we had "breached the fundamental law of our country" by proposing such a provision; he quoted from the preamble of the constitution, which stated, "Whereas Canada is founded upon principles that recognize the supremacy of God and the rule of law."

As the session drew closer, Jim Walding announced he could not support "a measure that would legitimize what I consider a perversion." Realizing that the bill might not gain the support of all our members, especially Walding, we introduced an amendment that said "nothing in the Code shall be interpreted as condoning or condemning any beliefs, values or lifestyles based upon any of the characteristics referred to in the Code." Although we did not consider it necessary, this amendments seemed a prudent step to ensure passage.

In the evening of the last day of the 1987 session, dark and menacing clouds congregated over the legislature. Inside, legislators were locked in a no-holds-barred battle over our amendments to the Human Rights Act. For over six hours the battle waged about the inclusion of the words "sexual orientation." Progressive Conservative Dennis Rocan roared his opposition: "I told my son, if I ever catch you wearing an earring, I am going to cut your ear off." The PC hitman, Don Orchard, dared me, "Do you want as your legacy that Winnipeg becomes the AIDS capital of Canada?"

It fell to me to have the last word in the early hours of the morning, as the session was finally wrapping up. I revealed my surprise at "the sense of hate one feels from across the way." This, of course, produced outrage from the Opposition benches. The legislation was finally passed by a 29–25 vote. Certainly, if I had not summoned the several dissident caucus members into my office and spoken to them, we could have lost this critical vote. Although I had been cautious at the beginning, I became more convinced about the rightness of our initiative as the debate raged on.

Speaking immediately after the vote, I said, "I don't believe I've ever been more proud, in eighteen years of elected office, with the speakers, the comments, and the deeply held feelings, regardless of politics, that are involved

The Pawley family celebrates the provincial election victory,
17 November 1981.

The first meeting of the Pawley government cabinet in November 1981.
Clockwise from left: Maureen Hemphill (Education), Leonard Evans
(Natural Resources), Laurent Desjardins (Health), Howard Pawley
(Premier), Muriel Smith (Economic Development and Tourism),
Vic Schroeder (Finance and Labour), Jay Cowan (Northern Affairs), Eugene
Kostyra (Consumer and Corporate Affairs), Wilson Parasiuk (Energy and Mines),
Roland Penner (Attorney General), Sam Uskiw (Government Services,
Highways and Transportation), and Bill Uruski (Agriculture).
Missing from the photo was Pete Adams (Municipal Affairs).

Addressing the Manitoba NDP annual convention, 14 February 1982.

Attending the First Ministers' Conference on Aboriginal
Constitutional Matters, Ottawa, March 1983.

First Ministers' Conference on Aboriginal Constitutional Matters, March 1983.
From left: Brian Peckford, Grant Devine, Bill Bennett, Richard Hatfield, Bill Davis, John Buchanan, René Lévesque, Howard Pawley, James Lee, Peter Lougheed.

Welcoming Pope John Paul II to Manitoba, July 1984.

Tour of the Limestone hydroelectric project, 10 September 1985, with
Hon. Jay Cowan, and the Hon. Wilson Parasiuk.

Howard Pawley, June 1986.

Speaking at the First Ministers' Conference on Aboriginal Constitutional
Matters, March 1987.

At the First Ministers' Conference on the Constitution
at Meech Lake, June 1987.

Left to right: Don Getty, Robert Bourassa, David Peterson, Howard Pawley, Bill
Vander Zalm, John Buchanan, and Brian Mulroney.

With Brian Mulroney at Meech Lake, June 1987.

Receiving the Order of Canada as Officer of the Order from Governor General Adrienne Clarkson, November 2002.

Discussing public auto insurance at press conference in Moncton, New Brunswick, 2004.

for the honourable members on my side of the Chamber who expressed their views from their hearts with deep conviction that this is right and proper and can make a more decent, more equitable society for all Manitobans—not just for some." Manitoba maintained its progressive reputation by becoming the second Canadian province to enact such a law. Quebec had preceded us in 1977.

The Environment Is Number One, 1986–1988

In the mid-1980s, Manitoba was operating under the first Environment Act, which had been adopted in 1968. This act dealt only with air, water, and soil, and only with actions that emitted contaminants. We believed it was necessary to prevent environment damage from occurring in the first place.

In 1986, the Manitoba Hazardous Waste Management Corporation Act was proclaimed, establishing the development, ownership, and operating responsibilities for Manitoba's hazardous waste management system, eventually located in southern Manitoba, near St. Jean Baptiste. By 1987, we would be ahead of the times in promoting progressive environmental legislation. I was pleased that Manitoba became the leader in breaking new ground on the environmental front; for this Gerard Lecuyer deserves much of the credit for his outstanding leadership.

Before the new Environmental Act was passed in 1987, documents were distributed throughout the province to all potentially interested groups—including municipalities, environmental groups, farming organizations, companies involved in the production and distribution of chemicals, etc.—so they could study the proposed legislation and consider making comments to us in writing or at meetings scheduled throughout the province in 1986. The consultation by Gerard Lecuyer was very thorough. Even those who were concerned about some new aspects of the legislation were very appreciative of the opportunity to express their views. It was an opportunity to build trust and convince them of the necessity of tougher measures in order to protect our environment and, over the long term, to create a healthier economy for Manitoba.

About 400 concerned citizens, business people, environmentalists, and farmers made comments at meetings, and sixty written submissions were also received. The feedback proved very useful. This was the type of legislation that might have given us a great deal of difficulty had we not involved a broad spectrum of Manitobans in the drafting process.

Governments today could learn much from this consultation process. Manitoba's new Environment Act was enacted in a new era of environmental protection for Manitoba. It was the most comprehensive, far-reaching, and up-to-date environmental legislation in Canada at the time, and even today it remains almost totally unchanged.

The new Environment Act was innovative and prevention oriented. It contained five basic principles. First, it had the scope to protect all ecosystems, whether human influenced or entirely natural. Accordingly, any project of environmental significance would be subjected to an impact assessment. Second, the act provided for efficient and effective control of contaminant emissions, partly through a new system of source licensing that was built into the act. Every development proposal that impacted the environment would be required to have a license. Through the licensing process, environmental standards would be set for specific developments.

Third, the Act provided for a unified process, one that rejected the type of artificial division between pollution control and environmental impact that is still the norm in most jurisdictions. The new legislation could assess resource use, impact on sensitive areas, the socioeconomic impacts of development, and other important factors. Best of all, the unified process meant a single application and a single environmental licence could be obtained. Other provinces can have three or more environmental approvals for a single development project.

Fourth, the Act, for the first time, provided for a strengthened public role in environmental decision making. The department's actions in granting or denying a licence to develop would be open to public scrutiny and be accountable.

Fifth, the Act strengthened the ability to enforce environmental laws, providing substantial fines and jail sentences for offences. Directors of corporations could be personally liable for violations; facing fines and jail sentences for their actions. Pollution would not be profitable and would not be tolerated.

The Manitoba High-Level Nuclear Waste Disposal Act

The Manitoba Government had been consistent in its policy of support for nuclear waste research at Atomic Energy of Canada because we had one of the world's first-class research laboratories. However, we opposed the disposal of high-level nuclear waste within our borders and near our borders in any drainage basins that drained into our province. Indeed, as premier, I intervened in the U.S. when an American site-selection process included a site in the Red River Valley, which drains into Manitoba.

In February of 1987, Gerard Lecuyer reiterated Manitoba's position on nuclear waste disposal to the House of Commons Standing Committee on Environment and Forestry in Ottawa. He also announced the government's intention to ensure that a nuclear waste disposal facility would never be established in Manitoba.

Our legislation in the area of the environment was intended to provide a present and future framework for environmental protection and enhancement that would benefit all Manitobans. Fundamental to this legislation were three principles: leadership, prevention, and stewardship.

Manitoba was the first jurisdiction in Canada to introduce this type of legislation. It was a clear statement of our intent to protect and maintain our ecological processes, including our watersheds, to keep them free from human-generated nuclear contaminants and thereby fulfil our stewardship role.

The new act made the disposal of high-level nuclear waste in Manitoba a violation of provincial law, and it required that the wastes emanating from research conducted at the Underground Research Laboratory be stored above ground to permit retrieval and provide for continuous monitoring. It also prohibited the storage of waste not intended for research purposes in Manitoba.

Nuclear waste disposal had provoked strong opposition from citizens in the affected area and from the many who travel to the area in summer. Some people felt that if the scientists had concluded it would be safe to dispose of nuclear waste underground, we shouldn't worry. We took a different view: although scientists can help us understand relative risks, it is our society that determines what is an acceptable risk and who should bear that risk. That is a socio-political decision, and it should be made by elected members, as lawmakers, after consultation with the citizens they represent.

National Task Force on Environment and Economy

Gerard Lecuyer would also chair a task force which allowed Canadians to respond to a report being prepared by the World Commission on the Environment and Development, which had a mandate from the United Nations. The commission released its final report, "Our Common Future," in April 1987. The report expressed optimism that the world can solve its environmental and economic development problems "in a more open, fair and just manner in a new era of economic growth." A few months later, Lecuyer remarked, "I was proud to sit in the imposing members' Chamber of the United Nation Assembly, where Mr. McMillan, as spokesman for Canada, tabled Canada's response to the world report 'Our Common Future.'"

As premier, I was proud that Canada had been the first country to respond and act quickly to the World Commission Report. Manitoba again had been a leader.

Labour: Final Offer Selection

One final issue stands out for me as a successful legacy of my government's progressive policies. The NDP is traditionally associated with the labour movement and the needs of working people, but less often have we been able to enact our vision and principles through legislation. After our 1986 re-election, leaders of my government and the labour movement met to discuss what labour initiatives could be advanced during our second term. There would be no surprises, no false expectations.[4] What would be feasible for the government to undertake in a single term with what was admittedly a slender legislative majority? It was important to recognize the importance of both short-term and long-term objectives. We discovered that we generally had similar long-term objectives, but we all knew that we faced short-term practicalities.

Many in the party and the labour movement preferred to push ahead with "anti-scab" legislation, but with our slender majority and the emotional divisiveness that this issue would undoubtedly provoke, it seemed to make strategic sense not to proceed with it. However, a great deal of support emerged for what most considered a reasonable compromise. This was Final Offer Selection (FOS). FOS appeared to solve many of the difficulties confronting working people. Its main advantage was that it provided an option for negotiators to settle a labour dispute without resorting to a strike. There were too many examples of employers being determined to hold the line at all costs, to turn back the clock, or to break the union. Too often, collective bargaining belonged to the "law of the jungle." FOS provided an alternative process.

FOS is a form of arbitration in which both the company and the union mutually agree to forgo their right to strike/lockout and submit their final offer to a selector, who then selects one or other of the offers in its totality. The list of selectors would be one mutually agreed on by representatives of the business and labour communities. Although FOS had previously been used in some cases on a voluntary basis, such as when it was included in collective agreement, it would now apply to all units covered under the Labour Relations Act. It could be used during a strike and serve as an incentive to the parties to bargain fairly.

The political and economic motivation for such legislation was grounded in the reality that the size of the workplace was changing. Units had become smaller and had less strength to bargain effectively. Larger numbers of the employees involved in such units were women and youth, whose pay and benefits were less than those in larger and more traditional units of employment. These economic inequities had to be addressed. From a political perspective, FOS appeared to me as a reasonable alternative to anti-scab legislation.

Not unexpectedly, the business community was united and ferocious in its opposition. They threatened to challenge the legislation under the Charter of Rights and Freedoms.

Most members of the Manitoba Federation of Labour (MFL) endorsed FOS, but important public sector unions remained opposed. These unions feared the undermining of free collective bargaining. What if a government unfriendly to the union movement assumed power in the future? A third party might become involved in the negotiations and undermine free collective bargaining.

After vigorous debate at the 1985 Manitoba Federation of Labour convention, 600 delegates voted by a two-to-one margin in favour of endorsing the concept. An articulate Wilf Hudson, president of the federation, identified the primary reason for the positive vote as the "provision of an option for negotiators to settle a dispute without being forced to call an unproductive strike." Hudson complained that Labour legislation permitted unions to be destroyed and working people to lose their jobs: "Employers take advantage of the situation and return collective bargaining to the law of the jungle. Final Offer Selection is an alternative which may be used by either of the bargaining parties." [5] We continued to stick to our guns despite substantial attacks on the legislation. It was finally enacted at the beginning of 1988.

Unfortunately, in 1991, a majority Progressive Conservative government succeeded in repealing the legislation. In doing so, it ended what was one of the most innovative attempts at developing an alternative to strikes or lockouts in the event of labour-management disputes. [6] Indeed, I think it's fair to say that for their time, the main tenets of our legislative agenda—a natural extension of the social democratic philosophy established in my first term as premier—were progressive.

During our term, labour saw other improvements that would have a long-term impact in favour of working people. Manitoba would lead the provinces in this regard. We refused to permit the recession of the 1980s to deter us.

But the recession was not the only obstacle we faced. As we had experienced with the crisis over French-language services, which took time and attention away from realizing our ideals, we would also be challenged and sometimes distracted in the late '80s by newly emerging issues, this time on the federal scene.

CHAPTER 8

Manitoba
on the Federal Scene

THE LAST HALF OF THE 1980S was a demanding period in my premiership. After a difficult 1986 election campaign, our government began vigorous action on several fronts to accomplish what we believed were important goals—establishing progressive environmental legislation, improving the mechanisms by which labour disputes might be resolved, and including sexual orientation in a strengthened Human Rights Act. This provincial agenda would have been more than enough to keep us busy. In the same period, however, equally challenging problems confronted us on the federal level. These were the years of the memorable CF-18 fiasco and the Free Trade Agreement, the deal that changed Canada.

Back in 1981, my aim was to reduce the tension in the difficult relationship between the Manitoba and federal governments. It was no secret that the liaison between the Trudeau and Lyon governments had been extremely adversarial. Nevertheless, I wanted to work fairly with the federal government, to look upon them as a senior level of government and trust that they would treat us with the same level of respect. Without doubt, assuming power after the bitter battles that had taken place during the 1981 constitutional negotiations would not be stress-free on the federal-provincial front.

Two incidents vividly depict this atmosphere.

At my first federal-provincial meeting in February 1982, I had, sadly, sensed the prime minister's growing disenchantment with cooperative federalism. After this summit, in a private conversation with me (as the new premier on the block), Trudeau expressed his frustration about the premiers whose only interest, he felt, was "to destroy the federal government." He added sorrowfully, "I once believed in cooperative federalism, but I no longer do." This was perhaps reasonable in the aftermath of the intense acrimony provoked by the negotiations for the patriation of Canada's constitution.

At the same conference, the premiers and the prime minister had been invited by Governor-General Edward Schreyer for dinner at Rideau Hall. A worried René Lévesque, the premier of Quebec, telephoned me at my room at the Chateau Laurier Hotel. "Pawley, I am not going to the governor-general's residence for the reception tonight. If there is anything said involving Quebec, please let me know." "Why me?" I retorted. "Because you're the new guy on the block. I know I can't trust the other guys but I don't know about you," he answered.

I had not realized that at the time of this formal dinner hosted by the governor-general the mood had been very tense. Recalling it, veteran Premier Richard Hatfield of New Brunswick described the occasion as having been very emotional, a function uglier than he had ever attended in his life. Some premiers refused to speak to other premiers. Trudeau was hostile because of bad service and contemptuous about the food. At one point, it was said, Trudeau instructed the governor-general to "finish his dinner quickly so he could get the hell out of there without breaking protocol."[1] No wonder Lévesque was not eager to attend!

Although cooperation among the Trudeau government, Lloyd Axworthy (Manitoba's representative in the federal cabinet), and our provincial government would be positive, little did I recognize how swiftly this relationship would erode in the remaining years of my premiership, during the Mulroney era. A succession of combative events would trigger a confrontational atmosphere. Nowhere was that more sadly apparent than with both the CF-18 and the free-trade battles.

The CF-18 Fiasco

In 1986 the Mulroney government announced that it was awarding a multi-million-dollar CF-18 contract to the Montreal-based Canadair Company rather than to Bristol Aerospace Ltd. of Winnipeg. This decision was made for the crassest of political motivations, without any regard for the respective merits of the competing bids. No other issue in contemporary times, outside the National Energy Program, aroused the fury of western Canadians as much as the blatant unfairness of this decision. Future generations of Canadians can learn much from this ugly chapter in federal-provincial politics.

Manitobans relied on the solemn assurances repeatedly given by the federal government and by their regional minister, Jake Epp, that this award would be based solely on merit, not political considerations. Whichever company submitted the lowest bid with the superior product would win the contract. The regional economic impact would be massive and permanent. Manitobans were thrilled with the federal government's commitment to fairness in the process. The province would finally reap the benefits of recent advances in technological growth, no longer condemned to being "hewers of wood and drawers of water." The Mulroney government's promises to stick to the merit of the bids were considered crucial because the Manitoba bid stood no chance if the decision was to be based on political clout: Quebec had seventy-five MPs while Manitoba had but fourteen. Mulroney's assurances were thus very popular in the keystone province, and Bristol's representatives were overjoyed. They were confident that they would surely win on an even playing field.

Perhaps we were unmindful of other factors at work in Quebec. As Peter Hadekel explains, "francophone nationalists saw Quebec's glass as almost empty. Yet the rest of the country thought it was far too full; to them the federal government bent over backwards to humour, please, and spoil Quebec."[2] Federalist politicians in Quebec were nervous about the separatist threat, and Premier Bourassa was using this chip to press the case for the CF-18 contract with Mulroney. The union representing Canadair employees and the management itself had come up with the clever ruse that the technology deserved to be in Canadian hands. The contract increasingly became a test of power and how the interests of Canadair, later Bombardier, were synonymous with those of Quebec. Pressure was mounting on Mulroney.

While in London, England, in October of 1986, I received a frantic long-distance telephone call from worried staff in Winnipeg. They urged me to immediately contact Prime Minister Mulroney. "Funny business is going on," they warned. "The Tories are toying with the bid," desperate federal officials in the bowels of the Ottawa bureaucracy were warning their Manitoba counterparts. The same Bristol officials who earlier had urged Mayor Norrie of Winnipeg and me to assume a low profile, cautioning that Manitoba "could never be the winners in a political tug of war with Quebec," were now in a frenzy about the real possibility of unfairly losing the contract. Indeed, a worried Bristol had purchased a full-page ad in the *Globe and Mail* claiming its bid was in the best interests of Canada.

That same evening, I attended a sumptuous dinner at Canada House, hosted by Canada's high commissioner, Roy McMurtry, the former Conservative Attorney General of Ontario. There, I was confronted by a deeply worried Sir Francis Tombs, who was the head of Rolls Royce, the owner of Bristol Aerospace. In these official surroundings, he forcibly counselled me that his company would have no alternative but to re-examine any future investment strategies they might undertake in Manitoba: "If this is the way Canada wishes to do business, we will avoid smaller provinces; they have too little political clout with Ottawa. It's better for us to choose provinces like Quebec or Ontario: they can pull the political strings."

Angered by this threat, I was vividly reminded why western Canadians have historically felt alienated by the lopsided political-economic power of central Canada. I was determined that they would not win this time without a good fight.

The following day, Tombs reinforced his conversation with me by writing a powerful letter of concern to Prime Minister Mulroney, in which he advised that he had taken the opportunity "of expressing my grave concerns over rumours of the forthcoming awarding of a contract for the support of the CF-18 aircraft." Ominously, Tombs warned, "we believe that we won the technical and financial evaluations, but that political considerations may result in the order being placed elsewhere. This would have a serious effect on our Bristol Aerospace plants in Winnipeg and upon our future investment intentions in Canada." Ironically, Tombs closed his letter with a request for the prime minister's "intervention."[3]

After several fruitless attempts to reach Mulroney the following day, I reluctantly left London for a scheduled weekend break in the county of Cornwall in western England, the site of my ancestral roots. There, on 23 October, I finally received the prime minister's telephone response. Neither I nor my wife Adele, who was accompanying me, was pleased by this procrastination. We had spent more than a day in this beautiful Cornish countryside stuck in a cramped hotel room awaiting his call—in my case, with considerable foreboding.

I started the telephone conversation by advising the prime minister about the rumours relayed to me from Winnipeg and the information I had gathered in London alleging that a decision had already been made. I reminded him of the tendering process. "Was it no longer being honoured?" I demanded. "Was politics superseding the above-board process that had been promised to prevent such abuse?" Mulroney responded in his usual smooth, charming way. Had he not always been fair to the West? he asked. An uneasy chill raced up my spine. I replied, "Brian, all that may be fine, but I hear worrisome reports pertaining to the CF-18 contract." The prime minister assured me that he had not studied the file, and that no decision had been made. He promised to call once a decision had been made, and to discuss it with me first.

Only much later did we discover the lengths to which the prime minister was prepared to go to mislead Manitoba about a decision that the federal government had already made. In his memoirs, Michel Gratton, who worked in the PMO from July 1984 to March 1987 (first as the deputy press secretary, and later as the press secretary), informs us that a decision on the awarding of the CF-18 contract had in fact been made for some time, but the announcement was delayed until Mulroney's good friend Grant Devine, premier of Saskatchewan, managed to secure re-election in 1986.[4] As Gratton reveals, Premier Devine was one of the prime minister's most "loyal allies." The awarding of the contract would certainly affect Manitoba Conservatives most, but Mulroney also knew that "the bad reaction there was bound to overflow into neighboring Saskatchewan," and since Devine was in a close race, "a negative gesture by Ottawa at this point could be devastating." This revelation is particularly interesting to me: my telephone conversation from Cornwall to Mulroney took place on 23 October 1986—three days after Devine had won re-election. In 2010, Mia Rabson, a *Winnipeg Free Press* reporter, obtained cabinet documents through an access-to-information request that prove that the prime minister had been fully aware of the contract, and the recommendations that it be awarded to Canadair, by 16 June 1986. The documents also reveal the prime minister was aware as early as 9 October that a decision had been made.[5] Regrettably, I was correct about my suspicions of the trustworthiness of the prime minister despite his condemnation of my remarks as "vulgar."

Although I remained uneasy after the Cornwall phone call, I did experience some relief. After all, the prime minister of Canada had just given me his solemn assurance. Surely I could depend on the assurances of a prime minister! Two days later, tired and anxious, I flew back to Manitoba where I would soon be enlightened about the real designs of the Mulroney government in this matter.

On the morning of 31 October 1986, during my daily forty-minute drive to Winnipeg from my residence, I was smacked with the lead item on the CBC morning news. Treasury Board chair Robert de Cotret had just announced that the federal government contract for the CF-18 maintenance work had been awarded to Canadair in Montreal. De Cotret explained that the government decision was based on the importance that it attributed to technology transfer. This was obvious bafflegab, coming as it did from a government that neither before nor subsequently demonstrated much interest in Canadian nationalism. Although normally slow to rise to anger, I was furious by the time I reached the premier's office.

Already, worried officials of the provincial trade department were assembling there along with their minister, Vic Schroeder. Hurried calls by various officials were put through to the union, Bristol Aerospace, and the City of Winnipeg, summoning their representatives to meet with us at once. As an increasing number of tense individuals huddled, it was agreed that there was no alternative but for Manitoba to go on an immediate offensive.

At ten o'clock, I stormed out of my office to meet with the media at a rapidly called press conference. Even the faces of the normally neutral reporters vividly betrayed their anger at the enormous body blow delivered so unceremoniously to their province. There, the electrifying atmosphere was the same as throughout the province. Barely containing my anger, I opened the press conference by denouncing the Mulroney government's decision.[6] I outlined the pledge given to me only a few days earlier by the prime minister and which his office had been reminded of on the "Wednesday of this week"—a promise to call me before the decision was made. I announced my decision to lead, the next day, an all-party delegation of business, labour, provincial, and city representatives to Ottawa to meet Mulroney and Tory cabinet ministers from Manitoba and demand the reversal of this horrendous decision. Irritated, I advised Manitobans of my frustration and added, referring to the breach of Mulroney's promise, "It's one more example of the shaft. I cannot trust this man." October 1986 may very well have been the first occasion that any person in public life expressly raised "the trust factor" in relationship to Mulroney. In the years to follow, however, many voices could be heard questioning the integrity of this former prime minister.

The immediate reaction throughout the province was furious. The provincial Tories were among the first to climb on board, denouncing their federal leader's decision unanimously and doing all they could to distance themselves from their federal colleagues. Frank Lawson, owner of Mother Tucker's Electronics in Winnipeg and a former president of the Manitoba Young Conservatives, erected a sign in front of his store that reflected the outrage within Conservative ranks: "Mullooney, Take Your Politics, Take your

Contract, Take your B.S. and shove it."[7] There was even talk about breaking ties with their federal counterparts, an idea that was encouraged by Filmon himself. During a tour through Conservative country after my confrontation with Mulroney, I discovered the persistence of the political storm. An election then would certainly have increased the slim margin we had won in the last election. Filmon denounced the decision as an "outrage." Musings began about the Progressive Conservative Party changing the name of its provincial wing. Another Tory MLA announced his intention to cancel his membership in the PC Canada 500 Club, whose members paid $1000 a year for the right to hobnob with senior cabinet ministers. Ads were taken out in newspapers, blistering editorials appeared, and a rush of letters was sent to the papers. The West was being snubbed. What was most ironic about this development was the reality that western Conservatives, nursing dozens of grievances against central Canada, had waited twenty years to come to power.

The morning after my press conference, the Manitoba delegation departed Winnipeg International Airport for an urgent meeting in Ottawa with Mulroney and his ministers from Manitoba. The Manitoba delegation included John Doole, Winnipeg Chamber of Commerce; Donald Henderson of the Manitoba Chamber; Wilf Hudson, president of the Manitoba Federation of Labour; and Randy Alleyne, head of the union representing the Bristol Aerospace employees. Mayor Bill Norrie went on behalf of the City of Winnipeg.

As I rushed through the Winnipeg airport, an angry resident of the Stony Mountain district accosted me, shouting "Give Mulroney hell!" and adding, "I voted for the Tories in the last election but never again." By coincidence, within a few moments I discovered myself seated immediately behind Felix Holtmann, the Progressive Conservative MP for that area. Burly and quick-tempered, he did not take kindly to the report I somewhat eagerly related to him about this incident. Obviously feeling the pain inflicted by his government's unpopular decision, he yelled, "I am sick and tired of your constant whining," physically making gestures that clearly indicated that he was not about to continue the discussion with me on this latest policy quarrel.

Landing in Ottawa, I had to work my way through a large and noisy crowd of reporters awaiting me at the city's airport, representing all sectors of the national media. The agreed-upon meeting with the prime minister was scheduled to take place at the Langevin Building. As the Manitoba delegation gradually made its way there along Rideau Street, we were surprised by the generous encouragement extended to us by several Ottawa citizens who met us along the way. Obviously, Mulroney had touched a raw nerve that went even beyond the boundaries of Manitoba and western Canada.

Arriving at the conference room in the Langevin Block, we were seated as a group, and we patiently awaited the arrival of the prime minister. Entering the room fashionably late, Mulroney was coolly received. He began the meeting on a sour note, hissing, "Premier Pawley, I have been made aware of your vulgar remarks." Evidently he was referring to the press conference the day before when I had dared to openly question the prime minister's trustworthiness. "They will be long remembered," he warned, ominously adding, "and I have made note of them." To these comments, I responded, "Mr. Prime Minister, it doesn't matter very much what you think of me, nor indeed what I might think of you; however what is critical is that you re-establish the trust from the Manitoba people that you have lost." My remarks did nothing to assuage his anger; he turned to Mayor Norrie and snapped, "Mr. Mayor, do you have a submission to make?" His snub was obviously aimed at me and was one that I could not let go unchallenged. "Mr. Prime Minister, I will be speaking on behalf of Manitobans," I firmly asserted. With obviously increasing discomfort, Mulroney was left with no choice but to listen to me.

I related to him the reasons for the anger we all shared at "this act of betrayal by the federal government." "The decision should be immediately reversed," I insisted. "It is unfair treatment of a province with less political clout. Smaller provinces should not be treated in this manner."

If the prime minister had expected the criticism from the Winnipeg mayor to be more restrained, he was sadly mistaken. Never before in his life, Norrie explained, had he heard as much anger directed at a prime minister from Winnipeggers as he heard at the past weekend's Blue Bomber football game. If Mulroney expected criticism to slack off when it came to the turn of the representatives of the Manitoba and Winnipeg Chambers of Commerce, he was in for bitter disappointment. Doole and Henderson both sharply chastised the federal government's actions. As the labour representative prepared to speak, Mulroney attempted to make his departure. I was able to delay his exit only when I implored him to remain and listen to what the spokespersons for the workers had to say: "Surely you can't walk out and not hear the representatives of the workers themselves speak." Mulroney slowly and reluctantly returned to the table.

The president of the Federation of Labour and the regional vice-president of the Canadian Association of Industrial, Mechanical and Allied Workers, the local union at Bristol Aerospace, spoke eloquently about the sense of betrayal and anger felt by workers at the plant. The Manitoba Mulroney cabinet ministers, Jake Epp and Charlie Mayer, sat stoically through the meeting. Not once did they intervene to support the Manitoba delegation or their own constituents. They had failed to head off the announcement so unfair to their own province. Indeed, Jake Epp had done much damage by repeatedly trying to reassure Manitobans that the CF-18 contract would be landed by Manitoba.

The bitter confrontation finally ended on a highly unsatisfactory note. The die had been cast, and for the Mulroney government there was no turning back.

I did my best in the press conference that followed to focus on the theme of fairness to the smaller provinces in the Canadian federation that, like Manitoba, lacked the political clout enjoyed by the larger provinces in central Canada. Little did I know at the time that Mulroney's anger about what he perceived as my insults led him to order that "all federal business in Manitoba would be done over Pawley's head" and that Pawley "should share none of the credit when the federal government had something favourable to announce." I "was to be kept in the dark as much as possible."[8]

That evening, a lively debate took place on CBC radio between me and Dan McKenzie, a Tory Winnipeg MP associated with the far right of the Progressive Conservative Party. McKenzie sneered that our opposition to Mulroney's decision was hypocritical: "Why is Pawley so upset? He leads the peace marches in Winnipeg against military expenditures. Why would he want the CF-18 maintenance contract in the first place in his province?" In response, I firmly advised the Winnipeg MP that the wastefulness of the arms race was not the real issue here. Whether or not military expenditures were a wise choice, the federal government had chosen to spend these monies, and consequently the tendering process had to be fair and above board. It was not. Manitoba was shafted by tampering with the bidding process. The real issue, I added, is fairness to smaller provinces. You and the government you support must bear responsibility.

I telexed my fellow premiers in western Canada asking for their support, but I expected little. Indeed, if I had anticipated it I would only have been disappointed. Only Premier Vander Zalm of British Columbia would express any support of Manitoba, and that was done solely by private communication. An interesting revelation is provided in Pat Carney's biography. [9] She relates how the former prime minister misled her into believing that British Columbia would be rewarded with an ice-breaker contract as some sort of quid pro quo for awarding the CF-18 contract to Quebec. "Tell Vander Zalm he will get his ice breaker," Mulroney assured Carney. A few weeks later Mulroney denied making any such commitment and appeared inflamed by the suggestion that he had. "I said no such thing! Retract your statement immediately," Mulroney demanded. Carney, perhaps unkindly, describes the statement as being accompanied by Mulroney's "CF-18 look—greasy skin, sleazy manner." In Carney's book, we get the first hint of the anguish of the West, which would shortly thereafter trigger the formation of the Reform Party.

Carney claims it was one of the few instances where Joe Clark, sitting to Mulroney's left, contradicted his successor: "Whatever you say, don't say it was in the national interest," Clarke cautioned. This is a telling comment coming from one who only a year earlier had identified the defeat of the NDP Manitoba government as a top priority for Conservatives in western Canada. [10] If that desire had been fulfilled in March 1986, the West would have been solidly governed by Tories who, like Devine and Getty, would rarely have raised any objections to selling out the interests of western Canada. I was not surprised when neither Getty nor Devine responded to my telex pleading for support from fellow western premiers.

Interestingly, Carney's revelations, like Gratton's and Rabson's accounts, further confirm the blatant misrepresentation Mulroney made to me. As I mentioned, he claimed he was not familiar with the file and that no decision had been made. But if he hadn't accessed the file, then who did make the decision? According to Carney's account, not only was the decision not made in cabinet, it had not been made in either the Economic Committee of cabinet or the Treasury Board of cabinet. There can be no doubt that Mulroney unilaterally made the decision, perhaps in consultation with a few personal advisors.

Peter Hadekel advances another reason for Mulroney's decision. [11] He shows how documents released under the Access to Information Act reveal that the "technology transfer" touted by Canadair was a fiction. The technology was proprietary to McDonnell Douglas and could only have been used on the CF-18 contract, so Canadair could have benefited from it only by "osmosis." Hadekel also points out that the documents "cited regional considerations" as the basis for changing the civil service recommendation, and that a senior bureaucrat pointed to how "historic Quebec sensitivity about Ontario getting more spin-offs from the fighter program at McDonnell Douglas" played a role in the decision.[12]

It is this type of prime ministerial abuse that is provoking disillusionment with politics in Canada today, as evidenced by steadily declining turnouts at federal elections. The same abuse of power has been seen repeatedly in Mulroney's successors. It substantiates the argument that a suitable place to begin democratic reform is to reduce the extent of the Canadian prime minister's power, which is perhaps unequalled in any other developed democratic nation today.

It would not be fair to ignore the disappointing stances adopted by both John Turner, leader of the Liberal opposition, and Ed Broadbent, leader of the NDP. Indeed, Mulroney relished the opportunity to repeatedly taunt both opposition parties. He openly dared both his counterparts to disagree with him on the awarding of the contract. When pressed by reporters on the issues, he delighted in urging them to seek out both party leaders and seek out where they stood on the issue: "Ask them whether they're for and against it"; "I understand they support the government," he would add.

With the Liberals seeking to regain support in Quebec, perhaps their waffling could have been anticipated. Ed Broadbent's lack of response was more surprising, since Manitoba was, at the time, the only NDP-governed province in the entire country. Instead, he urged the establishment of a commission to discover the truth of the matter. This disappointed Manitoba New Democrats who always held Broadbent in the highest esteem. Vic Schroeder, provincial minister of industry, trade and technology, wrote Ed a lengthy letter reflecting the concerns of Manitoba's NDP, expressing disappointment with the federal leader's position and complaining that he had been in touch with his office "a number of times." He felt compelled to add, "I don't think you have any idea as to the intensity of the anger."[13]

Having levelled this criticism, I must acknowledge in retrospect that Ed was sincerely attempting to avoid choking off what appeared to be phenomenal growth in support for the NDP in Quebec, shown in the polling of the time. Obviously, if Ed was to achieve a breakthrough in the next federal election, he needed to continue to nourish this trend. Mulroney recognized this and, wishing to place Ed in an impossible position, urged his staff to ask Broadbent, "if the contract shouldn't have gone to Quebec." According to Gratton, the prime minister was disappointed that the reporters had failed to "force Broadbent to stand up and contradict Pawley," but rather devoted their space to "Pawley's complaints."[14] Moreover, Broadbent did question the integrity of the government's tendering procedures. Although nothing arose from his efforts, Broadbent urged the Auditor General to "initiate immediately an inquiry into the details of the CF-18 maintenance contract."

This anger over the CF-18 contract continued to climb with desperate Manitoba Tories, who had enjoyed some political momentum picked up from their defeat earlier in the year. They even debated the possibility of separating themselves from their federal colleagues. In St. James-Assiniboia, Grant Russell, the famous anti-French-language leader of the Grassroots Manitoba movement, and the same person who had sued me for defamation during the French-language services controversy, angrily resigned his position as Conservative federal constituency secretary. Many other Conservatives were ripping up their party membership cards, and some were resigning from their elite fund-raising club.

The next occasion when the prime minister and I clashed over the CF-18 issue was in Vancouver at a first ministers' meeting on 20 and 23 November. Mulroney was greeted by placard-carrying Bristol workers. In the conference I vigorously attacked the Mulroney government decision: "The CF-18 was, and is, a symbol, a graphic symbol of the frustration we have felt over many decades—the traditional frustrations of western Canada seeing national policies favour the centre, seeing our own prospects and priorities put second, or lower, behind those provinces and regions that have greater electoral weight." I added, "This government promised to address them in a way that would be fair and positive."

Mulroney, visibly angry, retorted that I had not questioned his sense of fairness when he had flown to Manitoba to defend "Pawley's bilingualism policy before the local Conservatives." Gratton distorts this episode by suggesting that Mulroney got his revenge. Generally, the perception not only through the West but elsewhere in Canada was that he had acted intemperately and appeared only too desperate to dig up additional unsustainable excuses for his actions. Afterwards, several premiers approached me to advise how they respected my coolness despite his emotional outburst.

At the same conference, Mulroney came up with one more excuse for the contract's being awarded to Quebec: because of the province's high unemployment in contrast to Manitoba's rate of 6.9 percent. Accordingly, he argued, fairness had dictated the decision. This was the third excuse given for the government's actions in a little over a month. Others included the concern about technology transfer (i.e., keeping the technology in Canada with a Canadian company) and later the false suggestion, easily disproved by officials, that there had been little difference in the bid costs. Added to these excuses was the insinuation that the West was doing well from the Mulroney government. After all, there had been Mulroney's $1 billion to ease the financial crisis of western farmers, which had rescued Devine from defeat in the Saskatchewan election. It was at this conference that I began to realize vividly, for the first time, the extent of the anger felt by westerners outside Manitoba toward the CF-18 decision. At a reception held in conjunction with the conference, attendees who were mainly Conservative came up to me repeatedly, expressing their deep anger over the manner in which Manitoba had been treated by a government they had supported.

Against all this, it would have been easy for our government to play the Quebec card. However, all of us as government spokespeople went out of our way to avoid blaming Quebec. It was the Mulroney government and nobody else that was to blame, we would correctly argue. Of course, the Bourassa government had used its considerable influence to relentlessly lobby both Ottawa and powerful cabinet ministers from Quebec to award the contract to that province. That was to be expected, and it was not unreasonable. It was the Mulroney government, we argued, that should assume the ultimate responsibility for the action. There should be no mistake that the Mulroney government's actions were a giant setback for Manitoba, all of western Canada, and for the other smaller provinces in Confederation. This animosity would contribute considerably to intense resentment against the Meech Lake Accord, especially for its "Distinct Society" clause, throughout the West and particularly in Manitoba. Ultimately, it would prove fatal for the Accord itself.[15]

Free Trade: The Deal that Changed Canada

The CF-18 affair was only one of several battles I fought with the Mulroney government. Almost as intense was my disagreement with him over free trade. I objected not only to the contents of the proposed Agreement between Canada and the U.S. but also with the hard-line manner in which the prime minister was imposing it.

During the final period of my political career, I was heavily associated with the opposition to the proposed Canada-USA Free Trade Agreement. During the endless but generally unproductive series of federal-provincial meetings involving the prime minister and his aides and the premiers, I did all I could to resist whatever proposed changes I saw as contrary to the interests of Canada. My opposition was not doctrinaire; indeed, I preferred a freer system as opposed to one of protectionism.

I had earlier witnessed the deeply hollow masquerade that could exist in trade relations. A prime example of this was the export of hogs to the United States. In 1985, accompanied by Agriculture Minister Bill Uruski, I visited the governors of Iowa, Nebraska, and South Dakota to take issue with mechanisms the Americans had devised to thwart the export of our hogs into their states. Our tour met with limited success in opening up the barriers to this important Manitoba export. In our view, these states were hiding behind excuses, including claims that Manitoba hogs were unhealthy and unsafe. Their assumptions were totally self-serving, motivated by a desperate attempt to protect weak markets for their own producers. I vividly recall the governor of South Dakota advising us that their measures were comparable to a cancer patient's sucking at an apricot pit in a frantic effort to struggle with the disease; their ailing pork industry was suffering from a similar plight, he warned. This experience convinced me that protectionism was not in Canada's interest. Indeed, at a subsequent meeting of western premiers shortly after this experience, I endorsed the general principle of free trade.

Under the Mulroney government, free-trade talks commenced with the Americans. As premiers, we had been promised an integral role in the negotiations. We were assured that our opinions were valuable and, indeed, that a deal was possible only with our participation. This promise was to prove worthless. Although we met every three months, it became apparent that these meetings were exercises in public relations. The real decision makers were those on the inside. The Mulroney government, along with powerful business representatives, was carving out the Agreement behind closed doors, in keeping with the Holy Grail of free-market fundamentalism in Canada.

Despite requests to do so, the Mulroney government was not interested in seeking input through public hearings. In contrast, our provincial government arranged a series of public hearings to obtain opinions about the proposed Canada-U.S. free-trade agreement. These meetings were well attended, far beyond our expectations, and continued our tradition of seeking input from Manitoba's communities. Most of those attending felt that Canada was being sold out and questioned the federal rush job.

The eventual deal Mulroney proposed in a thirty-three-page preliminary text was one born of desperation. My main frustration was with the dispute resolution mechanisms. A mechanism of this kind—intended to guarantee the impartial application of Canadian and U.S. anti-dumping and counter-vailing duty laws and other aspects of trade-remedy laws—had long been proposed by Mulroney, but the one proposed here was extremely weak and ambiguous. Provisions pertaining to agriculture and deregulation of transportation were sure to seriously harm these sectors.

I denounced the dispute resolution provisions as "a case of smoke and mirrors," pointing out that the panel would be "powerless because Americans would bypass the mechanism and fight issues such as imposing tariffs on softwood lumber through U.S. federal courts." It would be the Americans who would interpret "what a subsidy is in Canada." Interestingly, Stephen Harper's trade minister, David Emerson, would finally (nearly two decades later) acknowledge this in respect to NAFTA: "You can win a legal victory today, and think you have established a legal precedent, only to have Congress change the laws affecting the industry and the ways disputes are litigated in the future."[16] The legal effects of all this have never been more evident than in February, 2009, when the Democrat-dominated Congress stipulated in an economic stimulus bill that all iron, steel, and manufactured goods purchased with stimulus money had to be made in America. Nothing in the Free Trade Agreement precludes this restriction. Canadians would find out how shoddily they had been let down.

In Ottawa, I was considered one of the most fervent foes of the government's proposals. On one occasion, aides for Mulroney taped my conversations with my aides; this became an issue in the House of Commons. The *Brandon Sun* charged that having a federal snoop following the premier around at the first ministers' conference was inexcusable, and it sneered, "fortunately for Pawley, the federal government operative was female so one assumes the Manitoba premier was able to have conversations in the men's room." The *Sun* was right on when it added, "Surely premiers should be allowed to whisper things to their aides without being spied upon."[17] Other journalists concluded that I had been the subject of over-zealous attention. The lines can sometimes be fuzzy about what is private and what is public, but there could be no debate about the ethics of a federal employee's taping conversations between me and members of my staff. Why such paranoia? One may only guess!

On one occasion, Canada's chief negotiator, Simon Reisman, snarled in response to a reporter's question, "I think you can spend an eternity with Mr. Pawley and not sell it to him." To me, it seemed strange that the debate had declined to this level.[18]

In December of 1987, during my last first ministers' meeting attended by Prime Minister Mulroney, the premiers met at a residence on the Governor-General's property to review the details of the recently negotiated Free Trade Agreement. Prior to our turkey dinner, Mulroney invited us all to an adjoining room and requested all of us premiers to pose for a photo. As the cameraman was preparing to take the picture he quipped to the assembled guests, "My mother can't understand why I can't get along with that nice Mr. Pawley." I replied, "I wish you had inherited the good judgment your mother obviously enjoys."

At the dinner, just before we were to discuss the details of the negotiated agreement, and just as Peterson and I were going to ask questions, Mulroney declared his need to immediately return to the House of Commons. His officials would answer my questions, he told me. I found his actions repellent. For several years, Mulroney had made much of the regular consultation meetings he was holding with the premiers. During these meetings I discovered little by way of concrete proposals for us to discuss. All we were able to do was voice our concerns about where the free-trade agreement should not go. I was worried about future establishment of Crown corporations like the Manitoba Public Insurance Corporation, involving public auto insurance. I repeatedly pressed for reassurances that farm-marketing boards would not be affected. I recall an eloquent appeal by Premier Joe Ghiz from Prince Edward Island that local procurement be permitted in some instances. In a province like Prince Edward Island this could be critical to the perseverance of small local contractors, few in number, who would primarily depend on the local business.

The summons to this meeting was the twelfth since the free-trade negotiations had begun and would be not without its share of fireworks. I had become increasingly angered by what I saw as the prime minister's attempt to seek our approval for political reasons. The real negotiations were being made by the political and economic elite of Canada and taking place behind closed doors.

I searched for ways to block the deal. Premier Peterson and I considered legal measures. This could possibly succeed in cases where any proposed measure impinged on areas of provincial jurisdiction, such as protecting the wine and grape producers though the Ontario Liquor Control Board. I even considered seriously withholding my support of the Meech Lake Accord. I believed that the free-trade agreement was weakening the powers of the federal government, thus defeating our efforts to protect its powers that had taken place during the Meech Lake Accord discussions.

When my government was defeated on a non-confidence vote in 1988, Simon Reisman boasted gleefully, "Pawley's defeat helps Free Trade." Earlier on various occasions, he had compared opponents of free trade to neo-Nazis. In another instance, Reisman described me as being its most ardent opponent. Subsequent events have justified the opposition of the dissenting premiers Peterson, Ghiz, and me.

Prosperity was promised. The federal election of 1988 was primarily fought on this issue. Although Mulroney received a mandate, the majority of Canadians expressed opposition to the direction in which he was taking the country on this deal. Today, the lofty expectations aroused by the proponents of free trade have not been realized.

Unfortunately, trade agreements like NAFTA have very little to do with trade today. Rather, they have created a whole new world of rights and powers for international capital. Manufacturing jobs are being lost at a record level, and more and more people are losing jobs and being paid less, often without benefits. Contrary to the commitment given by Parliament in 1989, the child poverty rate has not improved; it has worsened. The gap is widening between the rich and poor. Productivity is declining. There is continued reliance on resource exports. We have not significantly diversified our economy toward knowledge-based, high value-added activities. Free trade could be seen in a more positive light if it meant fair trade, with proper safeguards with respect to both environmental and labour standards.

There can be no doubt that my firmly held views, not only on the CF-18 and free trade issues but also on issues such as Aboriginal self-government and the Meech Lake Accord, placed me at odds with Prime Minister Mulroney and most of my fellow premiers, who were overwhelmingly Conservative. I was the "odd guy out," perceived by many of my colleagues as too left-wing and confrontational.

Over the long term, the political future of our entire nation was affected immeasurably by these two issues. It is true that in the short term, Manitoba's economy suffered the greatest damage from the CF-18 fiasco. But Mulroney's decision to award the contract to a Montreal-based company also had broader, more enduring impacts, insofar as it increased concern that the West was being treated as second-class citizens and heightened western premiers' wariness about the Meech Lake Accord and the Distinct Society clause. The process that led to the CF-18 decision also had long-term consequences. Characterized as it was by secretiveness and deceit—by decisions made behind closed doors and then justified by transparently false claims—it raised grave doubts about the possibility of cooperative, productive federal-provincial relations. Discussions over free trade did nothing to quell those fears; despite Mulroney's assurances that the premiers would play an important role in negotiations, the discussions leading to an accord were secretive and driven for the most part by the interests of the federal government and selective business representatives.

CHAPTER 9

The Meech Lake Accord

A Constitutional Endeavour

MY INVOLVEMENT WITH FEDERAL ISSUES in the late 1980s was not limited to my battles over free trade and the CF-18 decision. In August 1986, a few months before the CF-18 contract was announced, I also became engaged in the early stages of discussion about constitutional reform. It was, as things turned out, a discussion that was to extend well beyond my tenure as Manitoba's premier. It was also one in which I found myself yet again at odds with other premiers and in sharp disagreement with Brian Mulroney.

By the summer of 1986, both Ottawa and Quebec City signalled that a window of opportunity existed to negotiate a deal allowing Quebec to sign a constitutional reform package. Shortly afterwards, Mulroney met with Premier Bourassa to discuss the proposals and to strategize how to advance them. Ottawa officials advised their Quebec counterparts "to sound out the other provinces on the proposals over the next couple of months."[1] Subsequently, Canada's first minister asserted that getting a constitutional agreement on the Quebec question was one of his two top priorities, the other being the Canada-U.S. trade pact.

By tossing the ball into our court, the federal government couldn't lose. If the premiers agreed to go ahead with a formal process, then clearly the prime minister, as well as Quebec, would be winners; but in the event that other provinces, either collectively or individually, rejected a process to deal with the constitutional question, the provinces themselves could be portrayed as the villains while the federal government would be seen as at least valiantly attempting to advance the process of reconciliation. Any individual province blocking the process would be seen as endangering national unity. Clearly, it would not be in Manitoba's interest to be perceived as the spoiler in any reasonable effort to heal the 1982 constitutional wounds. Certainly, for all of us, the stakes were high; if we should fail, Canada could break up.

As the premier of Manitoba, the only NDP-governed province, I was anxious to avoid our being labelled as the province that wrecked the opportunity to address the Quebec question; nonetheless, I had grave concerns about engaging in another constitutional controversy. Re-elected to a second term after barely overcoming the fallout from the divisive French-language debate of 1983–84, I understood clearly the harmful passions capable of being aroused. I did not wish Manitobans to judge their NDP government to be more preoccupied with constitutional issues than with economic matters. I feared that the Tory opposition would opportunistically milk whatever benefit they might from the political situation. I feared that smaller and less well-off provinces would, like Manitoba, be adversely affected by a potential weakening of the federal spending power, and I suspected this aspect of the constitutional proposal was another attempt by fiscally minded federal Progressive Conservatives to diminish the role of government. The introduction of medicare would have been more difficult had the proposed spending limitation clause been in place. It would also lessen the chance of a national daycare program, as had been promised by the federal Progressive Conservatives.

My strategy in advance of any future first ministers' conference on the Quebec question was to maintain a low profile, avoiding any leadership role, preferring to wait in the wings until the prime minister himself articulated a clearer position. If he resolved the constitutional impasse, Prime Minister Mulroney would enjoy a mantle like that bestowed upon Pierre Elliot Trudeau, who had patriated the Canadian Constitution and enacted the Charter of Rights and Freedoms.

Debates about Quebec benefited Mulroney by diverting the public's attention from pressing national economic concerns, especially the fierce controversy expected over the proposed Canada-U.S. free-trade pact. Politically, the free trade pact could provide the potential for trade-offs with some provinces that would be otherwise leery of a new round of Quebec discussions, thus benefiting the federal government in its efforts to achieve both policy objectives.

By the summer of 1986, Senator Lowell Murray and Mulroney had devised a strategy that they believed would lead to success.[2] It had four elements:

1) Limit the agenda. It was important that the agenda include only items identified by Quebec, because any additional items would lead to a downward spiral going nowhere.

2) Do not commence formal negotiations until success could be assured. Visible negotiations would only limit flexibility and increase the prospects of failure. This risk would be minimized by advance pre-negotiations conducted in private.

3) Maintain the principle of the equality of the provinces. Thus, Quebec's demands would be met while generalizing the proposals to include the other provinces. The equality-of-provinces principle was intended to ensure that whatever Quebec received, other provinces would also receive, reflecting the political reality that any significant gains by Quebec alone would be unacceptable to the nation.

4) Act as an honest broker between Quebec and the other provinces, waiting until the end before advancing the proposals of the federal government. Quebec would have the responsibility for preparing texts and proposals; the federal government's role would be facilitative. This would allow the federal government "to gain the trust of their provincial counterparts and to gain a real understanding of what the bottom lines of the various provinces were."

Quebec set five conditions for constitutional reform: a veto over major constitutional changes; limitation to the spending power provision; recognition of Quebec as a distinct province within Canada; a guarantee that three judges trained in the Civil Code would sit on the Supreme Court of Canada; granting of constitutional control over immigration to Quebec. The summer of the 1986 Edmonton meeting of the premiers provided the forum to ascertain whether there was sufficient first-minister support to begin informal discussions of these five conditions.

Premier Bourassa warned that he would need to receive something on each condition; otherwise, a firestorm would result in Quebec. However, he also assured us that he was prepared to be flexible, recognizing the political realities facing each premier. The political risk of opening these discussions was seen as Bourassa's, because other premiers could simply walk if the talks should sour. The Quebec premier worried about too much publicity surrounding the talks. He counselled the other premiers that it was a propitious time to break the constitutional impasse, since he believed success could be achieved in short order on a short list of Quebec demands. Recognizing that an opportunity existed to resolve the Quebec question, the premiers, with admittedly varying degrees of enthusiasm, endorsed what was known as the Edmonton Declaration. Although I cooperated, I was more reluctant than the others, leery of a derailing of my government's focus on job creation.

A brief communiqué was issued by the premiers, symbolizing what Osgoode Law Professor Patrick Monahan called "a sort of starter's pistol," announcing to the country that the Quebec round had commenced and that a federal-provincial process would deal exclusively with the Quebec issue. Consensus existed among the premiers that this round would be followed by further constitutional discussions on matters raised by other provinces, including Senate reform, fisheries, property rights, etc., but only after the first round was successfully finished.

Shortly after the Edmonton Conference, Prime Minister Mulroney announced that he would work with the Quebec premier as a team to try to reach an agreement with the provinces to enable Quebec to sign the Constitution. Mulroney's intent was to create a "climate of confidence that will encourage the participants to want to reach a formula that was acceptable to Quebec and to the other Canadian provinces."[3] He stressed that we could not afford the luxury of failure in a constitutional initiative. Demands by other provinces should not "clutter up the Quebec issue."

Quebec's Journey to Manitoba

During the fall of 1986, Gil Remillard, Quebec's justice minister, and intergovernmental officials were in continual contact with the provinces, briefing them on the Quebec position. In October 1986, in a manner highly secretive, often bordering on the bizarre, they arrived in Manitoba, bringing negotiating drafts covering each of Quebec's five points. Afraid to give our officials copies of the drafts, they only reluctantly permitted our staff to copy down the wording—which, naturally, our staff would transcribe after their departure. If leaks should occur, the Quebec officials could say "with a straight face and a clear conscience that they had never before seen the working document and that it must, therefore, have originated elsewhere."

My advisors made a number of immediate observations about the Quebec drafts. They noted, for instance, that the veto provisions from Quebec appeared to repeat Premier Bourassa's offer in Edmonton as an alternative to a veto only for Quebec (i.e., that seven or more provinces with at least 75 percent of the Canadian population would also have veto power). We knew that this misnamed compromise would not sell in Manitoba. And they acknowledged that, contrary to Quebec's earlier assurance in Edmonton, the province sadly appeared to have retreated from any reference to strengthening the constitutional equalization provision. Quebec presumptively capitulated because of negative pressure from either the wealthier provinces or the Department of Finance in Ottawa.

Principally, Manitoba's concern was the process itself. Warnings were issued to Quebec that there was no getting away from linkages between the Quebec proposals and the Aboriginal negotiations, which were currently underway. The Aboriginal constitutional negotiations were critical and could not be sidetracked by the Quebec proposals. Our concerns that Aboriginal negotiations were in danger of being upstaged were conveyed to Quebec, and we stressed to the Quebec emissaries the necessity of public education if their proposals were to be eventually sold to the public.

———◦◦◦◦———

By November 1986, I was already in the eye of a storm when Quebec newspapers misinterpreted my remarks about how the Mulroney government's abysmal actions in the CF-18 affair might harm constitutional talks. The news reports alleged, "Pawley was threatening to block constitutional discussions." I had answered a reporter by pointing out that, "while the Constitution might be a priority for the prime minister, it's not a top priority for Manitoba. We will be interested in dealing with the issue of fairness to small provinces." [4] Intense emotions were fanned following the CF-18 decision, with charges and counter-charges exchanged. Anger grew in Manitoba and elsewhere in the West following the prime minister's silly attempt to compare federal contracts received by the West to what had gone to Quebec.

In December 1986, Senator Lowell Murray and Manitoba's Attorney General, Roland Penner, met as part of the senator's ongoing series of meetings with provincial intergovernmental ministers. Obviously, part of Ottawa's strategy was to get as much positive momentum rolling as possible through bilateral discussions at the ministerial level, thus avoiding officials poking holes in their drafts before governments could provide collective direction on the end result. Fearing Quebec might release its White Paper prematurely, Murray confided to Penner that the federal government still felt it could back away from the negotiations if it became apparent they would fail.

When Penner pointed out that the spending power limitation was our greatest concern, Murray replied that, in addition to the spending provision, the proposed immigration clauses troubled Ottawa. In private discussions at a Manitoba Strategy Committee of cabinet,[5] Penner cautioned us about the political difficulties the Manitoba government could encounter, including those to be expected from an opportunistic Progressive Conservative opposition. He described the expected controversy that would erupt in the province from the recently mandated legislative hearing process for constitutional amendments, which did not exist in any other province. This mandatory public requirement originated from the legislation enacted following the controversy that had swirled around the French-language services issue.

Senator Murray and Justice Minister Remillard of Quebec met in the middle of January 1987. Our office received a detailed debriefing. This was the first time we heard of plans for an informal meeting of first ministers for March or April 1987.[6] With the intent of avoiding a failure, informal discussions were to continue until then, at a cautious pace.

The last of the scheduled first ministers' meetings on Aboriginal constitutional issues was scheduled to take place in only two weeks. This final opportunity to define Aboriginal rights worried Manitoba officials. Manitoba warned Remillard and Murray that introducing Quebec issues into the Aboriginal meeting would be counter-productive. Quebec and the federal representatives wisely agreed that there would be no formal discussion of the Quebec proposals at the final meeting, for fear of upsetting the Aboriginal leadership. Premier Bourassa remained committed to not going public unless the proposals were leaked to the media first. Unfortunately, he failed to attend the Aboriginal meeting, thus Quebec was to be unrepresented.

Senator Murray and the chief of staff to the prime minister, Norman Spector, reported to the prime minister just before Christmas, and again on 17 January 1987, that although Remillard had run into some difficulties in the initial round of discussions, there were apparently no insurmountable obstacles. The question was how best to continue the discussions without attracting too much publicity. It was agreed that the best way to do this was to bring representatives from all the provinces together in the same room, in a low-key format that would allow everyone to assess any consensus that developed.

In March of 1987, at the NDP's national convention in Montreal, federal party leader Ed Broadbent and most of the party's strategists were keen to consolidate what appeared as substantial gains in Quebec public opinion. Could it be that the NDP in the next federal election might actually do what had always eluded it and its predecessor, the CCF, to finally win a number of Quebec ridings and become a truly national party? There had already been evidence of the strategic importance of Quebec to the parliamentary party, demonstrated by its low-key, ambivalent position on the CF-18 contract. So when a resolution recognizing Quebec as unique because of its French-speaking majority was presented to the party's convention, I sensed considerable unease, though no hostility, among Manitoba's delegates. The resolution also gave Quebec a veto on any constitutional changes to federal institutions like the Supreme Court and the Senate. It passed after being formally presented to the convention by Broadbent.

As premier, I was not enthusiastic about stoking the coals on this incendiary issue. Any perception that special status was being accorded to Quebec would be politically suicidal in Manitoba, and I was fully aware that a Quebec constitutional veto like the one supported by the federal NDP was not politically viable.

On 17 March 1987, the prime minister invited the premiers to the federal government's retreat at Meech Lake for a 30 April meeting to discuss progress on the informal talks taking place. Mulroney deliberately played down the prospects for success in the upcoming meeting, and he even cast doubt in the House of Commons about the chances for success. According to the prime minister, "We must find out whether or not there is sufficient political will to bring Quebec in to justify the undertaking of formal negotiations or whether it would be better to close the books and wait for a more favourable moment."[7]

Undoubtedly the federal government was highly uneasy about the possibility of failure. But it was a shrewd move on Mulroney's part to play down expectations. If there was success, the surprise factor, including his successful leadership as first minister in bringing his provincial counterparts to a successful completion, would all the more be positively highlighted. On the other hand, if there was failure, not much would be lost, as expectations would have been dampened. Despite the prime minister's public signals, his federal officials privately advised their provincial counterparts that the 30 April meeting would be a decisive step in the process.

In any event, nine months of quiet behind-the-scenes talks that had gone virtually unnoticed were now over. The invitation to Meech Lake was clear evidence of that. The media would be expected to follow the first ministers, and the public spotlight would be turned on. Every controversial utterance, even the slightest disagreement, would be carefully analyzed. This would, as Monahan points out, create "the inevitable hunt for winners and losers, and for villains and heroes."[8]

A few days after the prime minister's invitation was received, a letter from Senator Murray arrived, largely duplicating the earlier prime ministerial letter. Murray's letter dealt with each of the five points defined by Quebec. On distinct society, on the Supreme Court appointments, and on immigration, his proposals were eventually incorporated, with little variation, into the Meech Lake Accord.

The amending formula proposed the right to receive compensation for a province opting out of any amendment affecting its powers. To deal with Quebec's veto for changes to institutions such as the Supreme Court and Senate, Murray proposed that the level of consent for changes to these institutions be raised from 75 percent to 80 percent of the population. This change would permit either Quebec or Ontario to exercise a veto.

The spending power was more difficult. The senator's letter proposed that any new cost-shared program would have to be approved by at least seven provinces representing 50 percent of the nation's population. He also suggested that any province that opted out of a shared-cost program affecting education or cultural institutions would be entitled to receive reasonable compensation if the province established its own program consistent with national standards.

The senator's letter established the framework and the parameters for the discussion on 30 April. Mulroney, nevertheless, bit the bullet, and invited the premiers to his Meech Lake summer home to ascertain whether any success was possible. Stock of the progress would be undertaken in order to ascertain what the next steps would be. The meeting would begin over lunch and continue into the afternoon. On my part, and I suspect on the part of others as well, there was little hope of any significant progress.

A Day at Meech Lake

My arrival at the Meech Lake site as Canada's only social democrat and only NDP premier symbolically contrasted with that of the other first ministers. While most first ministers were chauffeured in their limousines and discharged in front of the Wilson House, an imposing pink granite mansion circled by the ten provincial flags waving in the breezy April day, the Manitoba delegation drove up in a rented van, parked short of its destination, and walked up the hill. The premiers were guided upstairs for the negotiations to follow, while their Attorney Generals and other officials were closeted downstairs.

Unlike the recent non-productive and public Aboriginal conferences, only first ministers were present, with two exceptions: Norman Spector, secretary to the federal cabinet for federal-provincial relations, and Oryssia Lennie, an assistant deputy minister from Alberta. Both took notes at the meeting. It was agreed, however, that no official, detailed note-taking would record the meeting's developments, to better encourage candidness. I was flabbergasted that our discussions would take place in such a non-transparent fashion after the very visible series of conferences we had held on Aboriginal self-government (1983–1987). The prime minister's strategy was to begin with the easiest items, hoping that the anticipated agreement obtained would then facilitate the momentum necessary to move to the more difficult questions. Nevertheless, complications arose early, with the first item concerning the appointment of three judges from Quebec to the Supreme Court of Canada. Finally, after two hours of debate, an agreement was patched together, with the federal government compelled to agree that the other provinces, as well as Quebec, would have the right to submit their own lists of nominees from which the federal government would make the appointment. The importance of this federal government concession was to underline the reality that other provinces would insist upon receiving whatever Quebec was able to secure from the bargaining table. This established, early in the negotiation, the important principle of equality of the provinces.

With the second item, immigration, an arrangement between Quebec and the federal government, on selecting immigrants, was agreed to. Other provinces would gain the same right, allowing them to negotiate similar agreements.

On the vital spending power proposal, the prime minister proposed that it be limited to the establishment of any new social programs and require the approval of at least seven provinces representing 50 percent of the population. Such a suggestion would have given both Ontario and Quebec, with their large populations, excessive clout, so I indicated that Manitoba could never accept the adoption of such a provision. After further debate, the proposed condition was reluctantly dropped and alternative wording was adopted, requiring the federal government to provide reasonable compensation to any province choosing not to participate in a program if it undertook its own initiative on programs compatible with national objectives. The changes assured the federal government's continued capacity to develop and design future cost-shared programs.

No province could prevent the federal government from launching such a program, as might have resulted years ago with regard to Canadian medicare if provinces had then enjoyed the right to veto. While this provision was later seen as deficient, it was a major improvement on that first proposed.

For me, the distinct society provision proved less difficult. It reflected the reality, not of a superior Quebec but of a province that simply was different and distinct.

Introducing the issue of the Senate, the prime minister advised that his personal preference would be to abolish the second chamber, which he referred to as "that bloody place." Not surprisingly, I signalled my preference for abolition too; but more unexpectedly, Premier Bill Vander Zalm of British Columbia also expressed sympathy for that position. Checking the support he might muster for his proposal, he was evidently disappointed that only two premiers would concur. With the option of abolition closed, a consensus emerged for Senate reform to be left until the Quebec question was settled; in the meantime, future Senate appointments would be made from a list of names recommended by the premiers to the prime minister. Looking back, I believe it was a serious error for such a proposal to have won our endorsement. Like the federal government, we appeared to be interested in lining up at the trough for political appointments. No system of democracy or federalism can justify an appointed legislative chamber accountable to nobody and with the power to block decisions of an elected chamber. The existing system makes abolition or meaningful reform a reasonable possibility. On the other hand, the accord diminished the potential for both future developments; senators appointed by the provinces would only lesson the likelihood of a new senate's deferring to the decisions of the House of Commons. Chances are that this could have led to future critical impasses.

The atmosphere was electrifying when success was announced. Staged to give the impression of an historic milestone not unlike the success by the Fathers of Confederation in 1867, the announcement caught the media off guard, and they failed to ask hard questions. Like the first ministers, they appeared caught up in the momentary euphoria, and took turns congratulating each other. Despite my own reservations, I too was uncharacteristically ecstatic over the outcome, joining in with the same enthusiasm as the others. Canadians watching the news that evening were understandably shocked but delighted at the appearance of their collective political leadership putting aside their political divisions to agree on such complex constitutional changes. At the time, there was little criticism about the in camera nature of the proceedings.

Since I had secured a major victory on the spending power provisions, many Manitobans applauded my achievement in derailing the earlier, unacceptable spending power proposal. The new proposal provided reasonable compensation to any province not participating in a national cost-shared program in an area of provincial jurisdiction if the province implemented a similar program that met national objectives. Notwithstanding the success, however, it would not be long before I realized that further significant improvements were required.

Throughout western Canada, where much opposition was later to emerge, the early reaction, like elsewhere in Canada, was a mix of either praise or indifference.[9] The earliest opposition came from Tony Penikett, the NDP premier of Yukon Territory, who understandably protested that the new unanimity clause for the creation of new provinces was unfair to Yukon. Neither he nor the leader of the Northwest Territories government had been invited to participate at Meech, although the proposals fundamentally affected their residents.

Upon returning to Manitoba, I announced extensive public hearings before the supporting motion would be introduced in the House for final voting. Sharon Carstairs, the Liberal leader and sole Liberal in the Manitoba legislature, was critical, claiming that Meech Lake represented a major change in Canada's direction. She warned, "Every time you strengthen Ontario, Quebec and the wealthy provinces who can afford to bankroll their own programs, this always leads to greater inequality."[10] Her remarks indicated a willingness to play to the traditional fears of the West about Quebec and Ontario and also demonstrated that she sided with the Liberal opponents of the Meech Lake Accord. It was about this time that I became increasingly aware that the dispute over the Accord was the issue that could propel Carstairs from relative obscurity to prominence. By standing on the side of the critics, against her national leader, John Turner, and thus rejecting Quebec's demands, she had potentially discovered a winning political formula. Filmon waffled, playing for more time although appearing to be more favourable than Carstairs to the Accord.

The Opposition leaders in Ottawa, John Turner and Ed Broadbent, endorsed the deal but reserved the right to study the agreement and propose changes to the legal writing before the final signatures. In some ways, their endorsement would prove too quick and easy. To the rest of Canada they appeared too willing to bend to Quebec's demands.

On 8 May, Prime Minister Mulroney, keen to firm up support for Meech Lake and bury the hatchet on the CF-18 flare-up between us, flew to Winnipeg for an eighteen-hour visit. The morning began with the prime minister hosting the Manitoba provincial delegation of several provincial cabinet ministers at a breakfast meeting at the Sheraton Hotel. Jokingly, yet I suspect with real meaning, he suggested that in flying over Manitoba and viewing the landscape it became obvious to him how our governments could serve each other through cooperative effort. Avoiding any crowds, obviously worried about any lingering negative reaction to his unpopular CF-18 decision, he was later whisked to the legislature for an hour-long meeting with me.

Meeting in my office, Mulroney was still euphoric about his Meech success. He read portions of a letter he had received from Canada's foremost authority on the Constitution, Eugene Forsey, who described the constitutional accord as "an extraordinary achievement." To Mulroney, the Forsey letter was critical, providing him credibility to ward off his many academic detractors. In the same discussions, the prime minister could not have been more effusive in his praise of my role. With great verbosity, he offered to commence a new era of maximum cooperation between Canada and Manitoba.

I was not about to reject such an overture if it stood any opportunity of working to Manitoba's advantage. (The mood radically changed later in 1987 because of disagreements between us over the Canada-U.S. Free Trade Agreement.)

The meeting ended with a two-minute statement to the media, after which Mulroney quickly extricated himself without answering reporters' questions. He was obviously fearful of being dragged back into the controversy over the CF-18 decision. The unpopularity of his actions regarding CF-18 would not only have ruined his visit but would have reflected negatively on his Meech Lake Accord efforts.

After his departure, to prove the advantages of cooperation over confrontation, the prime minister's regional minister and provincial point man, the Honourable Jake Epp, announced that the Mulroney-Pawley meeting could result in several multi-million dollar initiatives in Manitoba in health-related industries and rural development projects. As federal health minister, Epp appeared to be in an ideal position to deliver goodies to his home province and assist the federal government in overcoming the damage from the CF-18 fiasco. Delivering to Manitoba as well as to Quebec would firm up support for the Meech Lake Accord. The timing of that statement, coming within days of the signatures on Meech, revealed their uneasiness about the loyalty of the one premier, long considered around the premiers' circle as the "odd one out."

Trudeau Speaks Out

Later that May, just prior to the annual meeting of the western premiers, former prime minister Pierre Trudeau joined the debate over the Meech Lake Accord, contrary to general expectations. In a blistering article that appeared first in *La Presse* and the *Toronto Star*, Trudeau called Mulroney "a weakling" and the premiers "eunuchs." He accused Mulroney and the premiers of lacking the courage to stand up against Quebec nationalists, whom he referred to as "a bunch of snivelers" who should have been sent packing after the 1980 referendum on sovereignty-association.

If there was any doubt that reservations would be voiced at the western premiers' conference, it would soon disappear. Premier Vander Zalm alleged that Trudeau was simply "tasting sour grapes." Getty of Alberta bluntly said, "We never agreed with him. We had a period of trying to live with him; it was driving us out of Confederation." Devine of Saskatchewan, the host and chair, attempted to be more tactful: "It's one man's view of what the country looks like. Quite clearly it's not the view of the western premiers."

For my part, I regret that Trudeau had launched a personal attack on eleven first ministers rather than concentrate on the substance of the agreement. Obviously, the timing and tone of the attack hardened the premiers' resolve to press forward. If the message had been intended to dissuade the signatories, it was an abject failure. Clearly, however, the message proved more effective in influencing the Canadian public than any of us realized. It marked the beginning of a gradual decline in support for the Accord.

Trudeau's intervention intensified the worries of a number of high-ranking New Democrats throughout Canada, who believed that Broadbent and I had seriously erred. On the other hand, his entry into the debate was bound to serve the interests of Sharon Carstairs, who now basked in support from a powerful force. It would surely strengthen her position in the years ahead. I realized that I had to protect my political flanks and secure unequivocal protection for the spending power provisions.

I calculated that Ed Broadbent would be my best source of support. He was worried that a failure by the NDP to endorse Meech Lake would destroy the highest level of support the party had ever achieved in Quebec. Indeed, the NDP was running neck and neck there for first place. It was the chance of a lifetime for a breakthrough. Lacking the access to the prime minister that was enjoyed by the other mainly Conservative premiers, I called Broadbent and advised him that failure to secure clarification on the spending power would leave me in a politically unacceptable position. I warned him that I might have no alternative but to cut my losses and return home without signing the legal draft of the Accord. Broadbent was horrified at this prospect. Not only did he see his Quebec support eroding before his eyes, he also warned me that any Manitoba withdrawal would be blamed on the NDP itself, so I would be responsible for setting back the chance of a lifetime for a Quebec NDP breakthrough.

Fearing such consequences, Broadbent did what I had anticipated and entered into his own private discussions with Mulroney. Warning the prime minister that the Manitoba premier must not appear to be rebuffed at the upcoming Langevin meeting, Broadbent's message got through to Mulroney better than if I had delivered it myself. The first ministers set the stage for the next round in June.

On the Air Canada flight from Winnipeg to Ottawa, Donald Johnston, a staunch Trudeau supporter and former Trudeau cabinet minister, happened to be on board, and he urged me to withdraw my support for Meech. I replied that I intended to improve the Accord rather than destroy it. The task now before us was to sharpen the wording and remove any ambiguity.

Even if some preferred ambiguity to clarity, leaving the sorting out to the constitutional lawyers and the courts, I was not enthused about confusion in the meaning of the spending-power language. To social democrats, the spending-power provisions have been responsible for much that is the essence of Canada. Ambiguity had to be clarified. Comments by some premiers that they saw nothing wrong with taking federal money for one purpose and spending it on another, such as roads or bridges, did nothing to assuage my reservations. I would do what I could as one of the eleven to obtain more precise wording.

The reaction by premiers was varied, but there was little support for much rewriting. Bill Vander Zalm would have preferred to be home in British Columbia because of serious labour trouble there. He repeatedly threatened to walk out because the meeting was dragging on too long. He was finally checkmated by Mulroney's solemn pledge to fly him to Victoria as soon as the meeting was over. Don Getty, premier of Alberta, a province with a passionate dislike of Trudeau, was not about to be seen as knuckling under to the former prime minister's hectoring. Getty still thought he had secured a victory at Meech with the commitment to discuss Senate reform in the second round, after the Quebec issue was put to rest.

Certainly, no trouble for the prime minister would be expected from Grant Devine, perceived as a confidante of Mulroney. Some even referred to him as the prime minister's point man. He was not about to make any waves. Mulroney had bailed him out in the 1986 Saskatchewan election with a billion-dollar wheat aid program. Because Devine had made no secret of his support for the prime minister's CF-18 decision the previous fall, our relationship was, not surprisingly, cool. My staff would laugh at how many times Devine slipped out for coffee whenever it was my turn to address conferences. I never returned the favour!

Ontario's David Peterson, near a provincial election in which he hoped to attain majority government status, was pressured by Ontario's large ethnic community to get clarification on how the distinct society clause might affect them. Moreover, his powerful Attorney General, Ian Scott, had severe criticisms of the Accord and was prepared to press them forcefully. Premier Bourassa was serenely confident that he could just wait it out, calculating that the premiers could not afford to make major changes. While denouncing the Accord, Jacques Parizeau, leader of the Parti Québécois, had failed to ignite much opposition in Quebec.

Richard Hatfield, aware that he was only months from an election that he would probably lose, played the bon vivant role, never doubting that the Accord was right for Canada. John Buchanan was supportive of the federal government. Joe Ghiz, a Harvard constitutional law graduate, supported Meech for all the right reasons. A truly decent man, he wanted Quebec back in the constitutional family. Brian Peckford, feisty but for now tamed by the prime minister's pledge to include the jurisdiction of fisheries on the list for the next round, would not be any problem for Mulroney.

Finally, there was me. Andrew Cohen was probably right when he wrote, "To many of them, Pawley was too left wing on the environment, the economy, women's issues."[11]

I had made no friends, especially among my western colleagues, in my support for Aboriginal self-government during the four failed Aboriginal conferences that had taken place between 1983 and 1987. Accompanied by Roland Penner and Elijah Harper, I had from day one supported the enshrinement of Aboriginal self-government in the Constitution; unlike other premiers, we never wavered in our staunch support. Being the only New Democratic in power after 1981, I was usually on the opposite side of the rest of the western club on fundamental issues. There was, however, affinity among Peterson, Ghiz, and me, and this would play a part at Langevin.

Then there was the prime minister, heralded by many for his remarkable accomplishment at Meech Lake. Congratulated, perhaps too early, by his opposition foes, Turner and Broadbent, he was prepared to use his very superior negotiating skills to put a deal together—perhaps regardless of the cost. The appearance of a successful result would be crucial to him even if it should be at the expense of the central government.

Labelled a weakling by his nemesis and obviously stung by Trudeau's attack, Mulroney began the meeting by obsessively carrying on at great length about how Trudeau had been dead wrong in his recent criticisms. Reading at length from newspaper clippings, he described how the former prime minister had contradicted his earlier pronouncements. Mulroney was finally urged by Hatfield not to waste further time. "Will you forget about that bastard Trudeau," demanded the New Brunswick premier. As Joe Ghiz observed, "But there was another man in the room that day. We talked about him quite a bit.

He was there. He was there in spirit. He was Pierre Trudeau."[12] Ghiz said the prime minister would not let go. It was as if he was exorcising a ghost.

Mulroney's introductory remarks were intended to bind together the club. "Gentlemen, thank you all for coming. It's been an extremely difficult time, but we've made much progress at Meech Lake. As you know, since then, a lot of people have been criticizing us. One is the former prime minister, Prime Minister Pierre Trudeau." The attacks unquestionably stiffened the resolve of the far western premiers—Vander Zalm, Getty, and Devine—to stick together all the way. Despite the criticism, the prime minister had unwisely planned a ceremonial signing early in the afternoon. In case the discussion took a little longer than expected, the Langevin meeting earlier scheduled for 11:00 a.m. was advanced to 10:00 a.m. However, it was to be a marathon session as the meeting dragged on for nineteen hours, finally breaking up the following morning at 5:00 a.m.

Manitoba's team of advisors included Bryan Schwartz, constitutional law professor at the University of Manitoba; Stu Whitley, head of the Constitutional Law Section of the Department of the Attorney General; Cliff Scotton, chief of cabinet communications; Jim Eldridge, head of Manitoba's Intergovernmental Secretariat; and George Ford, my chief of staff. Attorney General Roland Penner had been compelled to leave early to fulfill a family commitment.

Everything certainly started well, as Mulroney, the ever-professional labour negotiator, settled the easy items first—the Supreme Court, immigration, and the Senate clauses—in less than two hours.

The distinct society clause was a hurdle. Peterson, with backing from me, wanted changes. Fearing that it was a threat to the Charter of Rights and Freedoms, we pressed for modifications. Ian Scott, a civil rights lawyer and Ontario's Attorney General, was especially worried; he felt that "if the Charter could not be protected, the entire deal should collapse." [13]

Peterson's repeated references to his experts' opinions agitated Premier Bourassa, who felt that nameless advisors from Ontario appeared to be running the show; he demanded that these experts be allowed to speak for themselves. Shortly thereafter, four of Ontario's advisors entered the inner room: Ian Scott, the Attorney General; Patrick Monahan, policy advisor; Ian McGilp, a constitutional lawyer; and Peter Hogg. Scott posed a question about what would take precedence in case of a court challenge—the collective rights of Quebec through the distinct society clause or the individual rights of anglophones under the Charter. Bourassa, still clearly agitated, snapped, "What is the interest of an elected Ontario politician in the language dispute in Quebec?" Richard Hatfield interjected, "It is none of our business." In response to such remarks, Scott became even more wary. He had never contemplated that Ontario's right to raise the concerns of a linguistic minority would be challenged in any constitutional talks.

Two federal officials in the room—Frank Iacobucci, Deputy Minister of Justice, and Roger Tasse, the former Deputy Minister of Justice—contradicted Scott's position on the legal impact of the distinct society clause. However, the most pivotal opinion came from Peter Hogg, an Ontario advisor, who also asserted that he did not share Scott's interpretation. In retrospect, if Hogg had sided with Scott, the outcome of the discussions would likely have been very different. The example raised by Scott was probably ill chosen, for it caused a number of premiers to become defensive on behalf of Bourassa. Using the example of an English-speaking province might have been more astute. Hogg's opinion that the distinct society provision would only marginally impact Charter protections appeared to the premiers as the most credible interpretation.

With my support, Peterson persisted in his objections and got Section 16 added, safeguarding Aboriginal and multicultural rights. Stung, perhaps, by some of the in-fighting at the recent Aboriginal conferences, some premiers didn't want Aboriginal Canadians even to be mentioned by name, and they insisted that this section refer to other sections of the Constitution only by number. Considering that just five years later, during the Charlottetown negotiations, the first ministers agreed to Aboriginal self-government, one could only marvel at how swiftly attitudes were to improve. As weak as the provision was, Peterson required it for political purposes, to show that he was protecting his ethnic constituency. Likewise, I was pleased to see the provision, as inadequate as it might be. Looking back, however, we were both wrong. The section did little to counter the future criticisms of those, especially in the Aboriginal community, who saw it as only a very cosmetic addition. A process to resolve the Aboriginal self-government issue should have been included to permit the resumption of talks. As premiers, we should have risen above the disappointments and bitterness of the failed rounds of Aboriginal constitutional conferences in the 1980s. In the end, the ambiguity of the clause prevailed.

Debate on the spending power provision was just as intense. While Peterson took the lead, with my backing, in questioning the distinct society provision, it was my turn to do the pushing with the spending power issue. For me it was essential for any federal government to utilize the central federal spending powers to create greater economic and social equity; to weaken them would surely defeat the objectives for which I had struggled.

Responding to my warnings about Manitoba's objections, Broadbent had met with Mulroney and proposed that the word "the" be added before "national objectives." Mulroney had agreed. Still displeased by the wording, I complained that it remained unclear who would establish either the program or the objectives. The provincial government that opted out could argue that it was meeting the objectives, while such a program could be at wide variance with the national program. For instance, on one occasion Premier Bourassa had mused aloud about establishing a program that would encourage births in Quebec and suggested that such an initiative would be compatible with a federal daycare program. I argued for the words "that is established by the government of Canada" to be inserted between "in a national-cost program" and "in an area of exclusive provincial jurisdiction if the province carried on a program or initiative that is compatible with the national objectives." Since the federal government implements shared-cost programs—in health care, post-secondary education, and social welfare—it was crucial to me that the program be one that met the objectives of the federal legislation. Otherwise, Canada could end up with a patchwork form of federalism, with disparate programs functioning in each province, reflecting the individual fiscal capacities of the different provinces.

In the event that the two largest and most powerful provinces opted out, there would be less political motivation for the federal government to proceed with any new initiatives in and for the remaining provinces. As a provincial premier, I wanted no part of any such arrangement. Canada's Parliament represented the totality, not just the parts. Although I would have preferred "standards" to "objectives," it nonetheless was clear that such a definition would not be realizable because Bourassa could not retreat that much and still retain credibility. Roland Penner and my other legal experts had earlier convinced me that the federal government could set out the objectives for any proposed program within the preamble of any proposed legislation, thereby ensuring general conformity throughout Canada. For instance, it could be spelled out in the enabling statute that a national daycare act program must be non-profit. Other conditions could be also included. Furthermore, I was aware of the danger of too little flexibility in reflecting regional differences in the launching of cost-shared programs. Peterson supported my move. Bourassa continued to resist.

Both Peterson and I argued that, in this matter, we were attempting to protect the central government against surrendering too much of its power. "You are ceding too much. Speak up!" we urged Mulroney. We thought it unbelievable that we as premiers were doing what would have otherwise been expected from the prime minister.

Opportunities continued for us to meet with officials or attend hastily arranged caucuses. Hatfield complained, "We basically had an agreement, but Pawley and Peterson were fussing." In fact, on one occasion, he was so impatient with what he perceived as our stubborn intransigence that after listening in at one of our caucuses, he shouted, "What you're saying is bullshit. If you're not prepared to go along with this, go in and say so." Premier Getty showed impatience with the discussion, arguing, "We are talking here about programs in areas of exclusive provincial jurisdiction." On another occasion, Mulroney called me aside and took a little walk to warn me vigorously, "if you don't agree to this, you will be responsible for breaking up our country."

Finally, at about 3:00 a.m., Bourassa agreed to the clarifying words I sought. Section 106A would read "compatible with the national objectives," which was much more forceful than the earlier hazy objectives. I was of the opinion that I had gained as much as was reasonably possible. We had come this far; the general objective in bringing Quebec back into the constitutional family was right for the country. Deficiencies remained, including the applicability of the unanimity provision for the entry of new provinces into Confederation. This would make it difficult in the future for the Yukon and Northwest Territories. To me, this was nonsense, but I could gain no concession. Recognizing politics as the art of the possible, I reluctantly gave in.

With some worthwhile gains in the spending power provision and with reassurances about the distinct society clause, I thought I could ward off the opposition I knew would eventually come. To walk out, even with Ontario, would have been unjustifiable; the federal government, two opposition leaders, and eight provinces were clearly onside. Still, I was conscious of the price of always being the odd one out at premiers' meetings. At the same time as Meech, I was, along with Peterson and Ghiz, fighting Mulroney's proposals for a Canada-U.S. free trade agreement. It would not have done anything for my credibility to oppose what was, at the time, a hugely popular constitutional deal concurrent with our opposition on the trade matter. The trade deal, in my mind, was more crucial.

Moreover, any Manitoba rejection would be viciously attacked throughout Canada as rooted in past emotional conflicts such as the infamous French-language debate and the CF-18 controversy. Last, but important to me, was the fact that since the French-language debate, there had been Manitoba legislative rules requiring public input. Even if they were alone in Canada, Manitobans would have a voice. I did not adhere to the doctrine that changes could be made only if they were to correct egregious errors. I felt I could still insist on changes before Manitoba's ratification. It is my opinion that such a process should have been extended to Canada as a whole.

With such thoughts, I huddled with Peterson early in the morning as it neared the make or break time. Earlier, we had agreed to stay together or go out together, so as not to isolate either province. Advising Peterson that I had gotten sufficient changes to warrant buying in, I added that there was a price we all had to pay. We both felt there could be improvements over what we had gained. But we decided, given what we had gained, that we couldn't withhold our consent. My decision followed exchanges between Whitley and Schwartz about the significance of the wording changes. Schwartz remained unhappy; Whitley was satisfied. As is not unusual with lawyers, I had two quite divergent opinions. I decided to go with Whitley's. However, returning to the room with the first ministers, I felt no euphoria, only a sense that all had been done that could be achieved, and that approval of the amended Accord was the best choice available.

Some have inquired about the length of the negotiations and the hour at which a decision was reached. Retrospectively, I view the process as flawed. It lacked credibility with the public. Rather than accepting or rejecting the Langevin deal, we might have been wiser to have walked out, agreeing to complete the negotiations only at a more reasonable hour. I know that other participants felt the same. There was no logical reason why we didn't. Perhaps drained of energy, we were collectively all too ready to conclude—not the way to build a nation in a pressure-cooker atmosphere!

While advising the prime minister of my approval, I warned that unless public input was obtained, the process could yet unravel before there was a completed deal. Emphasizing the legal requirements contained in the rules of the Manitoba legislature, I cautioned that it would be contrary to my nature and, more important, that of Manitoba, if such hearings were or were perceived to be a rubber stamp. If there is a demand in the province to renegotiate any additional terms, an ample opportunity must be provided. Even then, knowing there would be opposition in all parties, including in my own, I cautioned the prime minister once more: "Don't leave any required first ministers' meeting until the very end. An opportunity will be needed to pass the Accord in the Manitoba legislature and additional hearings might be required."

Stressing our experience with the French-language controversy, I urged Mulroney not to repeat the mistake we had made of appearing not to be seeking public input, or the Accord would never see the light of day. In response, the prime minister was conciliatory and assured all present that there would be appropriate public participation. Probably due to the lateness of the hour and fatigue, I did not insist that he flesh out this commitment. Regrettably, public participation turned out to be only perfunctory hearings by a Senate Commons Committee in Ottawa in August of 1987, where only invited submissions were allowed. Looking back, I'm still surprised by how my warnings about the outcome were more prophetic than I could possibly have known.

The path travelled by Mulroney in this respect was wholly inadequate and eventually self-destructive. Clearly, the process should have been more open, and the hearings should have taken place nationally and been readily available to everyone interested in making a submission, as occurred in Manitoba. The federal NDP must also bear criticism for its failure to demand hearings along the same lines as those that later took place in Manitoba.

Leaving the Langevin Block, I attempted to avoid the media, but it was not to be. They had waited for nineteen hours, occasionally receiving versions of what was happening from spin-doctors from the federal, Ontario, or Quebec governments. I advised them of my support. I would participate in the signing ceremony. Detailing the improvements in the Accord, I talked of the intended public hearings in Manitoba and further noted Mulroney's promise to do likewise at the national level. A restless two or three hours of sleep were interrupted by a call from Ed Broadbent, asking for details of the changes. Delighted with the progress I reported, he warmly congratulated me. Even then, I had an uneasy foreboding. There were, I realized, latent undercurrents that could be unleashed. Not since the French-language services issue had I sensed such unease about a controversy that was about to explode.

Nevertheless, the ceremony went well. All were finally onside. The *Winnipeg Free Press* heralded the achievements I had secured. Editorially, it wrote, "A good deal of the credit for [the] relatively good result should go to Premier Howard Pawley, who with Premier David Peterson of Ontario, offered the most effective criticism of the substance and style of the agreement reached a month earlier at Meech Lake."[14] Entering the legislature after my return, I received a standing ovation from my caucus members and applause from both the Opposition and Sharon Carstairs. Manitoba for the moment was proud! But it was not long before opposition surfaced.

Early on in the legislature, Carstairs expressed criticism about the negative impact of the distinct society clause on the Charter. My party and caucus colleagues feared that national objectives did not equate with national standards. As much as I tried, I would be unable to convince them that the compromise made sense. Francophone cabinet members Larry Desjardins and Gerard Lecuyer were disappointed by the lack of protection for the minority French-speaking population outside Quebec, and maverick MLA Jim Walding, later to bring down my government, disapproved. Most ominously, cabinet minister Elijah Harper, who three years later killed the Meech Lake Accord with procedural tactics, dropped into my office to privately confirm his opposition. He could not vote for it, he said, unless there were amendments on behalf of his people—the Aboriginals and First Peoples of Canada and Manitoba. I advised him that while I certainly respected his disagreement with the Accord, it remained my opinion that the prospect of enshrining Aboriginal self-government, as we had attempted to achieve together through our attendance at four constitutional conferences, would stand a improved prospect in the future if we could get the Quebec question behind us.

Yet not all was negative. Most members of the legislature, including Filmon's PCs, were endorsing the Accord. Ironically, a few weeks later, one of those too frequent procedural errors occurred—an ominous sign of more to come. When inadequate notice to permit the public hearings for the Accord to take place intersessionally was given to the members of the legislature, the Progressive Conservative opposition House leader, Gerry Mercier, failed to secure Gary Filmon's approval to waive the necessary notice. The House adjourned, without committee hearings, in the fall of 1987. In retrospect, one can only speculate about what might have resulted had the hearings proceeded promptly and the committee reported to the legislature before our government's defeat on 8 March 1988.

In late July 1987, Premier Bourassa made a point of hastily visiting Manitoba after the completion of the joint meeting of governors and premiers

in Traverse City, Michigan. Visiting the French-speaking community of
St. Boniface, he attempted to reassure residents of Quebec's support for
minority French-speaking people outside Quebec. He took issue with my
pledge to have meaningful hearings. The Quebec premier asserted what
was to become the seamless web doctrine—namely, only the correction of
egregious errors would be allowed.[15] Little did they realize at the time that
governments were no longer the only actors. As Alan Cairns observes in
Disruptions, "the elites of the groups with Charter recognition have stakes in
the Constitution. They have left the audience and are now on the playing field,
as are the Aboriginal peoples for whom the Constitution is a potential lever
to a less marginalized future."[16] At the September 1987 premiers' conference
in St. John, New Brunswick, another opportunity was missed. Feminist organizations were seeking minimal changes to ensure that they would have the
same protection as the multicultural and Aboriginal communities. Premier
Ghiz committed himself to raise the issue. Arrayed against Ghiz, Peterson,
and Pawley, a solid wall of opposition resisted even this modest amendment.
The strategy by the prime minister and Conservative premiers was to say as
little as possible and ratify the Accord as quickly as possible for fear of otherwise opening a Pandora's box. As later developments proved, it was an error to
proceed on the basis that no changes could be undertaken unless the mistakes
were egregious in nature.

After Hatfield's defeat, a New Brunswick delegation, including the
deputy premier, visited us. While they were opposed to the Accord and
Manitoba was onside, we were nevertheless able to agree about the need
for more openness in the process. On the weekend of 4–5 March 1988,
New Democrats at the annual provincial convention debated a resolution
urging Manitoba to withdraw support for the Accord. As I had feared, opposition was steadily building within the party. In an impassioned and anxious
plea to the delegates, I managed to sway a sufficient number of delegates to
cause the defeat of this resolution. Approved was a compromise motion that
hearings would take place and changes be proposed if they were deemed necessary. This followed mounting disagreement by many members of the party
including Gerry Friesen, a well-respected historian and long-time supporter;
Charles Bigelow, the former president and a senior statesman of the party;
and Andy Anstett, the capable former House leader.

But for the endorsements of the federal and provincial leadership, I sensed
that the Manitoba party would have rejected the Accord right then and there.

That intervention on my part was to be my last as premier on behalf of the Accord. On the following Tuesday, my government would be defeated in the legislature on a budget vote.

———◦◦◦◦———

In 1990 the demise of the Accord came about with the opposition of Elijah Harper, who prevented the Accord from coming to a Manitoba legislature vote in the final days leading up to its deadline for ratification. Among the few telephone calls Elijah accepted in these days was one from me, and it was serious: "Elijah, you know I disagree with what you are doing, because with all its defects, I think that we might be better to go ahead and make the commitment for further rounds on Aboriginal items. At the same time, if I were you, Elijah, I would continue to do what you're doing. If you back down at this point—and I am speaking to you now as a friend—I think you will lose credibility." Elijah listened and then responded in his usual quiet way: "I don't like this notoriety. I am looking forward to getting back to the trap line and looking at the stars at night." Incidentally, several other opposition members, including veteran New Democrat Len Evans, were also prepared to join Harper in refusing to provide unanimous consent to the Accord's coming to the legislature, but they refrained from doing so at the request of Ovide Mercredi, who preferred that the procedural victory be seen as that of the legislature's Aboriginal member. As a result of the Manitoba resistance, Premier Clyde Wells withdrew the legislation for approval of the Accord from the Newfoundland legislature. Efforts to resolve the impasse should not have been awaiting final resolution when only a few weeks remained in the three-year constitutional requirement. The demise of the Accord provoked an angry response in Quebec, triggering a train of events that eventually saw the re-election of the separatist Parti Québécois to government and Quebec nearly leaving the Federation in 1995.

CHAPTER 10

My Life as a Politician

I AM OFTEN ASKED about the life of a politician. Yes, it means early mornings, pancake breakfasts in community halls, hours of driving on lonely roads regardless of the weather conditions, missing family occasions such as birthdays and wedding anniversaries, draining endless Styrofoam cups of coffee, grabbing a hamburger on the run for lunch, snipping thousands of ribbons, touring schools, hospitals, seniors' homes, Aboriginal reserves, factories, and offices. You keep a smile on your face, spend many hours in motel rooms, and must be able to speak on any imaginable topic. I loved meeting constituents during regular office hours. I believe Lloyd Axworthy and I were among the first MLAs to open constituency offices, well before there was any financial support from the government to do so. Adele discovered that going grocery shopping with me would usually be a colossal time hurdle: what should take only a half-hour in the store would frequently drag into a couple of hours or so, as I carefully took down notes from constituents approaching me at the store on some problem or other. Understandably, these concerns were always to them the most critical issue of the day. Having said all this, I did enjoy my work immensely as I felt I could truly make some difference in somebody's life!

I mostly enjoyed entering a community hall packed with farmers or workers, and being able to circle the room shaking hands and encouraging people to discuss with me their real concerns. Adele would often accompany me. I enjoyed this much more than the endless hours of what was often pure verbosity in the legislature. I was always truly interested in people and their problems; occasions to talk with them were preferable to the tantrums regularly observed in the legislature. Some of my critics alleged that my apparent concern was only a political act, which I had continued for nearly twenty years. If it was, one observer wrote, I "should have been nominated for the Academy Award."

Sure, there is glamour attached to the job when you meet royalty and other heads of state. However, ceremonial occasions were not always my best performance. I recall once, suffering from jet lag, along with another colleague who had accompanied me on the flight, napping briefly in the presence of Princess Anne, who was seated between us, attending a performance of the Royal Winnipeg Ballet in London, England. She must have been wondering about the two of us. Once, contrary to etiquette, I jumped enthusiastically ahead of Her Majesty at Lower Fort Garry to greet a friend and constituent. I was firmly pulled back into line by the secretary to the Queen, who advised me not to do this again.

During the last year or so of my term as premier, Prince Andrew and his wife, Sarah, visited Manitoba. In the latter part of the afternoon, there was a reception on the grounds outside St. Boniface Hospital with the royal couple and thousands of Manitobans. We were to accompany the royals upon their departure for the airport at 5:30 p.m. At the reception, as usual, I was engaged in conversation—some distance from the royal couple—when suddenly they decided to leave earlier than expected. By the time word reached Adele and me, the couple, with police escort, had already left the scene. Our driver was delayed getting out of the parking lot, and though we tried to catch up to the royal couple, we became stranded in bumper-to-bumper traffic, able only to creep forward. Adele and I were thus unable to reach the airport to bid them farewell.

I feared the worst from the media. Why did the premier and his wife break protocol and common courtesy failing to see them off at the Winnipeg airport? I got little sleep that night. To my relief, the following day the press simply observed, in a bare afterthought to their lengthy coverage of the royal visit, "Premier Pawley and his wife for some unexplained reason were not present to see their Majesties off." Early next morning, though, Prince Andrew called me at home, apologetic about his early departure from the schedule at St. Boniface Hospital.

Transparency is Essential in Politics

I learned the importance of being always ready to be transparent in my dealings. I would always ask the question: if I do this, how would it look to the public if it should appear on the front pages of the media? An early example of this, as we have seen, occurred during my term as the minister bringing into being the public auto insurance system.

When I held the post of Attorney General, a rather humorous incident made me conscious that prairie socialists shared a sensitivity about the expenditure of public funds. While attending a national Attorney Generals' conference during the 1970s, Roy Romanow, the Attorney General of Saskatchewan, and I were taken aback by the extravagance of a suite we each were being booked into at the Sutton Place Hotel in Toronto. Together we went down to the front desk to book ourselves into smaller rooms, only to be informed by the night clerk that we need not worry, since the suite would be paid for by the Ontario government. Relieved that we would not have to explain the extravagant expenditures to our individual legislatures, we stayed put. After all, the taxpayers of Ontario were footing the bill and Ontario was a "have" province as opposed to our "have-not" provinces.

Another instance occurred shortly after my appointment as the Attorney General. I was driving home from the legislature when suddenly an RCMP cruiser cut me off, and a rather upset officer pointed out to me how fast I had been going. Suddenly he recognized me, and giving me a flustered look, said, "I know who you are, what do I do now?" I told him just to finish writing out the ticket.

Another occurrence involved Elijah Harper. In September of 1987, there was a minor car accident, and Elijah had been drinking. He telephoned me with the news early the following morning. I advised him it was "a no-win situation but you have the opportunity to come out of this looking very honest. Call a news conference before the media get wind of this and announce your resignation." It was a sad moment because he had been gaining momentum as an able and well-respected cabinet minister. Unlike others, however, he had not tried to dodge the incident or run away from it. The public response to his announcement was supportive. He pleaded guilty, paid his fine, attended a treatment centre, and voluntarily extended the term of his driving suspension. After a reasonable period, he was reappointed to cabinet and became an increasingly respected northern affairs minister. He did not blame the press or the prosecutor. It was Elijah who took a look at himself and said, "I've gained some strength as a person and I am able to share that experience with other people."

Solid Economic Accomplishments: An Economic Assessment

Except for the Yukon Territory, after the 1982 defeat of the Blakeney government, ours was the only NDP provincial government in Canada. For most of that period, the vast majority of provincial administrations were Conservative governments that shared a generally easy relationship with the Mulroney government. To some extent, our Manitoba NDP government did not enjoy equal footing with the others.

Our economic programs enjoyed pervasive public support. These included two programs aimed at assisting young people to achieve their first jobs: Jobs in Training and Career Start. We successfully initiated an assistance program for farmers to ameliorate the extreme difficulties inflicted upon them by the Bank of Canada's ruinously high interest rates. For similar reasons, the small-business community was assisted with interest-rate relief, venture capital, export promotion, research and development supports, information technology, one-stop shopping, and a favourable differential tax rate. Many of these initiatives had been made possible by a series of multi-pronged federal-provincial economic development agreements in the mining, manufacturing, tourism, and small business sectors. Regrettably these agreements were terminated in the mid-1980s when the Mulroney government came to power. In contrast to the federal government, the ability of Manitoba's provincial government to influence economic activity was constrained. Its deficits are financed externally, at least in part from offshore borrowing, making the province vulnerable to fluctuations in exchange rates and to the unpredictable whims and opinions of moneylenders.

The government recognized that much of the provincial infrastructure was in desperate need of either replacement or repair. The best time to undertake this—if the projects were labour-intensive—was during a recession. To accomplish this, a number of initiatives were undertaken, including construction of both the Earth Sciences building at the University of Manitoba and the University of Winnipeg field house. In Brandon, the Fire Training College was constructed. These projects took place during the winter months when unemployment was highest. Elsewhere in Manitoba, badly needed public works projects helped stimulate both short- and long-term employment. Many hospitals and community centres were aided.

Related to the success of the province's economic performance was our willingness to work cooperatively with the federal government—despite what were sometimes difficult relations. This would mainly benefit the City of Winnipeg. During the Trudeau era, the North Portage Development project was launched with the goal of stimulating the renewal of downtown Winnipeg, in grave need of revitalization.

Later during the Mulroney era, the NDP government, with Gary Doer as urban affairs minister, would work with the regional federal minister, Jake Epp, to execute an agreement leading to the highly successful Forks project, including the preservation of the riverbank and the development of pedestrian pathways along the Assiniboine River. Both projects reflected the provincial government's eagerness to work with the federal government, regardless of its political stripe, to transform the urban environment and give it a vitality it had not had for a decade. My government worked with the private sector and generated significant short-term employment both during the construction phase and in the creation of long-term jobs in many new offices and shops in the private, retail, and commercial sectors.

While the Manitoba NDP government's record in creating jobs and holding down unemployment was complicated by a rising participation rate and the return of workers from other provinces, it was clearly superior to the national average. In all honesty, it must be acknowledged that other provinces such as Ontario, Alberta, and Saskatchewan were hit even harder by the recession than Manitoba had been; the bust in the oil industry had played havoc with our prairie neighbours and Ontario was hit by a manufacturing decline.

The Manitoba Jobs strategy was, however, one of the success stories in Canadian provincial policy making in the 1980s. An economic assessment of the NDP term, as reported by Statistics Canada, has shown that more favourable results for the provincial economy were achieved than in other provinces where a pro-active economic policy was not pursued; and that the Manitoba economy, during our term, did better than during the two Progressive Conservative administrations immediately before and after.[1]

The province was able to boast of the lowest youth unemployment rate in Canada by the mid-1980s. Other data identified Manitoba as the only province without a significant increase in numbers of poverty-stricken Canadians during the early and mid-1980s. The NDP government, consistent with its overall philosophy, succeeded in distributing income a little more fairly. As to economic performance, the years of my government were highly successful compared to economic performance elsewhere in Canada, and in contrast with the record of the succeeding Filmon administration.

The province was able to boast of the lowest youth unemployment rate in Canada by the mid-1980s. Other data identified Manitoba as the only province without a significant increase in numbers of poverty-stricken Canadians during the early and mid-1980s. The NDP government, consistent with its overall philosophy, succeeded in distributing income a little more fairly. As to economic performance, the years of my government were highly successful compared to economic performance elsewhere in Canada, and in contrast with the record of the succeeding Filmon administration.

For example,

a) Overall, the Manitoba unemployment rate was 2.2 percentage points below the national average during the NDP years, only 1.5 points under during the Filmon years.

b) Youth unemployment was 3.2 percentage points below the national average under the Manitoba NDP but only 1.7 points under Filmon.

c) Inter-provincial population loss averaged 1191 per year with the NDP, but jumped sharply to 6102 under the Filmon administration.

d) Manitoba maintained an economic growth rate per year equal to the national average in the Pawley years but fell to less than 70 percent of the Canadian average during the Filmon administration.

e) Manitoba's total investment growth rate (in current dollars) averaged 8.3 percent per year during my administration, which was 1.4 times greater than the national average. During the Filmon administration, Manitoba's rate fell to 3.5 percent per year, only three-quarters of the Canadian average.

None of this was at the price of important social programs and advances, and beginnings were made to deal with the emerging environmental problems. It is true we were prepared to run a deficit, but this is not a fiscal failure when times are bad. We still have to learn that.

No wonder the *Globe and Mail*, no supporter of the NDP, ran a lead editorial reasoning that, "in the present national economy, it may be said that Central Canada starts at the Saskatchewan border," as Manitoba is the province with the lowest unemployment rate and the highest projected economic growth. The 1987 editorial spoke of the economic growth projection until 1995: "If not quite the Cinderella of Canadian provinces (too mature), Manitoba is looking pretty good." The same editorial applauded the momentum generated by the province's $1.94 billion Limestone Project on the Nelson River, then under construction and intended to supply 500 megawatts of power to Minnesota. It added that our government also benefited politically. Certainly, the Limestone Project had played a major role in our 1986 election win.[2]

Success on the Social Justice Front before the Fall

Fundamental to the NDP government's social democratic philosophy was the expansion of social justice. What distinguished us as social democrats was recognizing that, while social development could not come about without economic development, the reverse was equally true. Current doctrine argues for sacrifices on the social front to advance an economic agenda. As social democrats, we believe that this is wrong, because it results in regressive redistribution, from the less well-off to the better-off. The pursuit of a pro-active platform by the 1980s NDP government in Manitoba resulted in the gains of the Keynesian welfare state being preserved, more than in most other provinces. We also extended social services and programs in some limited ways, wherever costs would not be too excessive for the province to carry.

Preserving health and education programming was a key government priority. This was certainly not easy, because the costs of doing so usually exceeded the rate of inflation and therefore consumed a large and growing slice of the provincial budget. Having said this, it can be argued that we were slow to move on health reform measures, especially in areas of prevention. Insufficient measures were undertaken for the mentally ill. Major initiatives were taken, nevertheless, with the mentally disabled, to encourage a gradual move back into the community by ensuring appropriate supports for community living. Muriel Smith led the process of engaging all the community groups, professionals, and community and health workers in regional committees. Every person with mental disabilities in an institution, at risk of being in an institution, or at home was identified. Gaps and overlaps in services were identified and plans developed for comprehensive "birth to death" services to emerge over time. This also made financial sense; the old Manitoba Developmental Centre was financed entirely by provincial dollars, whereas community services (as a result of the Canada Assistance Plan) could be cost-shared with the federal government. Much work was also done to integrate such persons into local economies or into an expanded and improved network of occupational day centres, and a cross-section departmental secretariat was established to plan for the needs of Manitobans with all forms of disability.

Although considerably fewer units than had been built during the Schreyer years, affordable housing was provided at a higher rate than by the principally Conservative administrations in other jurisdictions. Regrettably, however, some of the reason for less housing being built in the '80s related to cutbacks in funding for subsidized and affordable housing by our federal partners: the Trudeau government during the 1970s was much more responsive in this area. Nevertheless, the concept of community economic development funds for neighbourhood regeneration was never pursued as thoroughly as it should have been, part of the reason being an inability to persuade the federal government to be sufficiently involved.

Our election commitment to extend children's dental care through the schools was a priority.[3] But we also focused on the needs of the elderly. Thanks to earlier provincial and federal initiatives in health care and pensions, they were living longer and in better health. They aspired to remain in their own homes as long as possible, so a network of supportive systems was developed to provide home care and congregate meals and other services in local communities. The Manitoba provincial supplements for the elderly introduced by the previous administration was substantially increased and renamed 55 Plus. Particularly helpful to single women in their late fifties and beyond, this program remains in place to day. Finally, some of the supportive housing units built during the Schreyer era of the '70s were converted into long-term care units for the socially needy of all ages.

The government, due to its philosophic sympathy with the plight of the disadvantaged in society, and because of its job creation strategy, increased welfare rates at a pace greater than the increase in the cost of living. Although costly, this succeeded in placing more purchasing power in the hands of those more inclined to spend it within the local economy, rather than offshore—as is the tendency of the more affluent, who today enjoy most of the savings from the broad tax cuts currently being introduced by most provinces and the federal government.

Greater opportunities were provided for women to fully participate in all aspects of work along with men. To this end, child daycare was expanded, permitting those previously unable to work, to do so, and recognizing the need for child care that would meet the needs of shift and seasonal workers. To build a child care system of both family and group care that would be good for the children, the parents, and the workers, basic standards were legislated, a licensing system introduced, training programs provided for

workers, community boards required to ensure close parent-centre cooperation, special grants made for equipment and wage supplements, and culturally
appropriate programming developed. Capital grants were given through the
public schools' finance board. The number of spaces and centres was gradually
increased throughout the province as resources permitted. Manitoba's child
care program was a recognized leader in Canada, only to be severely starved
during the Filmon era, with many centres operating on probation because of
below-standard staff qualifications.

Other important social programs included efforts to create sensitive procedures to help all family members break the cycle of violence. Emergency
help lines, women's resource centres, shelters, and second-stage housing were
introduced to increase family services in this area. Making children's services and facilities more culturally sensitive to Aboriginal people was another
priority of our government. Social Services Minister Len Evans halted the
practice of adopting out Manitoba's Aboriginal children to non-Aboriginal
families outside the province, a program taken to the next stage of repatriation
by Muriel Smith when she was the minister. We introduced a system of more
open adoptions through a registry process that allowed re-connection if both
the child and the natural parent chose to be registered. Finally, in 1987, the
government moved Child and Family Service agencies closer to the community and into preventive supportive service, rather than focusing on removing
children from families and placing them in treatment facilities.

In addition, our government enacted conflict of interest legislation for
members of the legislature and freedom of information legislation for the
public. Provisions were enacted to provide funding for constituency offices,
enabling Members of the legislative assembly to do a better job of serving
their constituents. Limits were imposed on what could be spent in election
campaigns by political parties and public funding was provided to assist in
defraying the cost of campaign expenditures. These measures, similar to those
enacted federally and in some other provinces, were major steps in reducing
the disproportionate influence of the rich and powerful on the democratic
process.

Ominous Storm Clouds Emerge

Our eventual defeat would not have been anticipated in 1987. Despite the
controversies, our popularity remained high. In a national editorial the *Globe
and Mail* wrote that "Mr Pawley now enjoys a pleasant thirteen-point lead

over a dour Conservative opposition and seems to hold the big bills in political currency."[4] After legislating a number of progressive changes in our highly successful 1987 session we were, nevertheless, witnessing ominous storm clouds emerging on the horizon. Our economic success certainly compared well to the situation in other jurisdictions, but a number of other issues were negatively affecting the popularity of my government.

First, a bad situation was exacerbated by the announcement of a 21 percent increase in auto insurance premiums by the publicly owned Manitoba Public Insurance Corporation. These increases had been caused by an icy winter that produced more crashes and ignited public protests and demonstrations. I was perhaps most affected, insofar as my personal popularity was concerned. I was always associated favourably with MPI as its first minister and chair. Now I would not escape the negative fallout.

Secondly, Meech Lake was becoming increasingly unpopular in Manitoba. Many in my party were hostile to it. It was reminiscent of the French-language services controversy. Nationally, the fallout contributed to the departure of seven of the premiers who had signed the original 1987 Meech Lake Accord.

Even our strong point, creating jobs and stimulating the economy, was no longer overwhelmingly topping the polls as the most important public issue. By 1988, the deficit, together with other fiscal and taxation issues, ranked high as major concerns in the polling. The mood was changing. It was argued that the NDP, described by its opponents even today as a "tax and spend" government, pursued too arduous a tax policy. Admittedly, the increase in taxes imposed in 1987 eroded the government's political support. One difficulty was that, although the NDP believed in progressive taxation, the linking of the federal and provincial tax systems meant that the "shape" of the system—a decidedly regressive shape—had already been set by federal deductions and tax expenditures.

The increase in income tax, although more equitable than a general sales tax increase, was bound to be controversial and misunderstood by the public. The cabinet spent long hours debating whether to impose a net income tax or to go the route of increasing the provincial sales tax. Although several preferred a sales tax, there was a clear consensus that despite the inherent political dangers, a social democratic government could hardly enact increases in a provincial sales tax that would hurt most those with low incomes. Although the announcement in the 1987 budget that we would use sizable tax increases to decrease the deficit was defensible, it was also politically naïve: income tax forms started to arrive in the mail in February 1988, when the NDP government held a narrow majority in the Manitoba legislature. There was little time for the government to explain the tax increase before its unexpected defeat. The Opposition, the media, and other powerful interests persuaded many Manitobans that we were spending excessively.

By the end of my administration, the debt service cost per capita was around the average of the ten provinces, showing that Manitoba was not out of line with the rest of the country. Compared to other provinces (including neighbouring Saskatchewan), Manitoba did a very capable job of managing its finances during the 1980s; Manitoba's deficit was the lowest on a per capita basis of any of the prairie provinces. Manitoba revenue receipts per capita were the third lowest in Canada, confirming a relatively low provincial tax regime overall. However, this was not the general public perception of what was taking place.

The public debt burden rose throughout Canada during this time because of the fallout from the recession of the early 1980s, coupled with what were sharp cuts in transfer payments from Ottawa to the provinces, and the fallout from double-digit interest rates, compliments of the Bank of Canada. Cuts in transfer payments had an immediate impact on the cost of both health care and education in the provinces.

Moreover, Manitoba was reducing its deficit at a much faster rate than the federal government despite sharp reductions in equalization payments paid to the province.[5] This reduction followed a decision by the federal government to alter the formula by which equalization payments are paid to the less well-off provinces, from a ten-province average to a five-province one. Manitoba's overall spending was the fourth lowest, almost $200 per person lower than the ten-province average.

Our outgoing NDP government would leave a $58 million operating surplus. At my final press conference as premier, I noted that throughout the 1988 election campaign we heard much about the alleged recklessness and irresponsibility of my government, when it was then the only government in Canada with its current account in the black; it was ironic too, I added, when you consider when we inherited the government from Sterling Lyon in 1981, Manitoba had the highest deficit among the western provinces. In 1988, it had the lowest.

When the provincial Tories assumed office in 1988 they siphoned off the surplus, adding an equalization payment windfall and putting it in as

$200 million fiscal stabilization fund, leaving the NDP supposedly burdened with a $142 million "deficit." The provincial auditor, Fred Jackson, subsequently appended an unusual note in the public accounts, giving (back) the NDP its rightful $58 million surplus and thus, provided an accurate account of the Province's finances.[6] Ironically, it was the Progressive Conservatives in the early '90s recession, under former Premier Filmon, that experienced a record deficit for the province. In the final year of my government, the province's net general-purpose debt per capita was $4,691, but by 31 March 1999, it had risen by 24 percent to $5,828.[7]

I believe net debt to GDP provides the best method of determining how well any government has managed the financial affairs of a nation or province, and in this respect, the NDP governments of Manitoba have an enviable record. According to a special report by the TD Bank, in 1987–88, the province's net debt to GDP was 21.7 percent, a figure reduced in the final year of our government, 1988–1989, to 19.7 percent. In subsequent years under the Progressive Conservative administration, the debt to GDP reached a high in 1998–1999 of 32.7 percent. In 1993–1994, only five years after our defeat, the debt to GDP had reached 27.7 percent. That figure was reduced to 21.8 percent by 2008–09 under the NDP during the Doer term.[8]

The Loss of Confidence

My government's unanticipated defeat on 8 March 1988 demonstrates the magnitude of human chemistry and its potentially catastrophic consequences in the real world of politics. Our defeat would, of course, set in motion other momentous consequences, not just with matters of provincial concern, but also with federal ramifications; the demise of the Meech Lake Accord is the primary example. The *Globe and Mail* editorialized, "It is depressing to think that Manitoba's stand on such matters will be shaped by the timing of a disgruntled backbencher whose pivotal role... 'gives people something to think about.'"[9] This was followed by an explosion in separatist support in Quebec, the formation of the Bloc Québécois under the leadership of Lucien Bouchard, the defeat in the national referendum of the proposed Charlottetown Accord, the re-election of the Parti Québécois, and the 1995 near defeat of federalist forces in that province.

Two people played key roles in the precarious legislative position of the NDP. Although the first of these, Larry Desjardins, did not intend to contribute to our defeat, he did precipitate it by resigning his seat and causing our situation to become numerically tenuous. The second person, James Walding, would deliberately and suddenly trigger our defeat.

Desjardins had strong personal beliefs, shaped by his close association with the Roman Catholic Church. Being passionately anti-abortion, he invariably tangled with NDP activists during both the Schreyer and the Pawley terms. This included clashes with various members of cabinet, who frequently engaged in tense and sometimes acrimonious disagreements with him about how best to deal with Dr. Morgentaler's application for permission to open a clinic in Winnipeg. And, of course, the annual debates at party conventions, endorsing the free choice position on abortion, would greatly irritate the health minister.

The government's financial assistance to Catholic schools was one of his pet causes. He was unhappy about Schreyer's unsuccessful effort to provide funding in the early 1970s, and resentment persisted when the Pawley government also refused to increase support for Catholic schools. Another issue which produced a grave predicament for him was our government's resolve to render protection under the human rights legislation for those who suffered discrimination because of sexual orientation. Larry repeatedly complained to me about this initiative, and I could not be certain that at some stage he might not bolt over this legislation. I was grateful that Larry remained on side and voted for the legislation.

However, tensions steadily grew in cabinet over Desjardin's leadership of the health department. There were recurring complaints from many of his colleagues that his anti-abortion bias was interfering with the operations of his department. It came to a head when a newspaper report forecasted that Larry Desjardin's days as a health minister were numbered. Coincidentally, Cam McLean, chair of the Manitoba Health Organization (MHO), approached Desjardins to serve as the new CEO of that organization, which represented the province's hospitals. The timing could not have been better for the unhappy Desjardins; he wanted out, and he accepted the offer. I was shocked when Desjardins approached me, advising that he was resigning his cabinet post and his St. Boniface seat. I worried that his resignation would leave the government in a most vulnerable and dangerous situation, our survival dependent on Walding's dubious loyalties. This unwelcome news from Desjardins arrived in late August of 1987 as I was leaving for the annual premiers' conference being hosted by Richard Hatfield of New Brunswick.

Shortly after my return, Desjardins suffered a serious heart attack and needed bypass surgery. Visiting him in the hospital, I discovered a distraught patient recovering from a life-threatening ordeal, and preparing for a career change. During a conversation with me, Larry toyed with the possibility of changing his mind and remaining with the government. Pleased, I offered him a lighter portfolio more suitable to his poor health. I suggested the position of minister without portfolio responsible for sports, because of his interest in sports, and Desjardins showed some interest in accepting. For the next month or two, Larry appeared inclined to return to cabinet, and we were lulled into thinking that he would remain in government. That was not to be. In late November, after my return from a trade mission to Japan and Hong Kong, I received a telephone call from Desjardins informing me that he was now going to assume the MHO post after all.

To my consternation, Larry would not, then or later, permit himself to be pinned down about a possible timetable for the resignation of his St. Boniface seat. If he was not staying, my preference was to call a snap by-election in the hope of bolstering our razor-thin majority in the House. Indeed in October of 1987, an encouraging party poll had revealed that the NDP enjoyed record popular support; chances were good that at that time we could have retained the St. Boniface constituency. Ron Duhamel, the well-respected deputy minister of education, had expressed an interest in seeking the provincial St. Boniface nomination in the event of Larry's departure. In fact, he later did run and succeed in winning, but it was to be in the federal St. Boniface riding, on behalf of the Liberals. (He went on to become a respected minister in the Chrétien government.)

On 23 December 1987, Larry met with me in my office and raised the possibility that he might hold on to his St. Boniface seat by sitting as an independent, thus avoiding the appearance of conflict of interest. I was puzzled, though, that he would even consider retaining his legislative responsibilities at the same time he was assuming the MHO obligations. Larry also complained that he was convinced that his son-in-law was "the victim of an evil vendetta designed to get even with him for shaking up the Lotteries Commission" while he had been minister in charge of that portfolio. Larry felt that he had been "abused with no support from his colleagues—and members of his family have been harassed, because they were related to me."

To my dismay, Larry delayed his resignation until just days before the House resumed sitting in February, when it was too late to call a by-election in St. Boniface. With the government's rising unpopularity—resulting from public hostility over Autopac rate increases exceeding 21 per cent—it was too late for us to avert a disaster in the House with a by-election. Maybe, if Larry had stayed on as an independent member, he might have sustained us in power. Only Desjardins knows!

James Derrick Walding arrived on the political stage in the spring of 1971 in a by-election made necessary by the resignation of an incumbent Progressive Conservative MLA who had moved to British Columbia. After his arrival in Canada from Great Britain with his wife, Val, Walding, a dispensing optician, had become interested in the NDP. The by-election in St. Vital was held concurrently with the one in St. Rose. Both were critical to the survival of the Schreyer government, which had been in office for less than two years. We had just gone through a vicious debate, engaging not only the members of the legislative assembly but also the public at large, over the establishment of public auto insurance.

Walding, after serving in the backbenches of the Schreyer government, eventually became chair of the NDP caucus. With the Schreyer government's advancing years, it was evident that stress in the party was developing around the colourful and dynamic natural resources minister Sid Green; this conflict soon consumed both the caucus and the party. It was evident that Walding's sympathies were with Green. As caucus chair, I noticed that Walding kept a Speaker's list that he would strictly enforce for everybody but Green; whenever this fiery minister signalled his intention to intervene, Walding always gave him a special nod so he could say his piece. In addition, Walding was never reluctant to espouse his strongly pro-British sentiments whenever the occasion permitted. For instance, he refused to acknowledge the new designation of Canada Day over the old Dominion Day.

At the time of the 1979 leadership convention, Walding publicly adopted a neutral stance and insisted that this stance was appropriate because of his responsibilities for the caucus chair. In reality, Walding and his wife supported my candidature and even hosted a small party for me in their home, which was attended by some of their local St. Vital constituency members and friends. In retrospect, I sense there was some expectation of being later rewarded, because I was favoured to win the leadership competition. Nonetheless, I had no doubt that the sympathies of Walding would have been with Green if there had been enough support for him to contest the leadership after Schreyer's departure.

As we have seen, during the 1981 election campaign, Walding revealed through some unfortunate actions that he was not interested in being a team player. At the ceremonial cabinet swearing-in, Walding was conspicuous by his absence. Clearly sulking because he had not been summoned to fill a ministerial role, he explained to a curious media that he had "other things to do." Only temporarily was this tension abated with his nomination as Speaker; it was a consolation prize. During the fiery days of the French-language controversy, with the Progressive Conservative opposition relying on the tactic of bell-ringing to defeat the legislation, Walding rebuffed all of our pleas to provide leadership by forcing members to show up and vote.

In the months leading up to the 1986 election, our relationship would further deteriorate. Walding faced a vigorous nomination challenge from two credible adversaries, Gerri Unwin, a St. Vital executive member, and Sig Laser, a member of my staff. Later I discovered that Walding was erroneously convinced that I inspired Sig's challenge to him, and thus I was responsible for nearly costing him his re-nomination. Sig Laser was obviously an extremely competent special assistant who worked closely with me, and, in Walding's eyes, would have enthusiastically responded to any call from me to seek the St. Vital nomination. Contrary to his belief, though, I did not encourage Laser; indeed I had insisted on his resignation from my staff during the contest. A cartoon in the *Winnipeg Free Press* would not have assuaged Walding's perception that I wanted him out; it depicted me lying on a couch telling a psychiatrist, "Doc, I have this recurring nightmare, in which Jim Walding is nominated, and later re-elected."

The contest in St. Vital was intense, with over 700 delegates attending the nomination meeting itself. Walding managed to scrape by with the smallest of margins. Walding attributed the narrowness of his win to his being the Speaker rather than a cabinet minister. A survey conducted among his constituents convinced him that they were holding that against him, that it had impaired his reputation among party members in his riding.

A few days after the 1986 election, I met with Walding to determine whether there was any chance that we could work together. Jim had already announced that he did not want to be Speaker again. I thought that we achieved an amiable compromise. Walding would be appointed to either the Telephone or Hydro boards, whose corporate statutes call for an MLA member. As Walding departed the premier's office, Cliff Scotton, my director of communications, suggested that Walding had been cheered by my willingness to work with him. I had less faith than Cliff. I sensed the next act was to be played soon.

I was not to be disappointed. The next day I received a letter[10] from Walding dated 3 April 1986, in which he argued that he had been the member for St. Vital since 1971 and that the riding deserved representation in cabinet. He complained that it was not he but the constituency that was disadvantaged by this grave oversight perpetrated by both Schreyer and Pawley. He claimed, "At every election, expectations are raised among New Democrats in St. Vital that at last they will have representation in the provincial cabinet, yet those expectations are consistently dashed." Walding drew my attention to the fact that he had "more seniority than three quarters of your cabinet," and warned that he wished to avoid "possible consequences of precipitous action." Of course, this implied threat did not go down well with me. Walding then moved on to list several ministries where he believed he could do a credible job, including urban, cultural, or consumer and corporate affairs. Sharing the letter with Cliff, I swore that there was absolutely no way I could surrender to such a manoeuvre.

The following day, making this harmful situation worse for Walding, excerpts from his letter appeared in the *Winnipeg Sun*. Although Walding insisted that he didn't believe in negotiating through the press and had marked his letter "Personal and Confidential," he was not beyond using the media to exert pressure. An intimate confidant was described by the *Winnipeg Sun* as saying that if Pawley agreed to change the speakership and establish a special riding to ensure continuity in the speakership, Walding would contemplate accepting such a post. Another newspaper reported that he was "re-assessing his position." A source close to Walding speculated on how his potential defection would affect the NDP, placing us in a precarious numerical predicament; nonetheless he blamed the situation on me for having insulted him. After such public utterances, any appointment, including to the Hydro or Telephone boards, were now inconceivable. Just as Walding managed to do himself out of a long-awaited cabinet position in 1981, he had again done himself in.

When I appointed four new ministers, Len Harapiak, Elijah Harper, Judy Wasylycia-Leis, and Gary Doer, Walding's resentment was evident. He made very few appearances at caucus meetings after this, and whenever he did arrive, he was usually late and took easy offence at his colleagues' remarks. The last time he attended, he smoked his pipe as he normally did; but unbeknownst to him, a previous caucus meeting had prohibited smoking during meetings because one of our members suffered from asthma. Sitting down in the far corner of the caucus room, Walding lit up and began to puff. Our colourful and spirited caucus chair, Marty Dolin, targeted somebody else who was also guilty of lighting up and with whom Marty was having a running debate, albeit a good-natured one, over the caucus rule: "I don't know how many times I have advised caucus that we have a non-smoking rule; that rule is now being broken and if any member isn't able to refrain from smoking, I ask that member to leave immediately." Although the comment was not aimed at Walding, he nonetheless misinterpreted it as being directed at him and as further evidence of caucus hostility to him. He hurriedly left the caucus room and to my knowledge, never returned.

On another occasion, the St. Vital NDP Association held their annual constituency dinner. It had always been a successful social and fund-raising event for New Democrats in that part of the city. With the dinner plates cleared away, Jim Walding gave thanks to all those who came out to support the constituency association. On this occasion, Jim had a special announcement to make: "I will not be running again to represent you in St. Vital," he advised those assembled. To my surprise, and without warning, a few clapped wildly at the table where Adele and I were seated; but the announcement created a hushed and rather tense silence throughout the room. Obviously irritated, Walding looked sharply toward our table, his eyes resting on those responsible for the applause. I do not believe they had intended to insult him—it was a spontaneous gesture—but as might be expected, Walding was not pleased.

On still another occasion, Marty Dolin was left with no alternative but to dispatch a letter to Walding's constituency association complaining that its member had neither been pulling his weight in caucus nor attending the regularly scheduled caucus meetings: of forty-three meetings held, he had missed all but six, and for these six he had been always late. Marty sought the constituency association's help in persuading its member to be a more loyal caucus member. Marty complained about one instance where Walding's vote had been urgently required and yet Walding was not even in the building. Marty called Walding's home at about 5:20 p.m. and found him there. The urgency was explained, and he agreed to return to the House. The bells were permitted to ring for only one hour, so, at 5:40, an anxious caucus secretary telephoned to check if Walding was finally on his way; to her amazement he had changed his mind and said he was not returning to the legislature. Marty then desperately called himself, only to be informed that Walding was now eating his dinner and was not available to come to the telephone. It was only because the Tories failed to have their full complement in the House that the government's measure passed. There could have been serious consequences for us. Marty begged the constituency association to help ensure better co-operation from their MLA.[11]

One can easily ascertain how these events—his not being appointed to cabinet, friction arising from his role as Speaker during the French-language debate, and bitterness over the departure of his friend Sid Green—would have contributed to Walding's growing alienation. His relationship with his fellow caucus members deteriorated. I could do little, unless I appointed him to cabinet, and I was not about to do that. It would have created a much worse situation and, in the process, greatly disaffected many caucus members.

In the latter part of 1987 and into early 1988, public anger intensified with auto insurance rate hikes. The pending departure of Larry Desjardins, reduc-ing our caucus to twenty-nine, created a precarious situation, which made the emerging crisis worse. Recognizing the steady deterioration of the situation, I asked some members to keep in touch with Walding to encourage him to re-main onside and then in turn to let me know what we might expect from him. Our situation was increasingly dangerous. Bill Uruski, Len Evans, and their wives were among the few that managed to continue some degree of relation-ship with the Waldings. Jim considered them friends, as he included them among the old-timers, and they thus escaped the suspicion he held about the new gang elected in 1981 and 1986. At my suggestion, Len and Alice invited Jim and Valerie to their home for a Saturday night social evening to get an impression as to his intentions. During the evening, they got the sense that the Waldings wished to move to Victoria, B.C., once they retired, but there was no indication this event would be imminent.

During the 1988 Throne Speech debate, Walding's extreme unhappiness aroused a pervasive air of suspense, and in his comments in the legislature he certainly made no secret of his displeasure. This fuelled speculation that he might bolt and vote against us. Amid this uncertainty, one could have carved the air in the House with a scalpel. Walding harangued the government for what he considered its flaws. Nonetheless, he remained loyal and voted with the government to defeat the Opposition's non-confidence motions.

A few days later, Eugene Kostyra, the minister of finance, introduced the annual budget. It was a hopeful budget, projecting a decrease of the projected deficit for 1988–89. Government spending per capita in Manitoba was lower than in the neighbouring, Conservative-governed provinces of Saskatchewan and Alberta. Eugene spent time with Walding, who had not attended the caucus briefing, and spelled out the budget's particulars; Walding appeared satisfied and according to him, the finance minister was "getting the deficit down."

On 1 March 1988, a week before the reading of the budget, I received a letter in which Walding complained about the role of the Speaker. He took up an old lament that he had publicly raised while he filled the role about the necessity for a Speaker who was independent, not a member of the legislature. In his view, an MLA should not be expected to serve as a Speaker. His earlier plea along these lines had been soundly rejected, not only by us but also by the Opposition. In this letter, he called for an immediate response from both Filmon and me about his proposal to investigate the feasibility of such an appointment. Although I disliked the notion, I was not about to estrange him further, and Walding was advised that we were prepared to act on his proposition by appointing a legislative committee, which he would chair, to examine the Speakership question.

Filmon replied with a letter dated 7 March, but was evasive as to his intention. Speaking to Walding the morning of the budget vote, I asked whether he had heard anything from Filmon. He replied, "No," and "If he knows what's best for him he will respond." Nonetheless, in retrospect, Jim's letter served its purpose; it lulled us into a sense of false security about his budget vote. To appoint him to the chair was a small price to pay, I judged, for the continuation of the government. Little did I recognize this as only a subterfuge.

However, even with Walding's remarks about Filmon fresh in my ears, I contacted David Chomiak, a friend of Walding's, and asked if he could have lunch with Walding on the critical budget day. Chomiak consented to test Walding out about his intentions for the vote. In the early afternoon, good news arrived. Dave assured me of his confidence that Jim was onside. During an afternoon radio interview, Jim indicated that he was satisfied with the budget and intended to vote with Government. All looked well.

My confidence, however, was to be shaken as we arrived at the 5:30 p.m. deadline for the vote; bells were already ringing to bring in the members. A clearly anguished Jay Cowan, methodical and hard-working government House leader, rushed up and announced, "I've just been speaking to Albert Driedger and he advised me, you guys are toast." "He must be kibitzing," I answered. "No," Jay responded, "Albert does not kibitz, I know he means it, he knows something."

In the moments before the page began to call the role for the non-confidence motion that had been moved by the leader of the Opposition, I felt more nervous than ever. So much rested on the outcome. After all, we were the only jurisdiction in North America, outside of the Yukon Territory, where the governing party was democratic socialist. Furthermore, we were only at the halfway point of our second term in government, and we had much to do. We had completed many difficult tasks during the first half of our term, and having already taken most of the difficult actions, we expected that we would politically recover in the second half of our term.

Only the weekend before the budget vote, the Manitoba NDP convention had been held. There, I had to plead with the delegates to resist their inclination to vote in opposition to the Meech Lake Accord. Thus preoccupied at the convention, I had too hurriedly dismissed growing media speculation that Walding might bolt. Because Walding had expressed an interest in a review of the role of the Speaker, I assumed incorrectly that he would remain loyal. Moreover, I knew that he had few financial resources to sustain him in case of his resignation. It was our mistaken assumption that he could not afford to forgo his MLA salary, the principal source of his income. Nor did I think he would be likely to cut the government adrift at this point, when he was still some time away from enjoying full pension entitlement. Our calculations were that if he left the legislature, he would have only about $21,000 per annum. For all these reasons, it seemed reasonable to assume Walding would stay on board.

Perhaps we would have been less confident if before the critical vote we had been aware of that "a backroom Tory" had phoned columnist Gordon Sinclair and said, "Circle March 8; the government is going to fall . . . I've been doing a lot of work." On March 9, "the backroom Tory" again phoned Sinclair and confirmed that his party had known the government was going down. He denied the Progressive Conservatives had anything to do with it because "bribery is against the law."

We were not the only ones on budget day watching Walding closely; the Tories were also keeping a close tab on what he was doing. Filmon later spoke about having carefully scrutinized Walding's every move before the vote. He described how Walding's hand would reach out for his glass of water, and how he would pull it back, before rising to vote against his own government. In the public galleries, about twelve wives of Progressive Conservative MLAs were coincidentally assembled in plentiful numbers to proctor the vote count, something they had rarely done. Before the vote, two PC frontbenchers called across the floor, "You guys are dead."[12]

Unwisely, we never contemplated Walding's leaving our ranks without providing some advance notice of his intention. It never crossed our minds that, having given both public and private assurances that he would vote for the budget, he would not continue his support at least for the time being. In retrospect, I with others can be criticized for a major miscalculation in assuming that Walding would do the honourable thing and give notice of any intention to defect. The question obviously must be asked: why should we have expected this? Why would the Tories permit him to do it? To give notice would have given Sharon Carstairs the option to vote with the Government, and thereby prop it up for the time being. In that case, we would have gained more time and perhaps succeeded in ameliorating our political position.

As the page read out the names of the Progressive Conservative members, and then called Sharon Carstairs "in favour" of the Tory non-confidence motion, Walding slowly rose from his seat and the name "James Walding" was announced. My heart stopped beating; the worst had happened. The bomb had finally dropped. Shock dominated our ranks. All we could do was to move adjournment. Jim Downey, a member on the Opposition front benches, hollered loudly at us to resign. In silent dismay, we assembled in the caucus room. A brief meeting took place where I asserted that I was prepared to continue as leader. Caucus members gave me a warm display of solidarity. It was at that time my intention to continue. The support in this time of crisis for me by caucus immediately after our defeat was inspiring.

Some of our members desperately rushed to the Walding home to try to persuade him to explain his actions. Unknown to us, at the time, was the fact that he had made reservations at a Winnipeg hotel to conceal himself from the press and his former colleagues. In addition, several members met with Sharon Carstairs to determine whether there was any way another vote could be taken. There was some speculation that a motion of confidence in the government could yet perhaps be taken; with Sharon's support it would pass. We were aware that she would likely prefer us in office to the Tories. Unfortunately, we concluded that we could not salvage the sorry debacle. We had no choice but to resign.

Speculation raged in the media and elsewhere, about Jim Walding's motivation for voting as he had. He had persistently complained about the province's Human Rights Code and affirmative action programs that he perceived as catering to "specific interest groups." In his response to the

Throne Speech in February 1988, he had made no attempt to conceal his resentment at the government, especially in respect to tax and auto insurance rate increases. Despite his objections, however, Walding had voted with the Government. Less than a month later during the budget debate, Walding had made no attempt to join in the debate and indicated he "rather like[d] the general tone of it." There was little to warn us of his pending betrayal.

That evening, I further considered what would be in the best interest of the party. Clearly, time was essential. An election called thirty-five days hence was the worst possible scenario. Our defeat would be uppermost in the public's mind, and we would have no opportunity to erase the impression left by our defeat. In the event that the election was delayed, the extra time might be of some benefit to us. Furthermore, a leadership convention with an attractive array of candidates would help to attract crucial media attention and might even succeed in shifting some of the focus from the circumstances that surrounded our defeat. Many of us recalled the leadership convention during the 1969 election campaign when Ed Schreyer defeated Sid Green and then went on to win. Could that scenario be repeated?

The next morning, I met with caucus, advising them that I thought it best if I stepped down as leader, and thus give the party more time to recover from its untimely legislative defeat. Before entering the caucus room, I had received a similar reading from some trusted members. A leadership campaign could possibly ignite the spark that would keep us in the ballpark. Moreover, I feared that my strong association with the establishment of public auto insurance would be a serious negative factor in the upcoming election campaign. It would be marked by deep anger directed at our government because of sharp increases of over 20 percent in auto insurance rates, which had ignited hefty demonstrations in front of the legislature, and severe fallout from increases in taxes; as they completed their annual tax returns in the critical weeks of the campaign, taxpayers would be emphatically reminded of these increases. Finally, my association with Meech Lake would clearly not be a winner on the campaign trial.

Personally, I discussed the pros and cons of resigning with Adele, Chris, and Charysse. It was the most difficult and hurtful political decision of my life. Suffering deep reservations and reluctant to leave at such a dreadful time, I agonized over the decision (one that would cause enormous inner pain for me for years afterward) in the hours and days following 8 March 1988. Finally, assuming the ultimate responsibility for what was a major miscalculation, I fell on my sword and resigned the leadership. It was my hope that in so doing, I would give the party sufficient opportunity to salvage enough members to become again, within a short time, the alternative party to the Progressive Conservatives. That had been the outcome, after all, in 1969, when the election of Schreyer in a leadership convention during the election campaign had contributed more than any other single event to the party's victory. Although history did not repeat itself by returning the NDP to government, twelve NDP members were elected in a legislature of fifty-seven, thus allowing the party to achieve official opposition status in 1990 and 1995 and eventually secure re-election in 1999.[13]

The *Winnipeg Free Press*, however, editorially suggested that I had blundered by resigning and attempting to assume all the responsibility for my government's defeat. They referred to polling done a few days after our downfall which showed a substantial number of Manitobans felt I had done a good job as premier (44 percent, as opposed to 47 percent who felt I had done a poor job). Twenty-seven percent of the electorate advised they were less likely to vote NDP because of my departure.

Needless to say, this was clearly the most dreadful time in my life. I wondered whether Walding's desertion on the critical vote could have been prevented. Had I been too intractable: perhaps I should have arranged a cabinet seat for him? Perhaps, recognizing the vulnerability of the government following the 1986 election, that would have been a wise decision. On the other hand, I would ask myself, what kind of precedent would this have created? Does the squeaky wheel always merit the grease? There were other alternatives: maybe I could have made an arrangement with Sharon Carstairs. Could I have done more to prevent Larry Desjardin's resignation? Perhaps we should have re-introduced a motion of confidence in the legislature and presented it to Lieutenant Governor George Johnson. This was done when the Pearson government was defeated in 1967. I believe Sharon Carstairs might have voted to sustain us in power, as she too was unaware of Walding's intentions to defeat us on the budget vote.

After Doer was elected party leader, he requested that I remain on as premier. I believe he was afraid that if he assumed the premiership, it would have been for a brief time only and would have adversely affected his future political aspirations.

Less than twelve hours after the fatal vote, a lone bullet from police officer Robert Cross's revolver would fatally wound Aboriginal leader J.J. Harper. Cross had stopped Harper as a suspect in a stolen car incident, even though the police had already arrested the two teenagers responsible.

One of the final acts of our government was thus the appointment of the Aboriginal Justice Inquiry. The recommendations of that Inquiry, whose commissioners included Justice A.C. Hamilton and Justice Murray Sinclair, addressed the severe problems confronting the Aboriginal community and the criminal justice system. Hamilton subsequently expressed disappointment that notwithstanding the Inquiry's work identifying these problems, successive governments had sadly failed to act on its recommendations.[14]

You Will Win

Life after Politics

Within months of my resignation as provincial party leader, I agreed to run for the NDP in the federal riding of Selkirk. Internal party polling showed that of all of the potential NDP candidates, I had the best chance of winning. I had always been interested in serving as an NDP MP in the House of Commons, and I considered such a move the best method of advancing the social democratic agenda. Before long into the campaign, however, I realized that Brian Mulroney and the Progressive Conservatives had placed a high priority on ensuring my defeat. The PCs were considered, on the basis of their comfortable margin of victory in 1984, sure bets in the constituency, but pundits acknowledged that I had a strong personal following in the rural part of the riding and was successfully turning the campaign into a close race. Making the outcome in Selkirk even more unpredictable was the popularity of the Liberals, which was strengthened by polarization over the free-trade agreement.

Mulroney personally visited the riding to provide support to the Progressive Conservative candidate, David Bjornson, as did Joe Clark, the foreign affairs minister. At the large Conservative rally in East Selkirk, Mulroney launched a blistering attack on my record as premier, describing his attendance at "Pawley's retirement." Unfortunately, my run for re-election in the political arena did indeed come to an abrupt end, as the PC candidate won the election (though he was defeated after only one term). Still, I swept the polls in the provincial riding of Selkirk, and I received the vast majority of the votes cast in the Brokenhead Reserve. To me this said much about the continued loyalty of those with whom I had worked most intimately through my years in provincial politics.

I was determined not to go back to practising law immediately but to wait until twelve months had passed since the end of my political career. Meanwhile, Adele and I spent a few months in various parts of Canada and the United States, visiting relatives and being tourists in our own country. A year later, I went back into practising law as an associate with the firm of Baker, Zivot in Winnipeg. Vic Schroeder, a friend and former cabinet colleague, was also a member of the firm.

It was around this time that I discovered my love for teaching at the university level. Professor Paul Thomas in the University of Manitoba's political science department telephoned me in the fall of 1989 to enquire about the possibility of my teaching a course there. During my political career I had enjoyed going into the high schools and universities to talk to students, and I looked forward to this new experience. It began with a labour studies course at the University of Manitoba on Saturday mornings during the winter term of 1990. If not for Paul's phone call and encouragement, I would not have had the opportunity to discover another career and an exceptionally interesting chapter in my life. My connection with the business community was limited, and an opportunity to lecture full time at a university in Manitoba was unlikely, as an appointment to teach there would have been seen as partisan rather than academic.

Several former premiers of Manitoba had been rewarded by prime ministers for their contributions. Following their premierships, Duff Roblin had been appointed to the Senate by Prime Minister Trudeau, and Sterling Lyon to the Manitoba Court of Appeal by Prime Minister Mulroney. Trudeau had also rewarded former NDP premier Ed Schreyer with a prestigious appointment, as Governor General. It was evident, however, that I did not enjoy the kind of relationship with Mulroney that Schreyer had enjoyed with Trudeau at the time of his appointment. Nothing could be reasonably expected there, not even a modest sinecure.

My appointment as an associate professor at the University of Windsor in 1990 was a source of amusement to some. After Adele had urged me to apply, regardless of the fact that I did not have a PhD, I responded to an ad in the Toronto *Globe and Mail* for a one-year teaching appointment in the political science department at the University of Windsor. In truth, I did not imagine I would remain there for longer than one year, as we considered Manitoba our home. Dr. Robert Krause, the department head at the time, called, asking whether the letter of application was a hoax. I replied, simply, "No." So I was invited down that week for an interview and was hired to begin teaching in September of that year. It pleased me to know that the university would consider my political experience as a former premier as a substitute for a PhD.

It was only a few months after my arrival at Windsor that Bob Krause confided to me that he had participated in the 1988 federal campaign. What's more, having worked out of the Conservative headquarters in Ottawa, he informed me that he was aware of a special committee set up to target several ridings throughout Canada where Mulroney and the Progressive Conservative Party were anxious to ensure that certain candidates would be defeated. I was one of their chosen targets. He now laughs about it, describing it as a plot to get me to teach at the University of Windsor and leave Manitoba behind. He has strongly supported my academic career.

The University of Windsor was very generous to me. I was appointed its Paul Martin Professor, a position that mandated my teaching in both the political science department and the Windsor Law School. At the end of my five-year term as the Paul Martin Professor, the university gave me tenure as an associate professor. During my final year of full-time lecturing at Windsor in 1999/2000, I was elected to the presidency of the University of Windsor Faculty Association for a one-year term. I found it rather amusing that I became a union leader only after my political career was over.

During a farewell tribute at the University in 2000, my colleague Jake Soderlund read from the local paper *The Room* about a tally from mail-ins that had identified favourite professors. I won! Jake also pointed out, however, that in the best lawyer category the winner was a defence lawyer then dominating the news—extremely skilled, yes, but better known at this stage as a fugitive from justice. (He was later prosecuted for fraud.) Wow! How the crowd laughed! How much credibility could be placed in my selection as the best professor if the same respondents had simultaneously selected this character?

After retirement—it was mandatory at sixty-five in Ontario then—I continued to teach courses on a sessional basis. I taught at the University of Windsor, completed a Stanley Knowles Professorship for a term at the University of Waterloo, and also taught two spring semesters at the University of Washington in Seattle and one winter semester at the University of Western Ontario in London, Ontario. In 2006–2007, I took on the position of acting director of studies in social justice. From time to time since the 1990s, I have also given guest lectures at the University of Toledo, Bowling

Green University in Ohio, University of Winnpeg, Wayne State University, and Michigan State University.

After a career in politics, one keeps bumping into people who have had previous contact with you, good or bad. During the mid-90s I was confronted by one angry former employee of the Manitoba Workers' Compensation Board who blamed me for his having been fired. I had no idea that my political reach had extended so far. On another occasion, while having coffee at Harvey's with several friends in September of 2004, I was confronted by an irate former Manitoban who complained that I had never returned a telephone call made to the premier's office in the 1980s. Wanting permission to visit the U.S. despite a criminal record preventing it, he had expected a reply from the premier in person, and some two decades later he continued to be annoyed that he had not gotten one.

This account doesn't mean that all such encounters are unpleasant; one does receive compliments from time to time. Once I was greeted in the mall in Windsor by a former Manitoban who had moved here. He told me that the Conservatives had represented the rich folks in Manitoba, but I had always represented everyone else.

In August of 1999 I was asked by the National Democratic Institute in Washington, DC, to go to Yemen with other representatives to meet with various political party leaders and the president. While in the capital city, San'a, I was booked into a rather small room, which turned out to be less than quiet. A day or two after I was there, I happened to run into a Manitoban in the lobby who recognized me. We exchanged some friendly conversation. Upon returning to my room, I received a call from the front desk advising me that I was being upgraded to the penthouse suite, with all its amenities. I was also advised that there would be no additional charges, plus a free dinner. When I booked out of the hotel, the desk clerk told me how wonderful it was to have a former prime minister of Canada stay at the hotel.

In May 2003, I was the guest speaker at a dinner at the Henry Jackson School for International Studies Lecture at the University of Washington. As I walked to the podium I heard an elderly guest sitting at a front table grumble, "He's a socialist." During the question period after my speech, he attacked me about Canada's socialist medicare system. Later, in a private conversation, he advised me that he had fled socialism in Manitoba (he had been born in East St. Paul). "When," I inquired? "In the1950s," he responded. "I saw the socialists coming." At that time, Ed Schreyer was already Manitoba's youngest ever elected MLA and I was the youngest president of the CCF, at age twenty-two. Gary Doer would have been a toddler! The gentleman, a retired urologist, had great foresight!

It is said that every lawyer and politician must have the ability to act in order to be successful in their professions. I have had the opportunity to test that assumption by taking on roles in plays performed by a local theatrical company. In 2006 I played the role of Reverend Jeremy Brown in *Inherit the Wind*, and in 2008, the role of Juror No. 9 in *Twelve Angry Men*. Since the box office receipts were donated to various social organizations and the university, it has not yet become necessary for me to obtain my actor's equity card.

I have also served or remain serving as a member of numerous boards of directors: the Douglas-Coldwell Foundation (as honorary patron), the Harry Crowe Foundation (as chair), the Association for Canadian Studies, the Council for Canadian Unity (as governor), the Public Advocacy Centre, the Erie-St. Claire Local Integrated Health Network, the Windsor Occupational Health Centre, the Canadian Liver Foundation, the National Panel of the Canadian Broadcast Standards Council (as vice-president), the Legal Aid Board of Windsor, the Windsor Art Gallery, the Windsor-Essex Alzheimer Society (as honorary director), and the Canadian Civil Liberties Association (as a vice-president).

Since Adele and I left Manitoba in 1990, our daughter, Charysse, and her husband, George Mason, have moved to the suburbs of Windsor. We now have two grandchildren here, Katrina and Aislinn. This has firmly grounded our stay in the Windsor area. We return to Manitoba frequently to visit with our son and his wife, Chris and Jennifer, and our other grandchildren, Scott, Mitchell, the triplets, Meaghan, Matthew, and Michael, and our step-grand-son Lucas. Finally, I returned to the province of my birth, Ontario, and opened another chapter in my life, a very rewarding and fulfilling opportunity to use the experience gained from my previous legal and political pursuits.

I have gratefully accepted honours bestowed upon me over the years. I am honoured to be an Officer of the Order of Canada, Order of Manitoba; to have been named the Social Justice Person of the Year in 2002; to be Associate Professor Emeritus at the University of Windsor; to have a Doctor of Laws, *Honoris Causa*, 1993, conferred upon me by the University of Windsor; and to have been given the Lucile Ono Manitoba Award from the Manitoba NDP in 2005, the Cesar E. Chavez Black Eagle Award, the 2008 Youth Parliament Achievement Award, and the University of Winnipeg's 2008 Distinguished

Alumni Award. I am humbled by these awards, but I see them primarily as symbols of the efforts of people who stood by and with me through the years in striving for social justice in our world. It is to them that I owe my deepest thanks and loyalty.

When I was given the opportunity to be a university lecturer, Adele and I were able to forge a new life after politics. It is a more private life, removed from nineteen years of the pressures of politics. Some people become addicted to drugs or alcohol; my addiction has been to interact with young people in their learning experiences at university. However, Manitoba remains my home province, and I will remain a Manitoban until my departure from this earth. I must add, though, that differences between Winnipeg and Windsor are not as pronounced as one might believe. They are moderate-sized cities, as opposed to Montreal, Toronto or Vancouver, but both have a splendid cultural mix. Just as Winnipeg considers itself to be part of the Manitoba region, Windsor considers itself part of the unique tri-county region. Both regions are progressive, caring, and unpretentious.

⚊⚊⚊❦⚊⚊⚊

In the early 1990s, while I was teaching a seminar class on Canadian federalism at the University of Windsor, I was asked to relate my political experiences with constitutional reform during my premiership in Manitoba. It was this discussion, followed by students' questions and the quiet of the room at the end of class, that led me to contemplate the various chapters in my life. A simple ad in the *Globe and Mail*, a desire to move on to another life experience, brought me to the city of Windsor, in the province of Ontario where I was born, to start a new career, much different from the one at which I had laboured for most of my adult life. In the silence of that room, I recalled the paths I had travelled to arrive here.

And as I left, I felt a deep sense of accomplishment and renewed energy to carry on with my life, strong in my belief that I have contributed just a little bit for a better world.

NOTES

CHAPTER 1

1 Walter Young, *The Anatomy of a Party: The National CCF, 1932–1961* (Toronto: University of Toronto Press, 1969), 180.

2 Douglas Fisher, "Voters Are in Activist Mood," *Toronto Sun*, 18 November 1981.

3 Library and Archives Canada, MG28-IV1, NDP New Party clubs 1959–61, 374–378.

4 Stanley Knowles to Carl Hamilton, 15 November 1960. In NDP files, Library and Archives Canada.

5 In a subsequent court case for damages, I was stunned and somewhat scared by the testimony given, not by my doctor, but by a medical specialist testifying for the insurance company that I might with the passage of time suffer from a permanent incapacity because of my fractured vertebrae. Fortunately, this has never happened.

6 In 2004, I received a call from a former Selkirk clergyman who advised that during the campaign he and the local editor of the weekly *Selkirk Journal* had felt sorry for me and they had plotted over a cup of coffee how they might aid my campaign, thus the front page picture. At the time, I thought both gentlemen were ardent Conservatives. How wrong one can be?

CHAPTER 2

1 Richard Simeon, "Studying Public Policy," *Canadian Journal of Political Science*, 1977.

2 *Winnipeg Tribune*, interview with Premier Schreyer, 5 July 1969.

3 The Terms of Reference read as follows:

To investigate the feasibility of instituting a program of public automobile insurance and to hear and consider representation respecting all aspects of automobile insurance;

To make recommendations deemed in the public interest; and

To submit draft legislation.

4 Brian E. Owen, "Business Managers' Influence on Government: Case Study of Participation in Three Processes of Government Policy Formulation in Manitoba," (PhD diss., University of Western Ontario, 1975), 118–119.

5   These included:

A basic $50,000 minimum liability insurance (Saskatchewan's was $35,000);

A schedule of benefits for injuries up to $6,000 for dismemberment, disfigurement or impairment (no fault); $200 deductible all perils (no fault); death benefits of up to a maximum of $10,000 (no fault); medical benefits to a maximum of $2000.00 (no-fault); lifetime disability payments of up to $50 per week.

While the rates would be determined after the legislation was passed and the plan established, the committee claimed that a government-operated plan could return eighty-five cents of every premium dollar to the motorist, while the current private enterprise system returned about thirty-seven cents from every premium dollar invested.

6   Manitoba, Legislative Assembly, *Debates and Proceedings*, 12 March 1970, 5 (Ed Schreyer, Premier).

7   Manitoba, Legislative Assembly, *Debates and Proceedings*, 16 March 1970, 29 (Walter Weir, MLA).

8   In "Business Managers' Influence" (see pp. 129–132), Owen outlines the steps taken by the IBC and the IAAM.

9   I recall one such radio talk show with John Harvard, the CJOB hotline host at that time, in which at least 90 percent of the calls were hostile. I sensed that the callers were organized and calling from local insurance firms.

10 I knew the effort was concentrated in the constituencies where the MLA was considered soft on the issue. I received fewer than six such calls in my constituency of Selkirk, north of the city of Winnipeg.

11 Advertisements in *Winnipeg Free Press* and *Winnipeg Tribune*, 27 April 1970.

12 George Froehlich, "Premier hints at Compensation for Agents," *Winnipeg Tribune*, 30 April 1970.

13 Manitoba, Legislative Assembly, *Debates and Proceedings*, 29 April 1970 (Bud Sherman, MLA).

14 Manitoba, Legislative Assembly, *Debates and Proceedings*, 7 May 1970 (Harry Enns, MLA).

15 Manitoba, Legislative Assembly, *Debates and Proceedings*, 31 March 1967 (Larry Desjardins, MLA).

16 In *Canadian Indemnity Company v. the Attorney-General of B.C.* [1977] 25 S.C.R., the Supreme Court of Canada dismissed a challenge on constitutional grounds to the Public Auto Insurance Plan passed in British Columbia a few years after the enactment of the Manitoba plan.

17 Manitoba, Legislative Assembly, *Debates and Proceedings*, 31 July 1970 (Larry Desjardins, MLA).

18 Herb Schultz, *A View From the Ledge: An Insider's Look at the Schreyer Years* (Winnipeg: Heartland, 2005).

19 A poll had been done in Beard's constituency of Churchill and it was discovered that a solid majority favoured the government plan.

20 Harroon Siddiqui, "Pawley: Manitoba's Man of the People," *Toronto Star*, 22 November 1981.

CHAPTER 3

1   Manitoba, Legislative Assembly, *Debates and Proceedings*, 18 May 1976 (Lorne Watt, MLA).

2   Philip Mathias, *Forced Growth: Five Studies of Government Involvement in the Development of Canada* (Toronto: J. Lewis and Samuel, 1971).

3   *R v. Catagas* [1978] 1 W.W.R. 282, Manitoba Court of Appeal.

4   *Murdoch v. Murdoch* [1975] 1 S.C.R. 423.

5   Manitoba, Legislative Assembly, *Debates and Proceedings*, 30 May 1977 (Frank Johnson, MLA).

6   Archives of Manitoba, ATG G0149 QO1254 Box 2.

7   This was certainly my experience from my law office days in the 1960s in Stonewall and Selkirk.

8   Standing Committee on Statutory Regulations and Orders, 1 June 1977, 461.

9   Ibid., 459.

10 Ibid., 442.

11 Manitoba, Legislative Assembly, *Debates and Proceedings*, 17 June 1977 (Howard Pawley, MLA).

12 Manitoba, Legislative Assembly, *Debates and Proceedings*, 28 November 1977 (Sterling Lyon, Premier).

13 The excellent book *A Partnership of Equals: The Struggle for the Reform of Family Law in Manitoba*, by Berenice B. Sisler (Winnipeg: Watson and Dwyer, 1995), was most helpful in preparing the section dealing with Marital Property and Maintenance Act legislation.

CHAPTER 4

1   My interest in and commitment to progressive change in Latin America were reflected on our election as government in 1981 by headlines in the *Globe and Mail*, which read "A committed socialist who admired Allende, Pawley is no dreamer."

2   Susan Ruttan, "Pawley interim N.D.P. Chief, Rivals Eye November Race," *Winnipeg Tribune*, 15 January 1979.

3   In *Wednesdays Are Cabinet Days* (Winnipeg: Queenston House, 1981), Russell Doern claims that Green had several reasons for jubilation: he had prevented a Pawley second ballot majority; he had stopped Pawley below 50 percent; and he had finally triumphed over Cherniack-Miller after a decade of sufferance.

4   Susan Ruttan, "Both Lyon, Pawley Happy with Survey," *Winnipeg Tribune*, 29 September 1979.

5   These quotes from the media are found in Doern, *Wednesdays Are Cabinet Days*, 181.

6   Frank Syms, letter to Peter Warren (CJOB radio talk show host), 27 August 1979. See comments about the Syms defection in Manitoba, Legislative Assembly, *Debates and Proceedings*, 3 March 1980 (Premier S. Lyon).

7   Manitoba, Legislative Assembly, *Debates and Proceedings*, 20 April 1981 (Wally McKenzie, MLA).

8   "League Favours Autopac As Is," *Winnipeg Free Press*, 5 December 1980.

9   Manitoba, Legislative Assembly, *Debates and Proceedings*, 18 December 1980 (Harry Enns, Minister of Government Services).

10   Manitoba, Legislative Assembly, *Debates and Proceedings*, 15 December 1980 (Warner Jorgensen, Minister of Consumer and Corporate Affairs).

11   Manitoba, Legislative Assembly, *Debates and Proceedings* (Throne Speech), 22 December 1980 (Premier Sterling Lyon).

12   Frances Russell, "Is the NDP Being too Democratic?" *Winnipeg Free Press*, 18 January 1982.

13   Manitoba, Legislative Assembly, *Debates and Proceedings*, 22 December 1980 (Opposition Leader Howard Pawley).

14   At the time of its defeat, the Lyon government left a debt of $251 million (Manitoba Budget, 31 March 1982).

15   Aldo Santin, "A Political Priest Helped the Poor," 7 June 2003, *Winnipeg Free Press*.

CHAPTER 5

1   Fred Cleverly, "NDP is Determined to Smash Progressives," *Winnipeg Free Press*, 18 September 1981.

2   Ingeborg Boyens, "Lyon brings Back 1977-Style Socialist Bashing," *Winnipeg Free Press*, 23 October 1981.

3   Richard Cleroux, "Manitoba Fall Vote a Good Bet; Lyon off and Running Already," *Globe and Mail*, 26 September 1981.

4   Unfortunately, the oil boom in the west declined in the 1980s and thus compromised our potential success with Man Oil. I regret this, as I earnestly believe that in the right circumstances, Manitobans would have immensely benefited from a boom in oil sales, as we now experience. After it had been established by the Trudeau government, Petro Canada was sold by subsequent Liberal and Conservative governments—an enormous blunder that we are paying for today.

5   New caucus members elected in 1981 included the following: Eugene Kostyra (Seven Oaks), overburdened with hard work right from the start; Roland Penner (Fort Rouge), a highly articulate and effective speaker; Maureen Hemphill (Logan), who would perform as no others could in turning various Opposition members' questions around to hurt them and whose response to issues was always rational and balanced; Muriel Smith (Osborne), the deputy premier, always level-headed in her persistent pursuit of social justice; Al Mackling (St. James), honest, principled, and forthright Attorney General and MLA in the 1969–1973 term; John Plohman (Dauphin), an appealing and colourful personality; Andy Anstett (Springfield), former clerk of the House and an expert on legislative rules; Elijah Harper (Rupertsland), a quiet but effective advisor on Aboriginal matters; Harry Harapiak (The Pas), known for his hard work and honesty; Gerard Lecuyer (Radisson), who would quickly establish himself as the most progressive environment minister in Canada; Mary Beth Dolin (Kildonan), a rapidly rising star who unfortunately died while still in office; John Bucklaschuk (Gimli), who had been the extremely capable provincial director of the NDP between 1977 to 1981, after serving as a special assistant to me between 1975 and 1977; he would hold many important cabinet responsibilities including Consumer and Corporate Affairs,

Cooperatives, Municipal Affairs, and Highways;" Jerry Storie (Flin Flon), who would become the youngest member of cabinet when he was appointed Minister of Housing in 1982; and Conrad Santos (Burrows), a PhD graduate originally from the Philippines. Myrna Phillips, who was the first New Democrat ever elected in Wolseley and would subsequently serve a stint as caucus chair and later as Speaker of the legislature (1981–1988); and Doreen Dodick (Riel), a faithful grassroots New Democrat who defeated Donald Craik, the powerful finance minister of the Lyon government. Also elected were Don Scott (Inkster), an extremely competent and able financial government analyst; and the youthful Steve Ashton, a former president of the students' union at the University of Manitoba who had also served on the University Senate and Board of Governors. An extremely conscientious Phil Eyler was elected in the marginal constituency of River East.

6   Five women were elected as New Democrat MLAs: Maureen Hemphill, Muriel Smith, Mary Beth Dolin, Myrna Phillips, and Doreen Dodick

7   Archives of Manitoba, P 941F 1969–76, Notes on Manitoba Situations, prepared by G.W. Cadbury, 1969.

8   A number of factors account for this difference between our experience and that of Ontario:

Trust existed at the leadership level in Manitoba.

Our negotiations involved the labour leadership and important cabinet ministers. The process contrasted with the one in Ontario, where civil servants played the major role in the talks.

Both parties adopted a low profile approach in Manitoba. Neither went to the media to get their message across. Neither side attempted to upstage the other.

My government did not impose superficially applied deadlines.

In Manitoba, the objective was to create jobs; the rationale given in Ontario was deficit fighting. This gave the appearance of a problem being imposed on the Rae government at the behest of the right-wing financial community.

The money saved in wage rollbacks ($10 million in Manitoba) was allocated to a Manitoba Jobs Fund. An advisory board consisting of government and union representatives was instrumental in determining where the monies would be spent.

The employees were given an assurance that, in return for wage adjustments, there would be no layoffs. In such situations, both parties need to benefit.

CHAPTER 6

1   Manitoba legislative debates, 32nd Legislature, Second session, 29 June 1983, 4046–4047.

2   Raymond Hébert, *Manitoba's French-Language Crisis: A Cautionary Tale* (Montreal: McGill-Queen's University Press, 2004), 205.

3   Hearings of the Legislative Committee on Privileges and Elections, Second session, 32nd Legislature of the Legislative Assembly of Manitoba, 29 September 1983, 941.

4   Legislative Assembly Debates, 2 August 1983, 4786. Raymond Hébert points out how all these theories relate to the dynamic of the French-language services debate: "the most plausible explanation of Lyon's scorched–earth approach to the

Pawley proposals can be found in right-wing authoritarianism theory: the self righteousness evident in many of the speeches made by Opposition members and their ad hominem depiction of government members as aliens allowed them not only to open the floodgates of unrestrained popular opposition to the Pawley proposals but also to push the Opposition to the extreme limits of socially acceptable behaviour. At this stage of the crisis, with one word from Lyon the true bigots might have rioted in the streets. For a few weeks in early July of 1984, democracy in Manitoba rested on this single thread, a very tenuous one indeed." Hebert, *Manitoba's French-Language Crisis*, 218.

5   Frances Russell, *The Manitoba Crucible* (Winnipeg: Heartland Associates), 428.

6   *Globe and Mail*, editorial, "Bad in any language," 28 February 1984, 6.

7   *Winnipeg Free Press*, 5 March 1984, 6.

8   Richard Cleroux, "Bells may toll a hollow victory," *Globe and Mail*, 1 March 1984, 8.

9   Ibid., 8.

10   Manitoba Legislative Debates, Fourth session, 32nd Legislature, 2920.

CHAPTER 7

1   Roland Penner, *A Glowing Dream: A Memoir* (Winnipeg: J. Gordon Shillingford Publishing, 2007), 210.

2   See Premier's Speech of Wednesday, 21 May 1986, Throne Speech debate. References are made to the favourable commentary by the Royal Bank of Canada and the Bank of Montreal.

3   The subsequent Conservative government gutted this provision and, sadly, it has never been revived.

4   It is also important to weigh the social and political price for any policy trade off. I recall a conversation with a senior Rae minister early in that government's term that appeared to indicate that enacting antiscab laws would be enough for the NDP without it also legislating public auto insurance during a first term in office.

5   *Winnipeg Free Press*, 5 July 1987.

6   Errol Black and Jim Silver, in an excellent chapter written not long after the appeal, illustrate how various data supports the conclusion that an "important benefit of FOS is that it provides workers in small units in some industries, and workers in rural areas, an opportunity to organize and achieve 'fair' working conditions without having to resort to the trauma and insecurities associated with 'suicidal' strikes." See Errol Black and Jim Silver, "Final Offer Selection: The Manitoba Experience," in *Hard Bargains: The Manitoba Movement Confronts the 1990s* (Winnipeg: Manitoba Labour Education Centre, 1991). They illustrate how FOS was born out of the need to assist the increasing proportion of the working population vulnerable to employers because of the decline in high-wage, unionized manufacturing sector jobs. This trend has intensified right up to the present time and unfortunately creative solutions to minimize the negative impact on working people have failed to materialize in the changing labour climate.

CHAPTER 8

1. Statistics Canada, Canadian Economic Observer: Historical Statistical Supplement 2006/07 (Cat. no. 11–210-XPB).

2 Peter Hadekel, *Silent Partners: Taxpayers and the Bankrolling of Bombardier* (Toronto: Key Porter Books, 2004).

3 Archives of Manitoba, Prem. CF 18 EC 0016 # 357 I 10spec Box 14.

4 Michel Gratton, *And So What Are the Boys Saying? An Inside Look at Brian Mulroney in Power* (Toronto: McGraw-Hill Ryerson Limited, 1987).

5 Mia Rabson, "Brian Really Was Lyin', Memos Prove Mulroney Was Totally Involved in CF-18 Debacle," *Winnipeg Free Press*, 14 August 2010.

6 Archives of Manitoba, Prem. CF-18 EC 0016 # 357, I 10spec.

7 "Tory backer tells PM to shove it over CF-18," *Winnipeg Free Press*, 4 November 1986.

8 Gratton, *And So What Are the Boys Saying?*

9 Pat Carney, *Trade Secrets: A Memoir* (Toronto: Key Porter Books, 2000).

10 Peter Newman, *The Canadian Revolution: From Deference to Defiance* (Toronto: Penguin Books, 1995).

11 Hadekel, *Silent Partners*.

12 Ibid.

13 Letter to Ed Broadbent, MP, from Honourable Vic Schroeder, Minister of Industry, Trade and Technology, 20 January 1987.

14 Gratton, *And So What Are the Boys Saying?*

15 Archives of Manitoba, Prem. series CF-18 Reference # EC 0016, Box 357, I 10 spec Box 14.

16 David Crane, "What Next for Softwood?" *Toronto Star*, 6 August 2006, A21.

17 *Brandon Sun*, editorial, 2 December 1987.

18 "Reisman writes off Pawley as lost cause but aims to snare Peterson," *Winnipeg Free Press*, 17 October 1987.

CHAPTER 9

1 Manitoba Intergovernmental Relations Secretariat, 1986. Discussion Paper, 3 July 1986, Archives of Manitoba, EC 0016.

2 Patrick Monahan, *Meech Lake: The Inside Story* (Toronto: University of Toronto Press, 1991), 51–53.

3 Fraser Graham, "PM and Bourassa work as a team on Constitution," *Globe and Mail*, 4 September 1986, A8.

4 Donald Benham, "Pawley Champions Fairness," *Winnipeg Sun*, 5 November 1986.

5 Manitoba Strategy Committee of Cabinet, Minutes of 5 February 1987, Archives of Manitoba, EC 0016.

6 Intergovernmental Relations Department, Memo from Jim Eldridge to George Ford, Clerk of Executive Council, from Diane Wilhelmy of the Quebec Federal-Provincial Office, 14 January 1987.

7 Letter from Prime Minister Mulroney to the Premiers, 17 March 1987.

8   Monahan, *Meech Lake*, 81.

9   *The Reid Report* (Angus Reid Associates), 2, 5 (May 1987).

10 Frances Russell, "Party Leaders All Have Doubts About Meech Lake Pact," *Winnipeg Free Press*, 9 May 1987.

11 Andrew Cohen, *A Deal Undone: The Making and Breaking of the Meech Lake Accord* (Vancouver: Douglas and McIntyre, 1990), 113.

12 Ibid., 103.

13 Ibid., 105.

14 *Winnipeg Free Press*, editorial, 4 June 1987.

15 Geoffrey York, "Bourassa and Pawley Disagree on Amending Meech Lake Accord," *Globe and Mail*, 29 July 1987.

16 Alan Cairns, *Disruptions: Constitutional Struggles, from the Charter to Meech Lake* (Toronto: McClelland and Stewart, 1991), 260.

CHAPTER 10

1   Source for numbers: Statistics Canada, Canadian Economic Observer: Historical Statistical Supplement 2006/07, (Catalogue no. 11–210-XPB).

2   *Globe and Mail*, "Manitoba's Fortunes," editorial, 19 March 1987.

3   When this came up in cabinet, experts in the field were telling us the problems were greatest with pre-schoolers, particularly in northern areas, where the cost of nutritious foods required for healthy tooth development was beyond the means of most families.

4   *Globe and Mail*, "Manitoba's Fortunes."

5   Manitoba Budget Address, 1988. The rate of deficit reduction in 1987–88, the final full year the NDP were in power, was 46.4 percent by Manitoba to 2.8 percent by Canada (See Manitoba Budget, 1988).

6. Manitoba, Public Accounts 1988–89, Vol. 1, Financial Statements for the Consolidated Fund, 9.

7. Manitoba, 1996 Manitoba Budget Address, Budget Paper B, Financial Review and Statistics; Manitoba, 2005 Manitoba Budget, Budget Paper B, Financial Review and Statistics.

8. TD Bank Financial Group, Special Report, "The Coming Era of Fiscal Restraint," 20 October 2009, p. 9, http://www.td.com/economics/special/db1009_fiscal.pdf.

9   *Globe and Mail*, "The vote that broke the NDP's back," 10 March 1988.

10 Letter to Howard Pawley from Jim Walding, 3 April 1986 (personal papers).

11 Letter to Jim Walding from Marty Dolin, Caucus Whip, 28 April 1987 (personal papers).

12 Frances Russell, "Odd events surround fall of government," *Winnipeg Free Press*, 15 March 1988, 7.

13 As a party it is true that we were heavily in debt but far less than subsequent reports repeatedly suggested: that we were nearly $1 million in debt at the time of our defeat; this was so at the end of 1988 after the heavy expenditures for the provincial and federal elections taking place after our defeat.

14 A.C. Hamilton, "Province Continues to Ignore Ideas to Improve Aboriginal Justice," *Winnipeg Free Press*, 12 August 2006.

INDEX